PIONEERS OF CHANGE

Experiments in Creating a Humane Society

The individuals and groups whose work is described in this book have all been recipients of the Right Livelihood Award. This annual award, widely known as the Alternative Nobel Prize, is presented in recognition of pioneering efforts in the areas of peace, sustainable development, environmental integrity, social justice and human rights.

The recipients include: Sunderlal Bahaguna (Chipko Movement); Dr Rosalie Bertell (Institute of Concern for Public Health); Ela Bhatt (Self-Employed Women's Association); Walden Bello (Food First); Stephen Corry (Survival International); Mike Cooley; Cary Fowler; Johan Galtung; Stephen Gaskin (Plenty International); Dr Inge Genefke (Rehabilitation and Research Centre for Torture Victims); Mohammed Idris (Consumers' Association of Penang); Robert Jungk; Ar Aklilu Lemma (International Child Development Centre); Jose Lutzenberger; Rajni Kothari (Lok-ayan); Petra Kelly; Hunter and Amory Lovins (Rocky Mountain Institute); Wangari Maathai (National Council of Women in Kenya); Manfred Max-Neef (Development Alternatives Centre); Bill Mollison (Permaculture Institute); Helena Norberg-Hodge (Ladakh Project); Dr Alice Stewart; Sir George Trevelyan; Professor John F. C. Turner; Theo van Boven; Patrick van Rensburg (Foundation for Education with Production); S. Wickremaaratchi (Participatory Institute for Development Alternatives).

JEREMY SEABROOK

PIONEERS OF CHANGE

EXPERIMENTS IN CREATING A
HUMANE SOCIETY

NEW SOCIETY *Publishers* • *Philadelphia*

ZED BOOKS • *London*

Pioneers of Change: Experiments in Creating a Humane Society was first published in 1993.

United States of America and Canada

New Society Publishers, 4527 Springfield Avenue, Philadelphia, PA 19143 and PO Box 189, Gabriola Island, BC VOR 1XO

Rest of the World

Zed Books Ltd, 57 Caledonian Road, London N1 9BU.

Cover designed by Andrew Corbett

Laserset by Yoram Tzabar

Printed and bound in the United States of America on partially recycled paper by Capital City Press of Montpelier, Vermont

A catalogue record for this book is available from the British Library

UK HB 1 85649 093 9   UK PB 1 85649 094 7

USA HB 0-86571-260-3   USA PB 0-86571-261-1

Canada HB 1-55092-198-3   Canada PB 1-55092-199-1

New Society Publishers is a project of the New Society Educational Foundation, a non-profit, tax-exempt, public foundation. Opinions expressed in this book do not necessarily represent positions of the New Society Educational Foundation.

Contents.

A NOTE ON RIGHT LIVELIHOOD

This book is based upon the work of those groups and individuals who have received the Right Livelihood Award between 1980 and 1990.

The Right Livelihood Foundation was set up by Jakob von Uexkull in the late 1970s. He had been dismayed to find, at United Nations conferences during the 1970s, that the amount of money spent on organising the meetings sometimes exceeded that allotted to the issue under discussion. On the fringes, however, he met many people whose work, largely unrecognised then, offered practical, hopeful solutions to the growing problems of resource depletion, environmental degradation, social injustice, infringement of human rights and the dispossession of indigenous peoples.

He wrote to the Nobel Foundation, offering to contribute towards the setting up of a new prize for the environment. The foundation had no plans to extend the range of its awards, even though the economics prize had been inaugurated only in 1963. Von Uexkull decided to go ahead with his own prize, to be awarded for 'right livelihood', in the area of peace, sustainable development, environmental integrity, social justice and human rights.

Jakob von Uexkull had been a translator, journalist and stamp-dealer. Over the years, he had built up a significant Middle East stamp collection, and when he sold his Saudi stamps to a museum in Saudi Arabia, this provided him with the bulk of the $100,000 with which the Right Livelihood Foundation was formed. Since that time, the capital has increased fourfold, mainly from private donations. No money is accepted from institutions.

In the first year, 1980, von Uexkull chose the recipients. The ceremony took place in a rented hall in Stockholm, before 35 people. By the following year, there was an international jury and a larger hall. Since 1985, the event has been hosted by the Swedish parliament. During its 12 years of existence, it has recognised over 40 individuals or groups, out of 250 submissions from more than 50 countries.

The work of these people is the subject of this book. Their vision and energies tend towards the definition of an alternative view of the world, a way out of an accelerating global industrialism that weighs so heavily upon the earth and upon its poorest people. The decay of Communism appears to leave uncontested the patterns of development determined by the West, which now offers its advice and prescriptions to the whole world. This is, however, an illusion: not only are alternatives vitally necessary, they also exist, coherent, hopeful and ready to release people from the immobilism, despair and violence which accompany the spread of industrialism.

In the beginning, von Uexkull was suspected of having been funded by the CIA or the KGB, in order to discredit the Nobel prize. But he was quite happy to disclose where the money had come from, and had nothing to hide. A Swedish newspaper ran a headline, saying that the money had come from stamps rather than from dynamite. Von Uexkull concedes that the Nobel prize has widened its scope in recent years, 'but the Nobel prize for medicine, for instance, is never going to be given to a shaman, a herbalist or a homeopath.'

The Right Livelihood Awards have achieved a high profile in some countries, especially in Germany, Scandinavia and India. Because the Greens have been so important in Germany, there is a recognition that alternatives are to be taken seriously. This is yet to happen in America, or Britain, which was, after all, the place of origin of the there-is-no-alternative dogma.

The more closely we look at the work of those who have received the award, the clearer it becomes that 'environment' is an incomplete way of describing their efforts and struggles. The Right Livelihood Foundation has encouraged many activists, researchers, scientists and social movements who have sustained their work in the presence of much hostility, and even of violent opposition. The issues with which they have been involved have now become central, and it can be seen that there are indeed hopeful alternatives that challenge the orthodoxies of the rich industrial countries.

For more than a year, together with Trevor Blackwell, I visited many of those who have won the 'Alternative Nobel' prize, and prepared a document for the 10th anniversary conference in Italy in 1990, which became the basis for the book. This can show only fragments of the richness and many-sided work of the people it deals with. In some cases. it was not possible to meet the individuals concerned. Others shared with me their insights, and stories, their lives and reflections, but since access to each was variable, this inevitably appears in the book.

I would like to thank all those I met, who were generous with their ideas, time and visions. Thanks especially to Trevor Blackwell, to Paul Ekins, Jakob von Uexkull, Helena Norberg-Hodge, Mohamed Idris, Winin Pereira.

Anyone who would like to contribute to the work of the Right Livelihood Foundation should contact:

The Right Livelihood Awards
P.O. Box 15072
S-10465 Stockholm
Sweden
Bank Account Number: 19 1824 1022 115, Nordbanken Stockholm, Sweden.

FOREWORD

The pessimists have long since given up on our collective ability to set the world economy onto a genuinely sustainable path; they have abundant evidence with which to demonstrate their case. The pace of destruction continues to outstrip our still paltry efforts to limit the social and environmental impacts of modern industrialism.

By contrast, the optimists point to a gradual but unmistakable growth in awareness, on the assumption that changed minds are a precondition of changed behaviour. And they point, too, to the growing body of best practice, to the example of thousands of individuals and organisations who are already out there *doing it* in one way or another, rather than simply talking about doing it.

Right Livelihood is no after-eight social theory for politically correct progressives: it is hands on, feet on, head and heart on every step of the way. Many of today's Right Livelihood practitioners are profiled here as the pioneers of change. Their work and ideas are grist to the optimists' mill, for what has been achieved is already astonishing, and the potential for replication is enormous.

But it is a long, slow haul. If these are the green shoots of a new society in the making, they are still very frail and very vulnerable. The economic climate in which they have to thrive is still profoundly inhospitable, and the politicians who could do so much to nurture and promote their growth still owe too much of their success to the vested interests of the past.

It is only in such terms that one can explain why the persistent gap between our knowledge base (the hard empirical evidence about the impacts of unsustainable growth and contemporary consumerism) and the policy response to that knowledge remains so enormous. From time to time, one begins to think that politicians really have seen the writing on the wall, and that the surging tides of green rhetoric heard at the Earth Summit in June 1992, or on a host of international platforms, genuinely prefigure substantive shifts in economic policy. But the tide soon ebbs, the media move on, the Micawberish muddling through reasserts itself.

In truth, the whole green alternative remains very much a foreign language for the majority of today's decision-makers. Some of it is getting through: sustainable development; biological diversity; community empowerment — such phrases trip lightly off the tongues of all but the most hardened defenders of the old order. But they are just that, select linguistic devices abstracted from the cultural and political context in which they speak of far deeper truths and far more radical changes in practice.

Armed only with their phrase books in Green Cliché, yet still weighed down by centuries of accumulated ideological baggage, mainstream politicians remind me of nothing so much as modern tourists who have learned just enough of the language to be able to ask the way in a foreign country, but are then quite incapable of understanding the answer they are given, let alone of acting upon it!

In one respect, all of us are now living in that unfamiliar and even frightening 'foreign country' — a country where the old maps are useless and the old ways of doing things no longer seem to get them done; where social problems multiply despite dramatic technological advance; where individual suffering deepens even as individual affluence grows; and where environmental degradation threatens to cancel out the future, all in the pursuit of so-called progress.

But therein lies the power of *Pioneers of Change*. For it is these voices, in all their breathtaking diversity, which not only show how the answers to such problems can be arrived at, but simultaneously encourage us all to learn more and more of their transformative language.

It is these voices, orchestrated by Jeremy Seabrook's cogent and compelling commentary, that will help to overcome the growing horrors of the 'foreign country' that has become the world today, and even to learn how to make it home for the whole of humankind.

Jonathon Porritt, 1993

INTRODUCTION

1. TRANSCENDING POLITICS

For radical social change to occur, at least two preconditions must be met. First, popular perceptions of the values and ideals of a social order must have ceased to be congruent with the language in which these are expressed; and secondly, the outline of an alternative must be discernible through the decaying structures. In Eastern Europe, it had long become clear that few believed in the sonorous vacuities of Marxism-Leninism, of the Party, the Proletariat, History. The rhetoric had come to mean little in the presence of actually existing humanity.

The West, too, is living in a moribund political culture, less glaringly detached from the experience of its people, but increasingly void of substance. It is the duty of those seeking change to articulate the words of renewal dissimulated behind the crumbling rhetoric with which those in power seek to maintain our acquiescence. It is not that the big words they use are themselves falsehoods; simply that these have become frozen, drained of vitality, with the result that we live in a permanent afterglow of ideals and struggles long realised, fixed now in an archaic and no longer flexible iconography. Social hope can be reborn only when a coherent and satisfying alternative becomes visible through the embalming fluid in which the received pieties are preserved.

Any attempt to characterise Western society ('our society', as it is called when there are problems to be solved or wars to be won, but not when it is a question of the ownership of wealth or the distribution of power), soon comes up with terms like 'secular', 'pluralist', 'materialist'. Its most cherished values will be said to be devotion to democracy and freedom; its primary purpose to optimise choice and diversity. Our way of life is governed by reason and pragmatism, but always following certain high principles from which we do not depart. We are tolerant of dissent, but retain an abhorrence of extremism of all kinds.

These clichés are the only things holding together the threadbare world view they claim to represent, and which is rarely called into question, perhaps because few of them stand up to a very searching scrutiny of the realities they are believed to evoke.

We are not even materialist, which is perhaps one of the less flattering descriptions we acknowledge. If we were, we would surely exhibit a greater respect for the material world in all its manifestations, from its 'raw materials', which is how we designate the resource base of the earth, to our own artefacts. The latter we hold in such contempt that they are destined to be demolished within the shortest lapse of time imaginable after their manufacture. The accelerating tempo at which we use up things and accumulate waste has nothing to do with materialism. It would be more accurate to see in it a kind of contorted mysticism, for it leads us to the conviction that, having torn through the material resources of the earth, these will nonetheless be inexhaustibly replenished. Perhaps the eagerness to destroy is a mutation of the search for transcendence: we cannot wait to see what lies on the other side of our destructiveness. However that may be, truly materialist societies are to be found among indigenous peoples, tribal people and forest-dwellers, for they respect and revere every material thing in their fragile habitat. They use everything sparingly and renewably, without impairing the reservoir of riches for those who will come after. It is no contradiction that these are also intensely spiritual cultures. Their preservation of the natural world is ensured, for they see it as the abode of spirits and gods. They sacralise what is indispensable, what is supremely useful. (Perhaps this is what we have done with money.) They are aware of the interconnections between human life and the living material base on which it depends; they recognise it must be shared with the rest of creation, and without dominance. Ours is a double rejection, of both the material and the spiritual. Perhaps this helps to explain the enigma of the multiple poverties that haunt our rich society.

Spiritual blindness, however, does not mean that we therefore occupy the secular society of our imagination. Secular societies do not exist. It is only that the faith of the people, evicted from its familiar spaces, sometimes migrates into some strange new abode, and loses the power to know or name itself. We reserve our superstitious reverence for the power of our own science and technology; and it is surely significant that the only realm in which our credulous people now expect miracles to occur is that of economic endeavour. Faith in the yield of purely material processes is still faith. Indeed, so strong is the belief in science and technology that it persuades us that we can be delivered from the consequences of our own actions by their workings; in fact, they promise that our promiscuous spillages of toxins, our incontinences and excesses can be cured by the very means that produced them. The superstitious, irrational beliefs which we see in allegedly more 'primitive' societies are merely the externalised contradictions of our own ideology, an ideology that is no less rigid, but alas, may well be far more damaging, for being unable to recognise itself as such.

But at least, it will be argued, we are pluralist. Yet the universalising mission of the West has seldom been held in check for very long. If it wavered earlier in the twentieth century, this was only under the shock of the universalising pretensions of another emanation of Western culture, Marxism. Throughout the industrial and colonial period, we have snuffed out alternatives wherever we have found them. We have subdued and ravaged societies from which we might have derived precious instruction in the meaning of sustainability. And what we once imposed upon much of the rest of the world through military conquest, we now filter through the more elegant and subtle conduits of economic necessity. The recolonising of the world by means of its subordination to the exigencies of Western interests admits of no alternative, and that system applies an astonishing *resourcefulness* in the ceaseless transfer of *resources* from poor to rich. Of course, earlier generations of colonists, empire-builders and bringers of truth have now abandoned their revelations, bibles and scriptures, and work through the prescriptions, conditionalities and orders that emanate from the World Bank and International Monetary Fund, from Western governments and the transnational corporations.

Nor are real alternatives much in evidence in the so-called 'metropolitan' countries. Economic dissidents do, of course, exist, and they exercise their freedoms by living in cardboard boxes under bridges, or begging on the city streets. Naturally, this does not involve the imposition upon individuals of compliance with the revealed certainties of absolute creeds; but the fate of those who elect to live outside the monetising monoculture is plain for all to see; indeed, they serve as warning and example to the rest.

'Freedom of choice', we tell ourselves, is one of our most cherished underlying principles. This fundamentalist slogan gains universal assent. Yet the conflation of these two elevated ideas actually deeply damages both. For 'freedom of choice' has come to mean something much diminished in Western society, namely consumer choice. In such a context, freedom of choice effectively eclipses wider liberties (not least, the freedom to choose other, possibly less destructive ways of answering human need), as well as choice itself, because consumer choice is actually won at the expense of natural biodiversity all over the world. Through the narrowing genetic base of food crops, the extinction of species, the wiping out of much of the heritage of plant wealth created by farmers over centuries, the monopolising of germplasm and its decay in gene banks, the homogenising of food-processing, the chemicalising of agriculture and the dispossession of subsistence farmers, we have lived through a rapid loss of variety, and hence of real choice, both present and future. By means of biotechnology, the processes of life can now be privately owned, patented by transnational companies. The really important choices in our lives have been superseded by the right to select from the 12,000 or so items which, we are told, adorn the shelves of 'our' supermarkets.

Even democracy, the holy of holies, has come to look less like active involvement of the people in decision-making than the superintendence of organised impotence. Perhaps the most commonly heard response of the people of the West to the forces that control their lives is a feeling of powerlessness; so much so, that in the United States, barely half the population takes the trouble to register any electoral preference at all. 'Who is going to listen to what we say?' people ask. 'What can you do about it?' 'What difference will it make?' 'They're all the same.' Whether confronted by crime, violence, addictions, fear on the streets, the breakdown of human associations and bondings, loneliness, psychiatric or social disorder, we have no influence on the direction or the shape of a society which produces these things; and neither are we expected to want it. No wonder people feel powerless. If few reflect that impotence is the last thing the happy inhabitants of a democracy are supposed to experience, this is doubtless because a distracting consumer choice has been seen as an at least temporarily adequate substitute for our lost liberties; the shotgun marriage of freedom with helplessness appears to have been consummated.

And yet, in spite of this, the totalising economistic ideology is beginning to fall apart. The 'externalities', not only of environment and of damage to irreplaceable ecosystems, but also of social justice and human well-being, can no longer be discounted in pursuit of archaic economic indicators that have less and less bearing upon happiness, security and well-being. Our devotion to 'the bottom line', even to 'the real world' (that figment in which the fantasists of economics would have us live), has been made redundant by the emergence of another, even more real, world, this time of skeletal trees, poisoned watercourses and altered climate, of mass hunger, and a displaced, frightened humanity seeking refuge under flimsy canvas in deserts or in fetid city slums; refugees from developmental violence. The bottom line is no longer the last, unappealable judgement of the ingenious and treacherous construct of our accounting system, but that of how much more of hubris and greed the planet can bear.

We can liberate ourselves from some of the debilitating clichés that caricature our lives and purposes, from words that have become so porous their meaning has leaked away. Nothing is any longer what it seems in this evasive vocabulary of a conservatism that seeks to conserve nothing, that only estranges us from our own experience and persuades us to abdicate the evidence of our senses. In a world of images and appearances, face value has become worthless.

Once the big words stand revealed as hollow, so many of the others also melt away. 'Resources' no longer indicates the treasures of the earth, but has become a synonym for the money which cannot measure them. 'Independence' is what people enjoy as they become more and more dependent on money, which undermines their autonomy by making them forget how to do and to make and to create things outside the encroaching cash economy. 'Sustainability' means maintaining the ideological fictions of industrial society, sparing it harmful contact with ecological reality. It also means sustaining the privileges of the rich and powerful. 'Survival' suggests not safeguarding the rights of threatened peoples in forests and jungles but the already-rich getting enough money to keep pace with the monetising of more and more areas of human activity. 'Defence' is the piling up of weapons of destruction, the manufacture of which actually undermines the most effective defence we have — the body's immune system, impaired by radioactivity and invisible contaminants. When we hear of our 'complex society', we should not be too intimidated: opacity is not the same thing as complexity. What is meant here is the social fog generated by a division of labour so extreme that we scarcely recognise our own function in it, let alone that of our neighbour. 'Efficiency' means the ever more effective meltdown of natural resources into commodities. 'Development' means reducing the breath-taking variety of forms of natural wealth in the world into money. 'Quality of life' is a genteel semaphore for the maintenance of privilege. 'Community' is a neighbourhood of strangers, while 'individualism' means the isolated pursuit of the collective illusion of mass markets.

Many of the dissatisfactions seething beneath the surface of these carefully protected falsehoods beat in vain against the ossified rhetoric that serves to submerge human purposes in the 'health' of the economy and the 'freedom' of the markets. But a new worldview is struggling to find expression through this malignancy; and this is what this book is all about.

The new view has at least three major objectives. The first is to *make visible* all that has been suppressed or elided in the existing ideology, giving true value to the work of women and children in the world, to count the true costs of the industrialising of our humanity, not only the pain and hunger of the poor, but the hidden price paid also by the most privileged, those undermined by toxins and carcinogens and addictions and violence, and especially by the damaged gene pool that may be our most enduring legacy to future generations we sometimes claim to be working for. The second focus is upon *empowerment*: not only the defence of self-reliance, but also giving a voice to the subsistence farmer and slumdweller, those who have been traditionally silenced. It means, too, the re-enfranchisement of people in the democracies, the rekindling of their creative powers and inventiveness, the reawakening of the human resources that have been put to sleep by the years of easy money. Empowerment means celebrating the local, the human scale. It means healing divisions, between consumers and producers, between women and men, First and Third Worlds. The third concern is the maintenance of real living *diversity* at every level. This means resistance to dangerous dependency on monocultures, whether of crops or social structures; protection of the rights of tribal people, forest-dwellers and fishing communities to the pursuit of their traditional life-styles and access to the resource base which ensures their survival. It means economic as well as political self-determination; chosen and not imposed patterns of development; human rights that value not only dissent and the defiance of prevailing orthodoxies, but also freedom from cultural dominance.

The alternative worldview seeking its way towards self-expression cannot be smothered by all the ideological managers of media conglomerates, nor by the guardians of privilege, nor by the exterminators of human richness and diversities, whether these take the form of the executives of transnationals or torturers trained in the military academies of totalitarian regimes. For what we are witnessing is a change of perception, that most subtle and irresistible of all revolutions; not so much cognition, but the shifting emotional force that drives it. Existing versions of the world, the old ideological taxonomies, are melting away. Only the words, heavy and useless as funerary monuments, still weigh us down.

2. OBSTACLES TO A COHERENT ALTERNATIVE

All countries are developing countries. The division between 'developed' and 'developing' suggests that in the rich world, development has already happened, and is now static and irreversible. This also serves as a deterministic model to those countries which are, presumably, in the process of being developed. It gives the impression that there is a single, inescapable (though unquestionably desirable) pathway, one which obliterates alternatives

Perhaps this is why the search for another worldview is so painful. There exist thousands of practical projects and endeavours in the world which represent a non-dogmatic convergence of the hopes of those people who understand that present patterns of development are no longer either manageable or desirable. The merging of these initiatives into a coherent alternative is already taking place in practice, even though a formulation of that alternative is not easy.

There are a number of difficulties in trying to express the new paradigm. For one thing, even this phrase hints at yet another set of fixed ideas, something that could readily harden into revelation, just as existing economic ideologies have done. Some have seen the state of the Green movement as similar to that of 'socialism before Marx'; and although there has been no such visionary of the Green movement, at least there is no danger of inflexible Green dogmas arising out of any definitive Green text. The possibility of 'Green fundamentalism' therefore also remains remote, although it is just possible to imagine how it might appear; and it would be unlikely to prove more benign than any of the other fundamentalisms — religious and secular — that threaten the world.

Secondly, a coherent expression of the new worldview is hindered by those in power, who have — among their multiple pollutings — also contaminated language. Many individuals and groups represented in this book stress the importance of language ('finding', 'inventing', 'rediscovering' a language), in order to revitalise the far from ignoble phrases whose meaning has deserted them with time.

Further, great efforts have been made by the monopolists of power to assimilate or neutralise new social movements. All governments now declare themselves Green, often, it appears, for purposes of camouflage or dissimulation of their purposes. Nowhere is this more treacherous than in the easy use of the word 'sustainable'. It means, of course, sustaining the industrial way of life in its current form. And further, as Anil Agarwal, of the Centre for Science and Environment in New Delhi points out, the existing industrial way of life *is* sustainable for a long time to come: it is simply that it will be paid for by the very lives of the poorest and by untold environmental destruction.

These subversions of meaning have been made easier by the recent reversal of an earlier relativizing of Western values, which occurred during the period of formal decolonization. The reassertion of the unique validity and sagacity of the West, and of the universality of its values, has been given fresh impetus, first of all by the conspicuous 'success' of an economic system which has the capacity to give its privileged people what they want; and secondly, by the collapse of socialism in Eastern Europe. What began as a celebration of the death of tyranny swiftly degenerated into a (perhaps premature) rejoicing over the extinction of alternatives, all alternatives.

This has reinforced the conviction of many that there is now no obstacle to the spread of that form of 'development' that has so benefited the West. This sometimes shows itself in a new-found tenderness for the poor on the part of Western politicians and economists: Who would now be so cruel as to deny the poor of the earth all the advantages which the rich so conspicuously enjoy? Such benign intentions successfully elide the issue of the relationship between the 'success' of the rich world, and the growing subordination to it of the poor, of those whose alternative and *sustainable* ways of answering need have been extinguished in the interests of the promotion everywhere of the industrial monoculture. It is clear that the West's prescriptions not only for Eastern Europe, but also for the South, to follow the same path cannot be realised. The experience of the West is not replicable in those places which are now coming under the amiable tutelage of its financial institutions. One is reminded of Gandhi's question, when he pointed out that it had cost the plunder of the whole planet to furnish Britain with its riches. 'How many planets does the rest of the world have?'

The expressed desire to share with the rest of the world the secret of the West's prodigious capacity for wealth-creation serves another purpose; and that is the maintenance of existing relationships, preserving the privileges of the rich, and the freedoms that attend them, however partial, fragile and provisional these may be. And since it is axiomatic for such politicians that the rich are unlikely voluntarily to surrender their version of the good life, it follows that the poor must go on paying for it, even if with their lives, as indeed they already do. Vandana Shiva, the Indian physicist and ecologist, says 'When colonialism was given the name of *development*, the processes of exploitation became all-pervasive.' Indeed, Anisur Rahman, Bangladeshi critic of development, has traced back the very idea of 'development' and 'development aid' as a Western response designed to forestall the threat of Bolshevik revolution in the Third World. (IFDA dossier, April-June 1991).

Development was exclusively defined as economic development, reducing the degree of progress and maturity in a society to be measured by the level of its production. The attraction of massive external finance and thrilling technology generated client states in the 'underdeveloped' world, where oligarchies able to capture the organs of State could enrich and empower themselves as a class relatively to the wider society, to whom 'development plans' one after the other at the national level, and subsequently, at the global level, were offered as a perpetual hope for prosperity.

If what Anisur Rahman says is true, then in the absence of threats of social revolution in the South following the dissolution of socialism, we should expect to see a decline in developmental rhetoric coming out of the West. And indeed, we are now seeing a more stern and inflexible insistence from Western financial institutions that countries now under their superintendence behave according to fixed and inflexible rules, no matter what violence this may do to their poorest or to their resource base.

Part of the exuberant self-congratulation of the neo-liberal revival in the West (which is, as Mohammed Idris, of the Consumers' Association of Penang says, a form of fundamentalism), comes from a sacralizing of the market economy, sanctifying it as the sole effective way of answering human need. Yet in spite of this triumphalism, there are consolations, in spite of the spectacle of an over-eager reconquest of Eastern Europe, and the didactic conclusion that no space exists between the destructive constraints of socialism and the emancipatory powers of the free market. The fact that so few people foresaw the rapidity of change in Eastern Europe, notwithstanding the considerable deployment of intellectual labour by Western 'experts' in such matters, is a clear indication of the ease with which even the most seemingly impregnable of human institutions can crumble. The response of the West may tell us more about its own insecurities and anxieties than about the obvious failings of its vanquished rival. The reassertion of the West's own universalizing mission may well be an indicator, at one level, of profound self-doubt. Lost without the buttressing presence of an alien, heretical creed, closer critical scrutiny might be turned upon the deficiencies of the West, and the crisis of faith in its own economic, political and social order. Hans Peter Durr, Director of the Heisenberg Institute of Physics at the Max Planck Institute in Munich, has pointed out that the work of change, before change actually occurs, is often long and arduous; but the ground is shifting all the time, even when the task of altering consciousness appears slow and thankless. Yet when a threshold is reached, where change is triggered, often by unforeseen events in an unpredictable way, everyone wonders why it didn't happen long before. However, on the face of it, the global picture is not particularly encouraging. The transfer of resources from South to North — what the 19th century more accurately termed 'tribute' — was in both 1989 and 1990 around \$50 billion. Martin Khor, economist with the Consumers' Association of Penang, believes this to be a considerable underestimate: when we add to this all the wealth that does not pass through the normal financial conduits, such as the effects of the brain drain, adverse terms of trade, capital leakages related to transfer pricing techniques, official and unofficial remittances of the transnationals, the total is probably four or five times that amount. Debt-servicing and low commodity prices force poor countries to export more, which in turn, leads to more intensive and industrialised farming methods, and places pressure upon the lands occupied by subsistence farmers and indigenous peoples. Many countries remain precariously dependent upon a single commodity — Uganda earns 95 per cent of its foreign exchange from coffee, Nigeria 95 per cent from crude petroleum, Guinea 91 per cent from ores and concentrates, Zambia 90 per cent from copper, Angola 88 per cent from crude petroleum, Congo 83 per cent from crude petroleum, Burundi 82 per cent from coffee, Rwanda 81 per cent from coffee, Botswana 78 per cent from diamonds, Gabon 69 per cent from crude petroleum, Chad 69 per cent from cotton and Mauritius 65 per cent from sugar and honey. At the same time, increasing industrial automation means that labour costs are falling in the North, and this is undermining the advantage to the transnationals of investing in countries where cheap labour is available. At the same time, breakthroughs in substitutes for raw materials in the North are likely to weaken the reliance of the rich countries upon basic commodities from the South. For example, the world price of sugar dropped from \$630 per metric ton in 1980 to \$89 in 1985, a reduction to which one company, Coca Cola (until then the world's largest consumer of sugar), contributed significantly by changing from sugar to corn syrup.

The G-7 summits, in Houston in July 1990 and London in July 1991, had major implications for the future of North-South relations. Behind the dispute between the United States and the European Community over farm subsidies, William Brock, former US Trade Representative and now lobbyist on behalf of some of America's top companies, revealed that 'Agriculture is not the issue...Rather it is the lynch-pin to agreement on matters of greater magnitude, like intellectual property rights, services, investments and subsidies.' The real purposes of the industrial countries have been evident in the Uruguay Round negotiations under the General Agreement on Tariffs and Trade (GATT). They want GATT to regulate a far wider range of economic exchanges than merely the trade in goods. Under the banner of 'free trade' (a quite different notion from fair trade), the extension of GATT is intended to give transnational corporations unprecedented rights to invest in Third World industrial and service sectors with minimal conditions, and to permit the to tighten their control further over industrial technology.

At the same time as the G-7 summits, however, alternative summits were held in parallel; an 'Envirosummit' at Houston, and an Alternative Economic Summit in London. The former called for environmental protection to be included as a major component of the Uruguay Round. The GATT negotiations could reverse gains made in the area of the environment, on the grounds that these are barriers to free trade. Governments would find it more difficult to ban the import of food products in the interests of human safety, and be prevented from banning the export of non-renewable resources like tropical hardwoods. The Envirosummit warned that 'free trade' was being promoted at the expense of the environment. In London in 1991, the alternative summit stressed the ideological nature of orthodox economics: this is an accounting system that is extremely selective about what it includes and what it leaves out. It simply omits all costs that might impair its unappealable 'bottom line' — the ruin of the ecology of whole countries, the eviction of people from their habitats, the alteration of land use, the violence and social injustice that accompany the creation of wealth. There is no longer enough room in the world to accommodate the 'externalised' costs of an economics whose fiduciary nature is masked by jargon and pseudo-science.

In August 1990, the South Commission in Caracas published its study of the prospects and problems of the South, the first time such a report has been drawn up by a group from the South itself. In spite of its contradictions — at times, its tone suggested that the South should replicate the developmental model of the North — it directly linked the needs of the poor with popular participation, democracy, freedom of the press and respect for human rights; and called for stronger action against corruption and for decreased arms expenditure. It stressed the need for food security and human resource development. A secretariat for the South should be set up, with a permanent research and back-up facility, as well as a South Bank. It recommended expanded trade between countries of the South, purposeful combined activity by commodity producers in order to secure fairer and more stable markets in the North.

It is clear that much of the work undertaken by alternative groups over the past 20 years ago, issues regarded as peripheral or even eccentric until recently, are coming closer to the centre of mainstream concerns.

In response to this, it is only to be expected that more subtle mechanisms of domination should be elaborated by the North. One of the most effective of these has been in the realm of ideology, in the efforts to universalise social and economic processes as reflections of 'natural laws'. How superior is the logic of economic necessity to the imposition upon recalcitrant human beings of revealed ideologies! By assimilating the workings of the dominant economic system to natural forces, the beneficiaries of its majestic necessities are exculpated from any responsibility for their effects upon the poor. For since they are advantaged solely by 'natural' laws, they cease to be objects of resentment, usurpers of the subsistence of the poor, and are transformed instead into a superior caste, to be both admired and emulated. The hopes which their showy life-styles bear are inscribed in the universal iconography of Western imagery that is flashed relentlessly across the globe.

The 'critique of economic reason', in the phrase used by André Gorz, for the title of his book, is a vital component in the formulation of alternatives. For economic forces are also political alibis; they are, as it were, the secret police of capitalism, whose arbitrary powers designate who will live and who will die. The 40,000 children who die each day in the world from malnutrition and avoidable disease are not casualties of natural scarcity. The constant triage, the silent suffering and extinction of the poorest in sight of global plenty, is determined by the same economic forces: only their remoteness and impersonality seem to absolve those decision-makers in their pyramids of marble and glass from any part in the fate of those whose lives are laid waste in this way.

What the classical economist Schumpeter called 'the pre-analytic vision' of economics omitted any account of environmental costs, as indeed, it was bound to do, at a time when economic endeavour seemed destined to remain insignificant against the perceived vastness of nature's reservoir of resources, and its seemingly inexhaustible capacity for absorbing waste. Recently, environmental 'externalities' have been discovered, and great efforts made to incorporate these into the existing economic paradigm. Whether this can ever be practicable has yet to be seen. But these are far from the only costs eliminated by traditional accounting systems. The costs of industrialization borne by humanity have never been adequately measured either, nor compensated within the industrial system, for they have occurred in a realm where economics is powerless to make good the damage it has inflicted. Monetary rewards for labour (no matter how generous) cannot discharge the duty of wealth-creators to those who are their instruments, and whose energies they command, because such rewards cover only a fraction of the true costs.

Arguments that raged in Britain over whether the early industrial period led to a rise or fall in the standard of living of the people, are echoed today in the experience of industrialization and urbanization in the South. Much of this argument centres upon the monetary gains which accrue to the people who undergo such change. But the real losses are rarely computed. Who can measure the cost to those whose psyche was broken and reassembled in the image of the manufactory in 19th century Britain? Similarly, who has costed the violence to the young woman, daughter of a rice-farmer in Thailand, who migrates to Bangkok or Pattaya to enter the sex industry? We have only to look at the disruption of settled ways of living, the abrupt reworking of the sensibility of country people the world over, the reshaping of the raw human material in the fabrication of city-dwellers, to realise that the social and psychological costs are borne not merely by the heroic survivors but also by those who perish each day, out of range of the crude instruments of economics which register neither their troubled lives nor their silent passing. We might also wonder about the costs involved in the remoulding of the people of the Western world into that sublime apotheosis of humanity indicated by the word 'consumers': the forfeit of function and purpose by a former working class is unlikely to incur no cost, although once again, this will not show up in those crude indicators that throw so little light upon human well-being or happiness.

One of the recurring themes to emerge from discussion with those engaged with practical alternatives is 'the uncanny resemblance between our behaviour towards one another and our behaviour towards the earth', as Wendell Berry wrote (Wendell Berry, *The Unsettling of America: Culture and Agriculture*, Sierra Club Books 1977). What costly inputs and additives the privileged require to maintain their urgent and accelerating passage through time; what irrigations of fantasy, what denatured fertilizing of need! The intensifying exploitation of natural riches for industrial purposes has its analogue in the mining and undermining of human resources. Human beings, too, can be opened up like territories ripe for development, ready for market penetration. Indeed, the language of advertisers and salespeople suggests a continuity of territorial conquest, of a piece with earlier colonizing thrusts, when fresh lands had to be subdued and annexed for the purposes of expansion of a superior power. So it is with the most recent extension of new markets: an 'internal colonization' has taken place; and it is this that makes the work of emancipation far more difficult, as has been recognised by, among others, Erik Dammann, in *The Future in Our Hands* (Pergamon Press, 1972). It is never easy to determine where humanity ends and the workings of social and economic systems begin: one is reminded of those images in the writings of Engels in the early industrial period, when he describes the victims of accidents, operatives caught up by their hair or limbs in the machinery they operated, and whirled round by it until mutilated beyond recognition. So it is that human need has been inextricably caught up in mechanisms, constructed ostensibly to satisfy it, but in which it is radically mangled and mis-shapen, so that we find it hard to distinguish between our need and the necessities of a social and economic system.

PART 1: PROTECTING DIVERSITY

3. BIOTECHNOLOGY AND GENETIC DIVERSITY

CARY FOWLER AND PAT MOONEY, RIGHT LIVELIHOOD AWARD WINNERS 1985. Cary Fowler has published much on the world food crisis and on the erosion of the world's genetic resources. Pat Mooney has spent most of his life on the Canadian prairies and in agricultural development work in Asia, Africa and Latin America. In 1979, he published a report *Seeds of the Earth*; and in 1983, *The Law of the Seed: Another Development and Plant Genetic Resources.* Fowler and Mooney have worked together since 1975. One of their proposals was the establishment of international seedbanks, which was adopted by the UN in 1985. Their book *Shattering: The Diversity of Life in the Age of Biotechnology*, was published in 1989 by the University of Arizona Press. Since 1978, they have worked for the Rural Advancement Fund International (RAFI), a small, non-profit organisation which focuses on the socio-economic impact of new technologies on rural societies. RAFI played a major role in stimulating the creation of the Food and Agricultural Organisation (FAO) Commission and Undertaking on Plant Genetic Resources and the International Fund for Plant Genetic Resources. Since the 1988 publication by RAFI of *The Laws of Life: Another Development and the New Biotechnologies* RAFI is developing a study/action programme dealing with the impact of biotechnology on agriculture; food-processing; basic community health; and the threat of biological warfare.

THERE HAS BEEN at least one more important consequence of the new confidence gained by the West from the decay of the socialist threat. The West can more readily pass off the novelties of its technology as a fresh source of hope to the poor. Like all previous economic miracles — intensified industrial farming methods, high-yielding varieties, wonder fertilizers and omnicidal pesticides — the most recent object of promotion, biotechnology, also promises to deliver people from hunger, want and disease.

One of the cruel ironies of this new technological escape route from the consequences of our own actions is that it is itself, in part, a response to of the damaging technologies of the Green Revolution — the loss of the soil's productive capacity, the forfeit of genetic diversity, the spread of monocultures and the dependency of farmers on increasingly expensive inputs. Those who now advocate the liberating potential of biotechnology claim that it will 'give humanity greater control over nature than anything that went before', thereby revealing the baleful cultural tradition in which it will be deployed, and demonstrating the persistence of the damaging myth of human 'dominion' over the earth and its inhabitants.

The danger from biotechnology is not that it is an act of hubris that threatens to modify creation, but that it will be used in a context where it can only exacerbate existing injustice. What could provide humanity with a real opportunity to relieve suffering is likely to become yet another weapon in the armoury used to oppress the poor, while at the same time, exposing the world to unforeseeable, grievous risks. Pat Mooney, of the Rural Advancement Fund International, says,

> People who believe that we should not interfere with the integrity of creation should not, by their own argument, eat corn (or maize), because this is a human-created crop. It would not have existed in nature without human intervention. In fact, agriculture itself is wholly artificial. Thousands of hectares sown to one variety is artificial to nature . . . Nothing has changed the environment more than agriculture. The smokestacks have done nothing to the world compared to what agriculture has done. But few people find agriculture abhorrent.

At this stage, the biotech companies, and the transnationals that operate in close association with them, are keen to stress only the beneficent outcome of their work, particularly in the areas of medicine and food. After all, they say, laboratory-made human insulin already protects many diabetes sufferers, and interferon is effective against certain cancers. But it is now possible to breed plants and animals for their most desirable characteristics, and in the laboratory, changes can be achieved in a fraction of the time required in the natural setting. Genes can be added to crops to help them resist blight, disease, mildew, insects, nematodes, drought or floods. The implications for productivity are not difficult to see. At the same time, bovine somatropin, a naturally occurring hormone, can now be more cheaply created in the laboratory, and could be used to produce monster cows, capable of 'giving up to 45,000 pounds of milk products a year. Pigs, with the addition of a human hormone, may have their fat content reduced by four-fifths. Microbes have been created that will decompose toxins in water, clean up industrial effluent and devour oil slicks. There is every prospect of creating nitrogen-fixing maize, of yield increases of 500 per cent for oil-palm and cassava, and coconut palms capable of giving 1000 per cent more by means of cloning.

It goes without saying, as Cary Fowler and Pat Mooney point out, that such intensive production could be sustained only through the artifice of extremely high-cost inputs of energy, fertilizer, pesticides, medicated feeds, hormones, antibiotics and capital. Among the more visionary possibilities unlocked by biotechnology is the idea of a 'green cow', one into the cellular structure of which plant chloroplasts have been introduced, so that it may use the energy of the sun directly, without the intermediate process of continuous and costly grazing. Something similar might even be possible for human beings, thereby, at a stroke, solving the problem of world hunger. In the long run, the creation of transgenic species is not technically ruled out: some have spoken of soldiers as ferocious as wolves, or labourers of bovine strength and placidity; (although the projection onto mute beasts of these wholly human characteristics probably renders any such exercise a priori redundant).

Resistance to the abuse of biotechnology has been conspicuously undertaken by Fowler and Mooney and their associates at RAFI. Indeed, they have drawn up a model draft law for countries to regulate the development of biotechnology. (See Development Dialogue, 1988; 1 & 2, publ. Dag Hammarskjold Foundation.)

At this point in its development, biotechnology remains strictly a private enterprise. As long ago as 1980, the United States Supreme Court decided that micro-organisms could be patented under existing law. The Patent and Trademark Office considered 'non-naturally occurring organisms, including animals, to be patentable subject matter'. Creation thus comes close to being regarded as the equivalent of manufactured goods: life can be OWNED. The first genetically altered animal, a mouse, was patented in 1988. It was given the patent number 4736866. In the same year, the Patent Office decided that farmers who buy or breed transgenic livestock must pay royalties to those companies holding the patents. The struggle was carried forward at GATT and the World Intellectual Property Organisation (WIPO) over changes to international conventions that would 'industrialise' biology. The right to ownership by private entities of genetically engineered material is strongly contested. Much of that material is based upon the genetic richness of the South, freely given to the North as part of the human heritage. The modification of crop plants and the resale of them to their countries of origin at high prices demonstrates the tendency of biotechnology to intensify structural injustices, already exacerbated by the Green Revolution.

Pat Mooney traces the debate on patenting.

We've always owned cows and dogs. Life has always, in that sense, been owned. But here, we see the processes of life can be owned, even a human characteristic, just as a plant characteristic can. It began with patenting fruits and flowers in the United States in the 1930s. When people said 'That's patenting life,' the answer was 'No, we're just patenting fruits and flowers, they're just ornamentals, it's not significant. We'd never think of patenting food crops or anything like that.' So the patent law was passed in the 1930s. Then in 1970, the companies came back and said 'We want to patent vegetables and cereals,' and people got upset about that. The answer was 'We're just patenting the plant breeding material, we're not patenting food products: no one's patenting peanut butter, just peanuts.'

By 1978, people were saying, 'Let's patent the end-product of breeding' — the example they gave was cut flowers. 'We'd never patent food.' But now, you can patent food, you can patent peanut butter now. But people still said, 'We don't want to have the patenting of animals, of course, or any higher life-forms.' Then in 1987 they patented the first mouse. It's gone up and up. You now have so many species with human genes in them. No one wants to say that they are patenting human beings. And of course, you cannot define human beings genetically very well. But if you take so many genes and stuff them into so many other things, as we joke in *Development Dialogue*, 'How many genes do you put into a pig before it starts to read the menu?' Ultimately, you'll allow for the patenting of human organs that are genetically created, perhaps livers in a test tube that can be put in stock for liver transplants. That will be very positive, but there'll be a patent on it. After that, the same will happen with other organs. No one's going to patent a human being, but we may well be filled with patents inside us. They'll cure us of genetic diseases, they'll prevent them. Then we'll be paying royalties on ourselves. 'The royalty we!' We'll be licensees of a life industry.

These lessons are not lost on the transnationals. Petrochemical and pharmaceutical companies which made such killings (not all of them metaphorical) through the Green Revolution, with fertilizers and pesticides, clearly felt threatened by the prospect of genetically engineered superstrains that might by-pass their products. This is why, in recent years, they have been buying up seed companies, a process closely monitored by the Rural Advancement Fund International. In 1987, the Imperial Chemical Industries (ICI) became one of the top ten seed producers. Between 1968 and 1988, Shell bought over 60 seed companies, Pioneer Hi-Breed 39, Ciba-Geigy 26. For them, this marks a logical extension of their control over the global food-chain. During the 1980s, Monsanto shifted from capital-intensive to knowledge-intensive activities, moving into 'life sciences' — agriculture, health care and nutrition. The Chairman of Occidental Petroleum stated that, 'Food resources in the nineties will be what energy resources were in the seventies.' As well as the pharmaceutical and agrochemical companies, the major food processors, such as Unilever, Nestlé, Heinz and Philip Morris are also moving into biotechnology, which may prove a crucial background for control of the world's food supplies. Squeezed between them are the poor farmers and consumers. Anwar Fazal, President of the International Organisation of Consumers' Unions, observes:

> Some 40 per cent of the world's manufacturing is based on biological materials. This 40 per cent is bound to be affected by the technology transformation. Whole industries are involved, and millions of human

beings will have to experience the effects. Concomitantly, power structures will be transformed and the rules of the power game changed. We already experience new systems of blackmail and corruption at the global level by governments in order to get their way. Biotechnology is a new, powerful tool on the way to controlling the world.

Simultaneously, the same transnational corporations have been increasingly investing in universities, financing research, and even whole departments. The possibility of commercial invasion of places of learning is often presented as a desirable marriage of 'the real world' with the cloistered seclusion of academic life. Fowler and Mooney fear that over time the integrity of the scientific process could well be threatened by this process.

Pat Mooney has monitored the logic of the growing concentration of power over which the TNCs are struggling.

> You can use plants or livestock as producers of drugs. There is the example of melanin, a human pigment, which can be bred into plants, soybeans or wheat, so that when you harvest the crop, the grain will go to make bread, but from the other part of it — the straw — you extract the melanin; so there are two harvesting purposes, one for food and one for drugs. Another example already in operation is with cow's milk: you take tissue, plasminogen activator, a human hormone, which is inserted into the genum of mice and then cows. It is extracted from the milk in increased quantity. You're using the animal as a bioreactor, to be the factory for your drug. It's very cheap. The pharmaceutical companies say 'We should buy food companies, as well as the pesticide companies, which already have the seed companies.'

> Then you come to the next level of extraction, whereby life becomes a matter of the control of information. DNA is a matter of genetic information, the DNA code is a code for life. Monitoring that information is a computer's task; so at the end of the day you have the drugs companies owned by the informatics companies, the IBMs and Siemens of the world, because it is that manipulation that is crucial. But then the response of the drug companies is that the real winners may be the life insurance companies, because life insurance is seen as a bargain, a bet between a company and an individual as to who knows best how long you're going to live. So the drug companies will propose that at birth the child's cell-line would be taken (a sample of the DNA of the child, which is replicated in each cell), and that would be analysed, and the company would say to the family, 'Well, here are the various dispositions of the child towards certain diseases, and we can breed drugs specifically for that child from the child's own cell-line, ready for when the child comes in danger of contracting these diseases. So we can develop flu vaccines, cold vaccines, from the

child's own cell-line, multiply it in a wheatfield, in a cow, in the belly of an insect, who knows.' So the drug companies are looking at the possibility of buying out the life insurance companies, so they'll have a wide capital base to guarantee the life insurance for the child, because they will know what the bargain is.

This is why you see all the mergers between pesticides and seeds, and between pharmaceuticals, pesticides and seeds, and in the last few years, the food-processing companies. And all the time, the size of the companies gets bigger: the average size of a seed company is less than $100 million in sales; of pesticides, $1 billion — $2 billion. The average pharmaceutical gets you into the range of $4 — $10 billion; and when it comes to food processors, they have between $10 — $20 billion. So the scope is still vast: information, DNA, is just another form of information, can only intensify the mergers.

There are other threats in the development of biotechnology, particularly to the countries of the South. Farmers and their products are more and more threatened with displacement by means of genetically-engineered, laboratory-wrought substitutes. One response to the charge that the rich world exploits the basic commodities of the poor has been the effort to create replacements which will render certain primary products superfluous. Such nature-identical substances can eliminate the livelihoods of millions of small producers. Of course, the development of technology has always and continuously displaces earlier patterns of production and reliance on natural materials; but the scale and intensity of present possibilities scarcely promises to set the poor free. If the 1980s saw falling prices for cash crops push more and more small farmers towards the edge of survival, the coming decades may see the total elimination of whole areas of traditional production.

One of the best known substitutes already on the market is thaumatin, a sweetener, indeed, the sweetest substance known. Derived from a fruit grown in the rainforests of West Africa, it is imported to Britain from Ghana and the Ivory Coast by Tate and Lyle, and marketed as 'talin'. Talin is now being produced in laboratories through recombinant DNA technology. Similarly, factory-made vanilla threatens the income of some 70,000 farmers in Madagascar, which exports three-quarters of the world's vanilla. Clonal production of oil-palms vastly increases productivity, but at the same time, lowers world prices. This jeopardises the living of small producers, who cannot afford the costly inputs, and it enhances the power of plantation owners and those companies which have patented the new strain of oil-palm. The vegetable-oil market is now worth around $35 billion a year. In the same way, the production of artificial cocoa-butter from inferior oils threatens to undermine a major export commodity of cocoa beans from several countries, including Ivory Coast, Ghana, Brazil, Malaysia, Nigeria and Cameroon.

Although the biotech companies insist that their laboratory tests are safe, and that fields tests are rigorously controlled (some even include a 'suicide gene', so that any micro-organisms that escape into the wild automatically self-destruct), it is difficult for governments to legislate, when even the law makers themselves are not always aware of the dangers. The worst possible occurrence would be what Rajni Kothari, publisher of Lokayan in New Delhi, calls an 'ecological holocaust', as a result of the narrowing of the genetic base of the world's crops. Varieties that are part of the common heritage of humanity are being privatised, the property of powerful interests concerned with the promotion of profitable monocultures. Biotechnology may lead to even swifter genetic erosion than occurred through the Green Revolution. (See Vandana Shiva, *The Violence of the Green Revolution*, Third World Network, Penang, Malaysia; and Zed Books Ltd, London.)

Some of the transnationals, far from creating crops that resist disease and pests, are simply modifying them so they become tolerant of their own brands of pesticide and herbicide. Ciba-Geigy markets its own brand of sorghum wrapped in three chemicals, one of which is to protect the seed from its own herbicide. It is, apparently, easier to change the genetic make-up of crops than it is to cause any mutation in the inherited characteristics of the system of commerce.

Public debate of these issues has been stimulated by the Rural Advancement Fund International. Without such work, 'discussion' would be conducted remote from those (all of us!) whose lives are going to be transformed, behind our backs and beyond the reach of democratic control. Those struggling for the preservation of genetic diversity, and for the people's right to control it, are resisting the entry of the ugly neologism 'bio-imperialism' into the language of domination.

The attachment of Fowler and Mooney to diversity is passionate. Indeed, they make explicit the connection between *crop* and *cultural* diversity. The wide varieties of traditional seeds were integrated with human cultures. Festivals and religious ceremonies were based on sowing, flowering and harvesting, embedded in cultures, language, thought and worldview. Fowler says 'We have altered the environment to suit the seed, rather than allow the seeds to develop out of the environment.' He points to the precise policy commitment of the United States, which led to the eager promotion of the Green Revolution, with the consequent loss of diversity. 'Of course, there were humanitarian reasons also, but US Aid Programmes pressured governments in the Third World to use high-yielding plants to produce more food as a means of stopping the spread of Communism. This led to food productivity, increased quantity, but fewer varieties.' How strange, that fostering one form of monoculture should have been considered an appropriate instrument to halt the spread of another!

Fowler sees the removal of more and more human beings from food production for their consumption as the beginning of loss of control over their lives. Certainly, this is borne out by the testimony of peasants and subsistence farmers at the point where they are forced to abandon the growing of food. I remember a meeting with some farmers on the island of Langkawi in Malaysia, whose rice fields had become silted up because of tourist development in the hills above their paddy fields: Pak Long Kassim, a man in his fifties, said, 'When you grow your own food you are free. How is a boy dressed in a uniform behind a hotel counter more free than a man who cultivates his own land? The last harvest a piece of land yields is a pocketful of dollars. After that, nothing. It becomes barren.' This suggests that those who are furthest from the source of their own nourishment, the richest people in the most 'advanced' parts of the world, are, in some ways, the most depowered, the most dependent of all.

Fowler says that the 'promise of biotechnology is that it can increase productivity more dramatically than anything has ever done before. But Third World farmers have been breeding new crop varieties for 12,000 years; Northern scientists work on genetic material for ten years, make a minor modification and are hailed as geniuses. And they 'own' the 'property' thus created. We are proposing a compensation mechanism for the Third World, and a conservation mechanism for genetic material, 'farmers' rights to balance 'plant breeders' rights. A fund has been set up under the auspices of the UN Food and Agricultural Organisation. We want contributions to be made compulsory. The South needs justice, not charity. A recent international conference, sponsored by the Keystone Foundation, was held in India and it endorsed the concept of a mandatory fund of three to five billion dollars a year, to be paid by nations which are recipients of germplasm from the Third World. The genetic diversity of the USA is far smaller than that of many other parts of the world; in spite of this, 85 per cent of all the varieties of apple in the USA have become extinct within a century. And by selling back seeds to the genetically-rich areas of the world, diversity can be wiped out there, too, very swiftly.

We have organised village-level conservation systems and regional international conferences. Both levels of work are needed. We were surprised at how quickly the United Nations structures were set up, and by the fact that some of the people we had been fighting have come round to see the importance of what we say. It may, however, be too little, too late. We have such a short time to gather material before it becomes extinct. And it must be protected *in situ*. Material stored in gene-banks becomes unusable, seeds fail to germinate, the material is spoilt. How can you save old seeds, unless you can find ways to save the old cultures which produced and protected them?

The linking of cultural and natural diversity in this way suggests a quite different relationship between the social and natural order from that which dominates the industrial paradigm. Cary Fowler insists that we are now at the end of the era of chemical agriculture.

The question is, Do we have the resources to reconstruct agriculture in an ecologically and humanly sensitive way? We give plants junk food, bad air, acid rain, and expect them to be healthy. Is it any wonder that cancer is one of the great scourges of the modern world, when what we eat has been abused in this way? We have already narrowed the genetic base of many crops. Indeed, some crops have been rescued from pests that would have destroyed them only by the use of wild genes — tobacco, sugar cane, tomatoes would not be grown commercially today but for the genes of their wild relatives.

The question of crops also impinges upon peace issues. The possibility of biological warfare against crops is a real one — you could destroy the economies of some countries by wiping out a single plant. Simply invade it with pests that will ruin the crop — coffee, bananas, cocoa — in some African or Latin American country, and it would be crippled.

The work of Fowler and Mooney gives new resonance to the words of Hannah Arendt, who wrote in *Between Past and Future*:

Without testament, without tradition — which selects and names, which hands down and preserves, which indicates where the treasures are and what their worth is — there seems to be no willed continuity in time and hence, humanly speaking, neither past nor future, only sempiternal change of the world and the biological cycle of creatures in it.

Even that biological cycle, it seems, can no longer be taken for granted.

MELAKU WOREDE, RIGHT LIVELIHOOD AWARD WINNER 1989. Melaku Worede was born in Ethiopia in 1936, and has spent his life as an agronomist. He obtained a Ph.D. in Agronomy in Nebraska, and returned to Ethiopia, where he became involved in the planning of the Plant Genetic Resources Centre in Addis Ababa, of which he became Director in 1979, a post he still holds. Ethiopia is one of the world's eight 'Vavilov Centres', noted for their great genetic diversity. This diversity is now under threat from drought and modern farming methods. It is this biodiversity that Worede has sought to preserve, and, going beyond this, to establish 'Strategic Seed Reserves' of traditional seeds that can be released to farmers for planting in times of drought, when no other seeds thrive. He regards local farmers as crucial partners in the conservation programme. Melaku Worede is also Vice-Chair of the UN Food and Agricultural Organisation's Commission on Plant Genetic Resources.

RESISTANCE TO THE MALIGN effects of monoculture is also being strengthened in the South. Dr Worede, at the Plant Genetic Resources Centre in Addis Ababa, speaks of retrieving the pride and dignity of Ethiopia, by restoring self-reliance.

It is a pity that Ethiopia should be seen as hopelessly poor, viewed as a basket-case, when in fact, it ought to be a bread-basket. We have a rich biological and cultural heritage which benefits the whole world. Seventy years ago, a scientist called Vavilov was travelling in Ethiopia by mule, and he surveyed or collected mainly cultivated food crops, and he designated Ethiopia as one of the areas of the world of greatest genetic variety. But until recently, we didn't know how to tap these resources. Some of our diversity was stolen from us. But now, we are in a position to safeguard our own interests. Other people saw us sitting on a bag of gold and crying, and they thought, 'These are fools'; so they took what we had, and used it for their own interests. For example, 20 or 25 years ago, scientists came here to explore plant-types, and they took some varieties of sorghum high in lysine, which is deficient in most cereals. The high-lysine gene was the only known source in the world. Our farmers knew a variety of sorghum by a name which in Amharic means 'milk-in-my-cheek'. Farmers in Wollo had recognised its value, and its highly nutritious properties. That gene is now widely used in all sorghum; but we could have used it to improve our own nutrition status. Many people have come here, taken materials which they subsequently work on and patent, and we find ourselves buying back the seeds. With biotechnology, the technique for genetic engineering exists in the countries where the diversity does not exist. They are keen to trap resources, which they then convert into monopolistic products. In our case, given the absence of the technology, the logic is to save and protect our resources first.

We are dealing with three levels of diversity — genes, species and ecosystems, which co-exist in an intricate symbiosis. We must halt extinction, and give priority to saving species, land ecosystems and natural habitats. The immediate question is how to maintain diversity, and at the same time, make progress in agricultural development.

Genetic erosion occurs for a number of reasons: the displacement of native cultivars by introduced new varieties, which are not necessarily adapted to the conditions in which they must grow, and are not very stable; they are superior in yield given high inputs, in terms of fertilizers and pesticides. The second main cause is the destruction of natural gene-pools. The wild relatives are often completely ploughed under, because of plantations, monocultures, or because of deforestation or drought. The most significant issue now is drought. Drought has always been there, but it was very serious in the early eighties; traditionally, farmers would always keep something for security, but what happened during this severe drought was that as food grain came through relief agencies, some farmers were consuming the seed they had conserved for next season's planting. We intervened in time, and prevented this happening, because if they had used the relief-grain for planting, they would have become dependent upon the high inputs which they could not possibly have afforded. Because famine was always here in Ethiopia, by tradition farmers would bury their seed, and disappear from the place struck by famine. Then 3 or 4 years later, some member of the family would return and claim it, and use it for seed again. That was how they saved the germplasm, not only for Ethiopia, but for the world. Those were the original gene-banks. It is not only nature, but our farmers, especially women farmers, who are bankers, born bankers, because they selected the seeds and adapted them to ecological realities.

The West sees our precious and irreplaceable genetic resources as *raw material*. Many breeders, scientists, in the West have never seen the landraces, the folkseeds as the farmers see them. To them, landraces are something you select from, for immediate use, and then throw the rest away like garbage. We need to keep control over our own resources. That is one reason for the establishment of the Plant Genetic Resources Centre. We have had 48,000 accessions of 72 crop varieties in ten years. We were able to mount a nationwide rescue operation since 1985; we have collected extensively, covering all crops in all ecological zones; not only food crops, but medicinal and industrial ones too.

We are now developing our own indigenous capacity. This means that agronomists, experts, breeders, must now take a holistic view, educate themselves by tapping and recording local farmers' knowledge of land, crops and cattle, must appreciate their knowledge and skill, and seek, with them, a point of entry into crop improvements.

The discussions within the FAO Commission on Plant Genetic Resources have led to the campaign for the recognition of the informal innovation systems of indigenous peoples. This concept should be introduced into the appropriate fora, including the World Intellectual Property Organisation, the Union for the Protection of New Plant Varieties, and the GATT negotiations on Trade-Related Intellectual Property Systems. It should be recognised that economically and socially valuable experiments are going on all the time, in unofficial and co-operative systems that are not recognised by existing intellectual property regimes. These were developed to acknowledge the contributions of Western, largely private or corporate processes of formal innovation. Third World farmers have always selected for certain characteristics, taken note of, and conserved mutations in their crops. In effect, they have always been plant breeders. They preserve biological resources *in situ*. This resource-base must be salvaged and enhanced. They are not living museums, but offer resources that can be developed for long-term food security. It is a dynamic process, evolutionary, not the passive storage of genetic material. Western gene-banks depend on finance from big companies. These simply isolate what they need now, and throw the rest away. A lot of potential is lost. If biological resources are protected in their habitat, variations will continue to develop, but the benefits from evolution in the environment may occur only in the remote future. If you simply control resources captured now, they will not represent the potential that exists in nature. You'll have a state of arrested evolution. As well as this, there is a deterioration in material due to handling — a genetic drift, when they are planted outside their natural habitat. There must be balance, the storage of assembled materials for easy access and immediate use, but long-term storage as well. There must be a back-up system which sustains diversity in a dynamic state.

Over time, there has been a damaging simplification of ecosystems in Ethiopia, the removal of forests to plant crops for cash, overuse of grazing land. When natural vegetation is removed, a chain of events is created, degradation and disturbance, the consequences of which cannot be foreseen. Weather changes, droughts and floods may occur. Conflicts arise out of this desertification, the abuse and deterioration of natural resources. Wars and conflicts should be seen as a result, not a cause of these things.

Melaku Worede first became interested in germplasm when a lecturer from Oklahoma visited Addis Ababa to lecture. 'I remember saying to him, "Why don't you give us some of your new varieties, so we can develop our agriculture?" He said, "Drop your bucket right where you are, you have a lot of resources which you should know about. Why do you want our varieties? You have more than we have."'

The relationship between North and South is sometimes inextricably complex. Many from the South have felt themselves and their traditions inferiorised by Northern technology. For alternatives to make their way in the South, these often have to gain approval from the North first, even when the new practice or insight itself originates in the South. Dr Worede was ridiculed when he first initiated on farm conservation programmes; but the idea gained ground with the support of RAFI, and the Unitarian Service Committee of Canada, and is now widely accepted.

Melaku Worede says that in Ethiopia, there is no clear-cut distinction between cities and farms.

> We never dissociate ourselves from farmers. In Addis itself, you will see farms, people growing things ... We are now starting on experiments on farming crops for Ethiopia and the rest of the world in case of climatic change. Drought may make us unable ever to grow certain things again. That is why we must urgently seek out what survives the droughts. We are starting a gene-bank of these things. There is a wild plant that grows on the Somali border, under the driest conditions, less than 200 mm of rain a year. It is called *kaga*, a kind of wild rose, a shrub of semi-desert, eaten by people and by goats and used also as a cosmetic. There are other crops, things people have known where to find in distress times. They go to the mountains and pick them and survive somehow ... But if you destroy the natural environment of such plants, you lose these resources; and your monocultures won't save you. There is food that I remember as a child: we used to dig out certain root plants and eat them, not because we were hungry, but because we enjoyed them. We knew them as famine crops, because our ancestors had used them during the war. Ethiopians have always fought; and the fighters knew where to find the plants they needed. My colleague, Legesse Wolde-Yohannes, and I were born in the same year; and when the Italians were bombing Addis, our parents fled to the same place, the valleys where no tanks could reach, nothing. That was where our parents had come from, and we survived for the first 5 years of our lives there. Although a lot has been forgotten, beyond the mountains not far from the city, you can still find a lot of the resources.

The disruption of traditional patterns of farming by drought, war, famine, 13 years of military Marxist rule, forced villagisation, has led to changes in eating habits within the country. Although *teff*, the staple, is still eaten everywhere, there has been an increase in bread wheat, as opposed to the durum wheat traditionally grown. In the rapidly expanding city of Addis, with its population of refugees from violence, hunger, civil war and environmental devastation, Western-style foods are becoming more conspicuous, especially with the educated young.

I visited Addis Ababa just before the downfall of Mengistu in 1990. The portraits of Marx, Lenin and Engels had been removed from the ceremonial arches of Africa Avenue, and only a few slogans remained on the archaically futuristic buildings of central Addis: only 'Peace, Solidarity and Friendship' still adorned the Hilton Hotel. Behind the monument to the Martyrs of the Revolution, some redundant metal red stars and giant hammers and sickles were rusting in the bushes.

Outside the *kebele* (neighbourhood) headquarters of one of the most wretched suburbs of Addis, the painted slogan still said 'Scientific Socialism is our Principle'. There are 1,300 houses in this kebele, almost 10,000 people. Many of them are recent arrivals in the city; and on every patch of overcrowded space, there are reminders of the rural background, an attempt to grow vegetables, to raise livestock, to keep alive a broken self-reliance. Stony lanes follow the contours of the hills, flanked by houses of nile-green corrugated metal, or wood-frame with mud walls. Prostitutes, some of them only 14- or 15-year-olds, stand in the mid-afternoon sunshine, satin dresses and jewellery incongruous splashes of luxury in the bleak city landscape. They charge 3 *birr* (about $2) for the room they rent, most of which goes to the men who control them. On the side of the roads, it seems, everyone is trying to sell something: bronze and raven-blue hens in wooden cages, cheese on banana leaves, dried chillies, cloves of garlic, purple onions, grain — maize, wheat and teff — in sacks, many of them labelled World Food Programme or Gift of the Government of Canada. The people must be registered with the kebele, in order to receive their subsidised rations — teff can be had for 70c a kilo, sugar for two birr. Many sell a proportion of their entitlement at a profit to those who can market it elsewhere. With the money, they purchase some other commodity which will yield them a profit — vegetables, saffron, pepper or *qat*, the mildly intoxicating leaf that is chewed by the unemployed men on the roadside.

There is more energy in the Mercato — one of the biggest markets in Africa — than anywhere else in the city; a living repudiation of a state control that was already in process of dissolution. Many traditional artefacts are on sale, material that has not been displaced by mass production. There are baskets and vessels of straw and grass, pottery, horn and metal, agricultural implements, wool and cotton fabrics, including the delicate white cotton *shemas*, the prayer shawls worn by both men and women of the Ethiopian Church, to which more than 80 per cent of the people belong. Children of seven and eight years old are working, as shoeshine boys, fare collectors in the shared private taxis; some are selling plastic carrier bags, chewing gum or Indian *agarbatti* (incense) sticks. Men hammer pieces of shapeless metal in small fume-filled workshops, skilfully working a panel of an abandoned car or an iron bedframe into utensils, lamps, tools. One man is cutting barbed wire, taken by night from some military installation; another is straightening rusty nails; a shoe-repairer is mending an incredibly derelict boot. A man sits on a bale of eucalyptus leaves on sale as fuel, embroidering a shirt in an intricate traditional design. Here, the human resources are stretched to their limits. The uneven stones of the streets are shiny with the swirling dust and the bare feet of passers-by. A boy trails the skin of a newly killed goat; from time to time, you come across animal remains — the jawbone of a dog, a dead fowl, some goat-horns. Women are making dishes out of dry cereal stalks that will serve as containers for traditional *injera* (teff pancakes). A rusty can on a stick in the earth indicates a distillery where *tela*, made from sorghum, is on sale. Hens, sheep and goats wander in and out of the compounds. Everywhere the children follow us. Half the two million people of Addis are aged under 20. They call out, the three words of English they know. These are 'Foreign', 'Father' and 'Money.' An old man picks up a rock, and says that if I am Russian, he is going to smash my head. 'Russians have brought nothing but poverty to Ethiopia. *Tebeda*. Fuck off.'

Everywhere, students are anxious to talk with foreigners, now they can do so without fear of being spied on and reported to the authorities. Dawit, an economics student from Gondar, says that neither the villagisation programme nor the kebele system in the cities was designed to help the people, but rather to control them. He points to the children whose clothes are more holes than fabric, the blind women outside St George's Church, the leprosy sufferers extending their stumps towards cream-coloured Landrovers bearing the logos of international charities, which dash between government offices and the Hilton and Ghion hotels. He says:

> If socialism had achieved anything, it would have given security to these people. Instead, it has brought us to ruin. There is nothing like a Marxist regime for raising people's political consciousness, even if only because it lets them know what they do not want. One effect of attaching Ethiopia to the destiny of a dying ideology was to make the young people turn to the West, its culture, its system. University students want to listen to Madonna and George Michael, Michael Jackson, Hank Williams. They grew tired of revolutionary Amharic songs about Development through Co-operation or International Proletarian Solidarity.

Dawit says it was a tragedy that Ethiopia should have become the site of an ideological struggle just at the time when it was losing momentum elsewhere in the world.

> There have always been bitter conflicts between the regions of Ethiopia, but in the past, the people have always united against external threats — as against the Italians in the 1890s. Feudalism and its overthrow by totalitarian Communism have both been disastrous. And now we can expect the West, with its self-interest and false promises, to take over. How shall we ever recover our confidence in ourselves, our capacity for self reliance, our own indigenous answers to violence, hunger and environmental breakdown?

4. REVALIDATING TRADITIONAL KNOWLEDGE

AKLILU LEMMA AND LEGESSE WOLDE-YOHANNES, RIGHT LIVELIHOOD AWARD WINNERS 1989. Bilharzia is a debilitating and eventually fatal disease, affecting more than 200 million people in 74 countries of the South. Existing treatment and prevention of the disease are too expensive for the communities that need them. In 1974, a young Ethiopian doctor, Aklilu Lemma, discovered that suds from the fruit of a common African plant, the endod, or soapberry, which African women had been using for centuries, act as a potent molluscicide. To promote research on this, he set up the Institute of Pathobiology in Addis Ababa University. He was joined in this work by Legesse Wolde-Yohannes in 1974. It has been a long struggle to gain acceptance by the mainstream international medical community for the use of endod. There was resistance from those who disparage research undertaken in the South; from commercial firms unwilling to invest in a product that is widely and freely available to the poorest; and from the World Health Organisation. Since 1976 Dr Aklilu Lemma has worked in the United Nations system, and is currently Deputy Director of UNICEF's International Child Development Centre in Florence. Legesse Wolde-Yohannes works at Ethiopia's Institute of Pathobiology, where he has co-ordinated endod research since 1980.

THE VITAL IMPORTANCE of farmers keeping alive the adaptive ability of plants and crops is allied to the survival of traditional cultures, wisdom and resources. A dramatic and practical example of popular use of plants is endod, or soapberry. No doubt, in the rich and as yet, uncharted biodiversity of Ethiopia, there are others.

When Aklilu Lemma returned to Ethiopia in 1964 after studying at Johns Hopkins University, there were reports of an epidemic of schistosomiasis, or bilharzia, in Northern Ethiopia, around the city of Adwa in Tigre. The then Minister of Health asked Lemma (who had studied lashmaniasis, another disease of the poorest, and therefore also under-researched and under-reported), if he would go with a medical team to investigate the extent and severity of the outbreak.

It was my first assignment. Adwa, you know, has great significance for Ethiopians. It was there, at the battle of Adwa, that the Italians were defeated in 1896. This was the first time that an indigenous African army had ever defeated a highly mechanised foreign invader. The Ethiopians were gracious winners. The Emperor escorted the defeated Italians to the seaport in safety, but he insisted that they should take no particle of

Ethiopian soil with them; accordingly, he made them clean their boots before they embarked, so that they should take away nothing of the country they had invaded. So we went to Adwa, studied the ecology of the region, and made observations on the water-contact of the people.

Bilharzia is caused by a microscopic worm, or schistome, solely transmitted by water snails, which release large numbers of the organism into rivers and irrigation canals. To be infected, one has only to be splashed by the water, since the organisms can bore through the human skin, and take up residence in the bloodstream. There, each pair of male and female worms can live for 20 or 30 years, laying up to 3,000 eggs a day. There are about 200 million sufferers from this disease in the tropics.

The river was the centre of much activity. Coming from the top of the stream, starting from the spring in the rocks, people were washing, children were swimming, women were cleaning clothes. In one area, where clothes were being washed with endod, we noticed more dead snails below the surface than at any other point in the stream. Where conventional soap was being used, there were fewer dead snails.

I went upstream, collected some live snails, put them in a beaker. I asked the washing women to put some suds in the container. In a few minutes, all the snails bubbled up, bled and died. I repeated it; and that led to 25 years of research into the plant, and of struggle for recognition of our findings.

We looked at other parts of the plant, roots, leaves and bark. The berries proved the most effective. We undertook a range of analyses — the active ingredients were concentrated in berries, although they were also present in bark and leaves. We studied the effects on fish and other water creatures. Endod is popularly used not only for washing clothes but also for killing lice and tics on clothes. When we published in World Health Organisation bulletins, we made our mark. The was the first plant molluscicide.

Meanwhile, scientists had come from the United Kingdom in 1966-67, from the Tropical Products Institute. They were interested in collaboration, and offered to carry out chemical work in the UK, while we did the biological work here. They took sacks full of the endod berries. I heard nothing from them, and it wasn't until I went to London that I discovered they had developed an extraction procedure which they had patented, with no reference or acknowledgement to me anywhere. They told me they hadn't wanted to publish until they had patented the method and protected it. I asked why no credit had been given to me. They tried to butter me up, took me to expensive restaurants and hotels. I went to Washington, where the Office of

Naval Research was interested in protecting men who had to wade through water which might well have been infested with bilharzia-bearing snails. They gave me a good grant, and at Stanford Research Institute, they developed an extraction procedure far better than the British one, and this was patented in my name.

Some of the scientists involved with the British process had meanwhile gone to the World Health Organisation. When they got there, they immediately dropped their interest in endod. From being a miracle plant, it was transformed. They said it was poisonous, it kills fish. The World Health Organisation poured cold water on the whole project; and it has taken almost 20 years more to prove its worth, to complete toxicology tests. Only in 1990 was it finally cleared for use in the field.

The most widely used commercial mollusicide, Baylucide, is very expensive, and was found in 1990 to be mutagenic. It seems that the efficacy of people's remedies and knowledge is not recognised until it has been commodified and marketed, often by the transnationals. The active ingredient in endod was identified as saponin, and named by scientists at Stanford Research Institute 'Lemma-toxin'.

Not that we were idle all the years we were waiting. We had two international workshops, one in Zambia, and the other in Swaziland. Ten sub-Saharan African countries have formed a network to import established strains of endod. Brazil, the Philippines, Sudan and Egypt have also shown an interest. Some of the most important work establishing the most effective strains of endod was carried out by a Dutchman, Charles Lugt, in the mid-seventies. He lived like a hermit, collecting 67 different strains from the Highlands and Lowlands. He cross-bred and isolated three strains, known as 23, 17 and 44, which were found to produce the most berries and to be the most hardy.

Legesse Wolde-Yohannes has been working on strains of endod that are resistant to pests and nematodes. He is also working with germplasm at the Plant Resources Centre at Addis Ababa University, on tissue culture and vegetative propagation, to speed up the breeding of resistance to pests, and a higher yield of berries with enhanced molluscidal properties. There is a small plantation in the grounds of the University, where endod bushes are monitored for productivity, resistance and effectiveness of their berries. The three most useful types kill 100 per cent of snails at 7 to 10 parts per million.

Endod was widely used in Ethiopia as a contraceptive before the spread of more recent birth-control techniques. In-vitro experiments showed extracts of berries to be an active biological spermicide. It has also been popularly used against ascaris, tapeworm, skin fungus and ringworm. It is said to be effective against anthrax and black-leg in cattle. Cooked young shoots and leaves are used for food in times of scarcity. The fruits and leaves in water intoxicate fish, and make it easier to catch them. And for centuries, endod has been known to be effective against aquatic leeches.

The spread of schistosomiasis through irrigation canals has been one of the unforeseen costs of development, borne by the poorest. It was monitored through the impact of the Aswan Dam, later in Gezira in Southern Sudan, and in Ethiopia in the Awash Valley, following large-scale irrigation to support sugar-cane, bananas and cotton in the 1970s. It is now a city disease too, because of the large-scale migration of people from the countryside.

Dr Wolde-Yohannes has worked closely with the Ethiopian Industry Ministry, in an effort to develop endod as a commercial detergent. At Stanford Research Institute, tests have been conducted, comparing clothing washed with endod with that washed in commercial detergents produced by Lever and Proctor and Gamble. There are some comparative advantages. In Ethiopia, in spite of the traditional use of endod, many people are tending to turn to commercial soap, partly because the availability of endod berries is seasonal, and partly because the use of soap is seen as more 'modern'. This is a reflection of a worldwide tendency to disgrace the traditional and familiar, and its replacement by industrialised goods and services.

Endod is a symbolic product. Dr Wolde-Yohannes says that there is great resistance on the part of the Western scientific establishment against products from poor countries. He observes,

> The West offers aid for *survival*, but not to *overcome*. After two decades of post-colonial struggle, I believe that the best future course for Africa is to invest in efforts to build the endogenous capabilities of its own people. Self-esteem can be raised by creating a sense of respect for the wisdom and experience of traditional societies, perhaps through the integrated application of old and modern technologies for the alleviation of local problems.

It was discovered within the last two years that endod may also be effective against harmful organisms in the West, for which at present no remedy exists. In the later 1980s, the Great Lakes saw the rapid spread of the zebra mussel, dumped in ballast water, probably in the St Clair River. The population of this mollusc, an inch and a half long, has exploded, and now threatens to be the most damaging biological invader ever seen in the Lakes. In two or three years the zebra mussel has polluted water pipes at municipal and industrial plants, interrupted water supplies, and disturbed the ecosystem in ways that have not yet fully been measured. It seems that, after all, the West may yet have to turn to the Third World for aid in combating this invasion.

5. PROTECTING CULTURAL DIVERSITY

SURVIVAL INTERNATIONAL, RIGHT LIVELIHOOD AWARD WINNER 1989. Survival International was founded in 1969, to help indigenous peoples exercise their right to survival and self-determination; to ensure that the interests of tribal peoples are properly presented in all decisions affecting their future; to secure for tribal peoples the ownership and use of adequate land and other resources and seek recognition of their rights over traditional land.

Tribal peoples number some 200 million, just 4 per cent of the world's population. too often treated as obstacles to progress, objects of study, the exotic showpiece of tourism or potential converts to another religion, they are in fact, members of complex and viable societies, with a sense of purpose, fulfilment and community that many in our 'modern' societies might envy. Through their intimate relationship with their environment, their dependence on its resources and identification with it, they are indeed the best custodians of the natural world. (Survival International publication.)

Survival International has over 8,000 members in 60 countries, and works through projects, campaigns, education and publications. It publishes a quarterly newsletter, books and reports on special themes, and Urgent Action Bulletins, calling on its supporters to act in defence of tribal people against specific threats.

THERE IS A DYNAMIC relationship between the loss of crop, genetic and species diversity in the South and the simultaneous erosion of cultural diversity. The assault on the inhabitants of the rainforests — or of the tundra, the rivers or the plains — is a direct consequence of pressure upon their resource-base.

The ruin of traditional habitats is directly linked to patterns of development that reach into the furthest redoubts of tribal and indigenous peoples. Third World governments, under pressure to service bottomless debts, must turn into cash every resource they can lay hands on, even if this means ravaging the last enclaves of ecosystems on which human communities depend for their survival. In the Philippines, for instance, the original 14 million hectares of virgin forest has now been reduced to around 750,000 hectares; and still this is being felled as an export commodity. The resistance of forest people has led to intensive militarisation of their areas; to human rights abuses and wholesale evictions and displacements.

The justification for such actions is familiar, and is of a piece with earlier colonial thrusts that destroyed the indigenous cultures of Australia and the Americas. It is not that we lack evidence as to the effects on traditional cultures brutally exposed to, and contaminated by powerful outsiders. The diseases that rage among the Yanomami in Brazil are not only physical, even though these are murderous enough; but their resistance is weakened by the abrupt relativisation of their cosmos and their beliefs. They have been wounded by a sudden loss of faith in ways of life that have sustained them for millennia. Many native peoples are dying of grief, at the violent disruption of a habitat that has always been an integral part of their belief system. It is not only that tribal peoples have been dispossessed of commons and forests, and have become malnourished and disoriented, as has occurred with the Penan people of Sarawak; their sustaining vision of the world has also been wiped out, the preservation of which is as basic a human need as food or shelter.

In June 1991, there was a dramatic example of this, when Mount Pinatubo erupted in the Philippines. The slopes of the volcano had been the home of the Aeta people for many hundreds of years. Those who lived on the lower slopes had adapted over the years to the modern world; indeed, many were employed on Clark USAF base. But those who still occupied the higher slopes had withdrawn deeper into the mountain; the spirit of the mountain was Apo Mamalyari, part of the aetiological myth of the habitat that was sacred to them. The destruction of their environment was complete, and they were compelled to move down the slopes of the hill to the evacuation centres set up by the government. Between June and October 1991, more than 500 Aetas died in those camps. Some fell prey to sicknesses to which they had no immunity, others were weakened by unfamiliar food, the charitable diet of sardines; some died of shock.

This was the result of a natural catastrophe. Elsewhere, it is a consequence of economic activity, initiated by outsiders. Of course, the rationalisation of such violence has been modernised since the bolder justifications of an earlier colonial period. Then, the rhetoric was of a mission to bring those who lived in ignorance and darkness into the light of truths vouchsafed to the West alone. In our time, the apologists are seemingly more benign. Now, they argue, no one must be excluded from the benefits of modern industrial society. (Just how totalising an imperative this is, is rarely perceived by those for whom it is an axiomatic truth, an act of faith, in fact.) This melancholy endeavour has been made easier by the reversal of a certain humility that had touched the Western expansionist project earlier this century; ascribable, no doubt, to the formal decolonisation movements, as well as to the work of those liberal anthropologists whose research showed some of the received certitudes of the West in a new relativising light. Thus, Ruth Benedict, in 1934, in *Patterns of Culture*:

> The psychological consequences of this spread of white culture have been out of all proportion to the materialistic. This world-wide cultural diffusion has protected us as man has never been protected before from

having to take seriously the civilizations of other peoples; it has given to our culture a massive universality that we have long ceased to account for historically, and which we read off rather as necessary and inevitable. We interpret our dependence, in our civilization, upon economic competition, as proof that this is the prime motivation that human nature can rely upon, or we read off the behaviour of small children as it is moulded in our civilization and recorded in child clinics, as child psychology or the way in which the young human animal is bound to behave.

The contemporary colonising impulse of the West exhibits itself in the concern of Western leaders and their surrogates and representatives in the South, not to permit any peoples to languish in 'backwardness', 'ignorance' or poverty. Dr Mohathir Mohammed, Prime Minister of Malaysia, declared in 1990, 'We do not intend to turn the Penan into human zoological specimens, to be gawked at by tourists and studied by anthropologists while the rest of the world passes them by.' With this benevolent objective, Sarawak has logged about 270,000 hectares of forest annually in the past decade. About three million hectares have already gone, which leaves perhaps six million hectares of untouched primary forest. The intervention of the Prince of Wales in February 1990 stung the government, not into admission of error but into a vigorous defence of its policy. In fact, Dr Mohammed defended the right of Malaysia to dispose of its forests as it chose. He made the issue one of 'national sovereignty', even though the benefits to Malaysia are likely to be short-term and not repeatable. He pointed out that Britain had destroyed all its own forests, and was, therefore, in no position to dictate to other countries how to dispose of their own. He might have added that Britain's recklessness in this regard had been compensated only by its violent predations upon the forests of its extensive empire: as early as the 1860s, the teak forests of Malabar had been stripped for British naval construction and the Indian railways. The question of where all the other industrialising countries are to turn when their forests have been used up did not arise.

Indeed, the denunciation of conservationism and the advocacy of a more sustainable resource-use as a neo-colonialist conspiracy, designed to prevent the Third World from 'developing', is a very sensitive issue. For this interpretation suggests that the rich world is really seeking to safeguard its own wealth and to prevent a more just distribution of it; and in this there is much truth. The trouble is, that those who declare that the Third World must follow the Western path thereby cast themselves in the role of friends of the poor. Yet, as we have seen, that experience cannot be repeated. Such rhetoric, therefore, serves as concealment for the quite different project of opening up the Third World to Western capital. This means making Third World resources freely available, and permitting the export of all raw materials, including tropical hardwoods. In return, the West can clean up its own environment and, in the name of 'development aid', is free to export dangerous and damaging technologies to the Third World, many of them now banned in the West.

SAHABAT ALAM MALAYSIA — SARAWAK. RIGHT LIVELIHOOD AWARD WINNER 1988. The Sarawak Office of Sahabat Alam Malaysia (SAM, Friends of the Earth) has been involved since 1986 with the Penan people of Sarawak in a struggle against logging in the province. In 1983, this logging was proceeding at a rate of 75 acres per hour, which was destroying the culture and lives of the Pelabit, Kaytan and Penan peoples. The SAM Sarawak Office is run by a 30-year-old Kayan, Harrison Ngau, who has been working with indigenous communities fighting problems caused by logging: pollution, soil erosion, land spoilage, destruction of forest resources. When petitions to government departments brought no help, the Penan people began in 1987 to blockade the logging camps and roads, bringing much of the logging to a halt. In June 1987, SAM Sarawak arranged for a delegation of native leaders to talk with the Malaysian government. Though this proved fruitless, the blockades generated much publicity abroad. In October 1987 Harrison Ngau and dozens of tribal people were arrested and the blockades broken in a police crackdown, but they started again the following year, especially affecting the operations of the Limbang Trading Company, owned by the Minister for Environment and Tourism. Ngau was released after 60 days, but is still bound by a restricted residence order.

SAM REPORTS THAT the intervals between the felling of trees in Sarawak have been shortened, and that the protected *engkabang* tree (illipe nut), which provides an income for the Penan people, is also being cut. The loggers take only the biggest trees, and as these are dragged from the site, they wreck everything else that grows in the vicinity. The protests of the Penan against the loggers, has caused them to be stigmatised as 'criminals', 'anti-government', 'anti-development'. This, too, has a long historical precedent, and is reminiscent of the British colonial authorities in India. When tribal people there resisted attempts to raise revenue from their forests, they were declared to be 'Criminal Tribes'. The Penan have no option but to resist the violent encroachments on to their lands: they simply have no other source of livelihood. Those to whom the government grants lavish logging concessions have no conception of the function of the forests in the life of the people. Rivers have been polluted; rattan, which provided material for handicrafts, is no longer available; fruits, herbs and medicines that supplemented diet and helped the self-provisioning of the people, have been swept away; and the resting-places of their dead have been disturbed by bulldozers. Friends of the Earth Malaysia has been supporting groups of indigenous people in the Sarawak High Court over their claims to native land. The verdict is expected to set a precedent; although in 1987 the Deputy Prime Minister had assured them that the government recognised the continuing rights of the native people. Indeed, many countries have passed legislation protecting the rights of indigenous peoples; it is simply that these are constantly overridden by the higher laws of economic necessity. In Sarawak, the constitutionality of logging concessions is also being contested. Politicians have, for many years, been giving away tracts of land, up to 50,000 hectares, to family and friends, with no public questioning of their actions.

Survival International is clear on the issue: it is not a question of preserving only the forests, but a whole ecosystem, of which human beings are an integral part. 'To talk of bringing them into the mainstream', a member of Friends of the Earth Malaysia says, 'means driving them into city slums. It means addiction to alcohol, it means loss of purpose and meaning. It is not that there is something romantic or picturesque about the jungle; it is a question of whether people are to live or die.' This also confronts the West with its much proclaimed belief in diversity, pluralism and choice. For if these things have any meaning, that must include the right of people not to enter the industrial way of life. And if they are prevented from pursuing their chosen culture — even if the agent of that prevention is economic necessity, rather than more conventional forms of brute force — then they are unfree. One of the effects of the universal acclamation of the market economy as the only admissible means of answering human need, has been to sanction the baleful consequences of its workings upon those peoples considered 'marginal' or 'backward' or 'primitive'. Economics is now the vehicle of diffusion of Western universalism.

It is an epic irony that, at the very moment when some people in the industrial world have come to acknowledge the importance of *sustainability* in its profligate economic system, these living examples of secular, sustainable practice should find themselves everywhere on the verge of extinction. As yet, there has been little sign of diminished demand for those resources which indigenous peoples have husbanded and harvested with such care, and which are still being wrested from them to feed a global industrial system with raw materials.

Many of those looking for an alternative to wasteful forms of industrialism have spoken of the need to learn from indigenous peoples. This has been interpreted by apologists of the existing order as a desire 'to turn back the clock', as a symptom of nostalgia, an attempt to reverse the march of material progress. There are two separate, but linked, issues here. One is the right of those people who choose to retain a life of harmonious integration with nature to do so. The second is, what, if anything, can the industrial world learn from the life-ways of tribal and forest peoples? It is not a question of compelling the rest of humanity to live in forests, to 'return' to some other version of 'unspoilt' or 'simple' ways of life, for that would also involve violent imposition of yet another ideology upon reluctant humanity. But there are certain principles, among them, respect for the natural world, the use of material resources more sparingly and in a more imaginative combination with our human resources, an awareness of the intractable finiteness of creation, which might be a source of precious and sober instruction to the North, a subject for fruitful reflection and inspiration.

How the Western way of life might be enhanced and liberated by some of these insights ought to be the focus of urgent and passionate discussion. Such discussions are taking place, but only at the margins. What we hear is, for the most part, a caricature of what the indigenous peoples want to say to us. Their voices are easily drowned in the reassurances of Western politicians who tell us what we want to hear — that we can have it all, more growth with environmental protection, and that the whole world can effortlessly have the same.

Renewed pressure on the resource base of tribal peoples has been exacerbated by debt: this creates a need for countries to export more, to cultivate more land more intensively, to realise immediate pecuniary gain. In the Philippines, for instance, in 1990, 44 per cent of the budget was set aside for debt-servicing. In the same year, Survival International reported widespread killing of the Lumad people on Mindanao by the private armies of logging companies. Ever since the arrival of the Spaniards, the Lumad have been pushed out of their ancestral lands. In North-East Mindanao, Lumad land was leased by the government to the Nasipit Lumber Company; and the military have joined forces with the loggers and developers, under pretext of 'counter-insurgency operations'. Governments often invoke a struggle against 'subversives', 'Leftists' or 'terrorists' when they want to seize lands or resources from their traditional owners. This effectively obscures the issues, and opens the way to more human rights abuses. Indeed, in the Philippines, much 'development' seems to take place at gunpoint — perhaps the most dramatic negation of what development means.

Third World governments are themselves in the grip of an international finance system from which there is no escape. It is, for them, a natural step to turn this politics of despair against the weakest, who are, of course, the most ill-defended sections of their own people. In the Philippines the anti-Communist rhetoric of the Marcos years was so virulent that it has continued to colour the vision of the regime's successors, with the result that even modest reformers are readily branded extremists and outlaws. In any case, and not only in the Philippines, what is often hailed as 'the return to democracy', turns out to be simply a restoration of the old oligarchy, who can scarcely be expected to translate their professions of sympathy for the marginal and the poor into action that might diminish their own wealth. There is a living connection between the efforts of countries to honour their debts to a dishonourable economic system, and the violation of human rights to which those efforts give rise.

In Brazil, Jorge Terena was employed in the office of Jose Lutzenberger, former Minister of the Environment, in March 1992. From the Terena tribe, he represents the Alliance of Forest People, which consists of the Union of National Indians with the National Council of Rubbertappers.

> Indians, tappers and river-dwellers have ancient ties with the environment. Spirits dwell in forests and rivers, and when these are destroyed, it is a destruction of the sacred. The equivalent would be if we were to come and lay waste the Vatican and St Peter's in Rome. We'd be jailed and calumniated. But that is what has happened to us, and no one in the West recognises it. Our sanctuaries have been trampled. One old shaman said to me he could no longer dream, and could therefore no longer guide his people, because the animals had fled and the spirits departed from the damaged landscape.

Jorge Terena's work is concerned not only with the recovery of the degraded ecosystems, but also with the recuperation of broken ways of living. Two years ago, the Jaburu project was set up in the *cerrado*. This is the Brazilian savannah, a landscape widely regarded as expendable, because it lacks the immediate appeal and dramatic appearance of the rainforests. Yet a day spent in the company of Jose Lutzenberger in the cerrado would soon convince anyone of the delicacy and wonder of the ecosystem: the variety of grasses bleached by the desiccating wind, the trees twisted into irregular shapes, where their branches have been scorched by fire, and have simply grown at right angles to the burn; the brilliant gems of gold and blue wildflowers shining in the dryness, the presence of marsh plants that tell of water running just below the surface, even in the driest season. The highest point in the landscape is marsh: a spring and coarse grass, where water forces itself up on to a small plateau, a reddish mound with even a few insect-eating plants at its rim; a wild, enchanting terrain, which was occupied by native people even within living memory. Out of this landscape, Brazil's new capital was constructed in the 1960s — a place far more arid and desolate than the austere beauty of the cerrado.

The Jaburu project aims to study the plants and animals that lived here, to reintroduce them, and to restore the livelihoods of the Shavante people, whose home was in the cerrado at Pimentel Barabosa. Two other degraded environments are also being restored, one in the pre-Amazon, belonging to the Suruni people, and the third in the Amazon itself.

At the Indian Research Centre at Goias, linked with the Catholic University of Goiana, students are studying biology and technical skills alongside the indigenous people, and experimenting with the plants and animals required to revitalise the ecosystem. Some are studying law, in order to defend the rights of native people in the courts.

FUNAI (the government agency which is supposed to safeguard the rights of indigenous people) was actually accessory to the destruction of the Shavante and others, especially during the time of military rule. FUNAI suborned the leaders, gave money to some and not to others, in order to divide the community. The people became dependent on money. My own community lost everything, except our language. Men now leave the villages for three or four months each year, to work on the sugar plantations. They become cheap labour for farmers. That has been the fate of ancient cultures and civilizations that lived at one with the forest. When they come to depend on money for survival, they no longer plant rice, manioc or corn in the village. They rely on the store to buy the *farinha*, which they no longer grind from their own manioc.

The health of the Yanomami is now critical. Over the last three years, more than 1,750 have died. Slaves originally brought malaria and yellow fever to Brazil, but malaria was unknown in Yanomami areas until the miners came. Even where the government has blown up airstrips, which is what they have done to discourage the prospectors and miners, these can quickly be rebuilt, or the *garimpeiros* (prospectors) simply take off elsewhere. The Yanomami are also suffering from anaemia, malnutrition, respiratory and skin infections and TB. There are now only around 7,500 in Brazil, though more remain in Venezuela. In 1989, the government tried to carve up Yanomami territory into 19 separate enclaves. This would have reduced their area by two-thirds. It is now accepted that they need contiguous territory. The road that cut through their land came in 1973, and since 1980, there has been continuous conflict between the Yanomami and miners searching for gold and casserite. In the gold rush of 1987-90, 45,000 miners invaded their territory.

There are now only 250,000 Indians in Brazil. In 1900, there were five million, 3.7 million of those in the Amazon. There were 900 nations then, some of them very small; 176 languages remain. Government must not only demarcate land, but also assure security. The constitution of Brazil states that Indians have exclusive rights to the soil in their areas. But the government has given land titles to individuals among them, and it then becomes private property. The Terena people did not know the meaning of individual ownership. Government says that we ask for too much land: but to sustain harvesting and hunting, wide areas are necessary. This is still not always understood. If people are enclosed within too small a space, they will damage their own environment. Then the government will say that they themselves are the cause of the damage, even though those same people have been protectors of that environment for thousands of years. What happens is that government demarcates the immediate surroundings of the Indian village as Indian land, but that confines them, denies them access to the space they need. Between these small zones, corridors remain, called 'national forest', which are open to exploitation for economic purposes. Yanomami territory was easily invaded in this way, and the Yanomami trapped. Now they are outnumbered by miners. The miners themselves are small, desperate individuals, working for Alcoa, BP, the Western Mining Corporation of Australia; they do the dirty work for the big corporations. I want to say to the government, 'You should do what the United States did to its Indians — shoot them. What you are doing is genocide, but an agonising genocide.' In the colonial period, they took Indians as slaves. They became sad and depressed in captivity, started to drink alcohol. Some killed themselves. When President Collor announced his economic plan, he confiscated the people's money. Money is to the mainstream what the forest is to Indians — the element which they see as indispensable for their survival. Now people all over Brazil are depressed; the consumption of drugs and alcohol has gone up; maybe people in São Paulo are killing themselves because they have lost their life-support system, just as the Indians have.

Development for Indians is death. In order to protect the Western system, human sacrifices are made. Which is the more irrational, superstitious? How can such spiritual blindness be called civilized? Once you destroy the spirit of the environment, people go wandering in search of that spirit; the psyche is messed up, the spiritual part of human beings ruined. People then start to question their own self-worth. The West believes only in body and soul, they don't understand the importance of cherishing the spirit. In the village where I grew up, there was no prison, no child-care provision, no home for the elderly. When I first went to São Paulo, I was looking at lost people, kids on the streets, beggars, the desperation for money. You could see what these people had lost, and it was frightening, because they didn't know what it was. Victims of development. That is why the relearning of the traditional ways is a matter of survival, not only for the people themselves, but also so that the rich and powerful may become wise and recognise the errors they have made.

EVARISTO NUGKUAG IKANAN, RIGHT LIVELIHOOD AWARD WINNER 1986. Evaristo is a Peruvian Indian leader, who has dedicated his life to organising indigenous people in the Amazon Basin to secure their human, civil, economic and political rights. In 1977 he was one of the founders of the Aguaruna and Huambia Council, which, with its comprehensive development programme, became one of most successful indigenous organisations in Peru. In 1981, he helped set up, and became President of the Inter-Indian Association of the Peruvian Rainforest, which brought together 13 jungle groups, representing half the 220,000 rainforest Indians of Peru. In 1984 AIDESEP hosted a meeting in Lima, which brought together Indian leaders from Colombia and Ecuador as well as Peru, and the Coordinadora, the co-ordinating body for the Indians of the Amazon basin, was formed. This group now has representatives from Colombia, Brazil, Peru, Ecuador and Bolivia.

THERE ARE NOW only 5,000 Huitoto people from whom I come. Our land is beautiful; small streams run through the hills down to the big river. Our forefathers lived in the upper reaches of the hills; and they were able to shout to one another from one hill to the next. On the margins of the rivers, we cultivate plantain, maize and rice, manioc in the higher areas. We always build our houses near a spring. We live on large expanses of land, so there will be sufficient space for animals and birds to live without being disturbed by human presence. When our fathers wanted to hunt, they could go freely into the forest and find the animals. And certain fish came up the rivers at different seasons. Particular parts of the rivers were divided up for particular families. Our fathers managed this extensive system, between the forest and the river. Now the area is being reduced. We have been invaded in the Amazon for centuries, from the conquistadores, missionaries, rubber merchants, commercial oil and gold prospectors and tourists. All came to take something from us. The lands of the Amazon are not a fertile paradise. We live in an environment that has retained its ecological balance only because we have applied our knowledge so as not to destroy the land. Only two percent of the land of the Amazon is suitable for agriculture. Governments have abused the rainforest as a means of avoiding agrarian reform.

The government wants the people to settle, so that we no longer have room to fish and hunt independently. This is why we have organised — to demand rights over the land we have traditionally occupied. Once the people are all concentrated into one place, they say all the rest is state land; and then they negotiate to divide this between cattle and timber companies. Once the land has been given to a colonist, it is difficult to recuperate it. The extent of colonisation depends on the strength of the indigenous community and its power to resist. If they are passive, obedient, because they've been dominated by religion, they let the colonists come in; and they suffer, because they are going to get their reward in heaven. There are other indigenous people who want to keep their own beliefs, and these are the people who have maintained their customs and defended their territory.

The Aguaruna are strong resisters. We are historically warriors. We were never 'discovered', and never beaten. American evangelical missionaries and also Jesuits came, and they fought each other as to who would gain more souls. When we saw this, we rejected both of them. We don't want anyone to fight for our souls apart from ourselves. This struggle went on from the mid-fifties to the seventies. There are still Jesuit missions, but we have told them they may not speak in the name of the Indian people, nor about the problems of the Indians.

The government of Peru had forgotten that we exist. They have been reminded of it now, because we are making our voice heard. We tell them that they must recognise us and respect our existence.

Each Indian people has its own beliefs, culture, language and religion. We, the Aguaruna, believe in hero figures, whose strength gives us spiritual vision. What the hero figure was is transmitted through us to the future. There are birds such as condors, animals such as jaguars, which are very strong: they also give vision to people when they consume certain plants. We don't believe that people die from illness. We die in struggle or in old age. When a young Aguaruna dies, we believe someone has harmed him or her, and we investigate it. We do not believe that a young person can just die from an illness. We believe that after death, there is another place where we live. It is not heaven, but it is another place. Our religion, which existed before there was a New or Old Testament, gave us discipline and meaning. The Bible talks of ten commandments, but we have many more. Although Christians have it all written down, they are constantly committing great sins. A priest comes here to win souls and to control a parish. We see he acquires cattle or business interests in wood, and to us he is not a parish priest, he becomes simply a cattle rancher. This is why we do not believe in their religion.

We had to organise. We had seen so much damage and so many failures to resist the greed of merchants, entrepreneurs, gold prospectors. Our fathers didn't know how to discuss with white people, how to deal with them because they had not been to their schools and didn't understand Spanish. So when they came from the forests with their products, they were stolen from right in front of their eyes, because they didn't know how to count or read scales. After some years, we children who had been to school, saw the suffering of our parents; we saw them captured, imprisoned and tortured because they didn't speak Spanish. They were called incapable, animals. If they died, it didn't matter, it didn't mean anything. There was no justice. The soldiers violated our women. So the young people who had been to school saw all this, and we realised that one day we would have to face up to it. We learned to read and write Spanish, because we had no kind of help. We succeeded. This was our decision and our desire. So when we came back from school, we discussed with our fathers how we could face these problems; and one way of doing it was to organise ourselves communally. We spent six months going to different communities, talking to people. Then we called a general assembly to discuss everything, a whole week long. That is how the Aguaruna and Huambia Council was formed. Nobody came to tell us how to do it, it was our own initiative. And this has spread to other Indians, because they have the same troubles.

The Aguaruna and Huambia culture is a living one; only the weakening of ethnic power has impeded its development. Once the bonds of dependency are broken, the culture will recover its vitality. It is a long process. Our original tribal identity became defined as 'Indian' with the coming of colonialism, and later, as 'peasant' with the coming of the market economy.

Many leaders have died defending their land, because some governments consider that Indians who have a political or educated background are subversives, and they can seek them out and kill them. But leaders who really believe in their people don't have fear. If that is our destiny, if we die defending the majority, if we have done this for our brothers, then we can die well. And it is not ourselves who will say what we have done, but history.

WANGARI MAATHAI AND THE GREEN BELT MOVEMENT OF KENYA, RIGHT LIVELIHOOD AWARD WINNER 1984. Professor Wangari Maathai was born in Kenya, and trained in veterinary anatomy. She became Associate Professor of Anatomy at Nairobi University in 1977. She has also long been active in the National Council of Women of Kenya, of which she has been Chair since 1980, and it was in the National Council of Women that the idea of the Green Belt Movement, a broad-based, grassroots, tree-planting activity, was born. Its first trees were planted on June 5th, World Environment Day, 1977. By the mid-1980s, Maathai estimated that it had around 600 nurseries, involving income for 2,000-3,000 women; had planted about 2,000 green belts of at least 1,000 trees each; and had assisted some 15,000 farmers to plant private green belts. Later, Maathai spread the successful Kenyan experience to twelve other African countries.

THE GREEN BELT MOVEMENT has also been rediscovering the value of forms of farming and forest maintenance that were in use long before European farming practice displaced them. Sixty per cent of the land of Kenya is degraded, and when the movement began, forest cover had been reduced to 2.5 per cent of the land area. With an annual population growth rate of 3.8 per cent, the woodfuel crisis that has been growing since independence was exacerbated by industrial users of wood — the tobacco, tea and sugar industries, saw mills and paper-pulp mills. Agricultural production dropped in areas where firewood was no longer available, because cow dung and organic residues which had previously been applied to crops as fertilizer, were used instead for fuel.

A large proportion of Kenya's foreign exchange goes to pay for the country's energy needs, but not for the energy needs of the poor, who have no alternative to bio-energy. With a lack of woodfuel, women must alter the eating habits of their families, using tea, bread, rice, maizemeal, which are refined carbohydrates. The disruption of balanced feeding patterns soon leads to malnutrition. Kwashiorkor becomes more visible among children, with the characteristic distended stomach, listlessness and reddish discoloration of the hair. Women must produce food from the impoverished soil of the *shamba* garden, and expend more and more of their own energy in lengthening journeys in search of fuel.

In this context, the Green Belt Movement has gained a high level of community participation, for it is clearly identified with survival. This calls forth a powerful response from women. What is more, Wangari Maathai demonstrates that older traditions can be reanimated, without this becoming yet another expensive input enterprise. For traditional knowledge is perhaps the next area of common human resources most likely to be taken over by the enclosers of many other resources, and sold back to the people as commodity. Already the transnationals employ 'ethnobotanists', seeking out traditional medicines and remedies, with a view to synthesising the active ingredients and patenting them as private property. We can foresee the self-defeating circularity of a value added commodification of wisdom and knowledge that has always existed, but which have to be forgotten first, in order to be 'rediscovered', and to make their triumphal entry into the market place.

The Green Belt Movement shows that this need not happen. Quite the reverse. Forest techniques are not the sole prerogative of experts, but are embodied in the popular practice of women. Green Belt is a truly mass movement. Before plantings, the promoters talk to the communities about the problems of desertification, they listen to suggestions and consult with the people about local issues. There is a follow-up afterwards by nursery attendants and Green Belt rangers, many of whom are poor and handicapped, and this provides them with employment which would otherwise be unavailable. Indigenous trees are used, not pines or eucalyptus, nor other exotic species likely to lend themselves to being turned into woodcarvings for tourists. Before planting trees, the commitment of the Green Belt Movement is recited:

> Being aware that Kenya is threatened by the expansion of desert-like conditions, that desertification comes as a result of misuse of land by indiscriminate cutting down of trees, bush-clearing and consequent soil-erosion by the elements, and that these actions result in drought, malnutrition, famine and death, WE RESOLVE to save our land by averting this same desertification by tree planting, wherever possible.

'In pronouncing these words,' says Wangari Maathai, 'we each make a personal commitment to our country, to save it from actions and elements which would deprive present and future generations from reaping the bounty which is the birthright and property of us all.'

The capacity to care beyond the answering of immediate needs involves a powerful spiritual content in the work. The creative capacities of women are drawn upon at low monetary cost, and with synergic effects. Green Belt offers both short- and long-term benefits: it recreates readily available sources of energy, and nutrition for both humans and livestock. It restores damaged environments, conserves soil, encourages rational land use and provides work. At the same time, tree nurseries and afforestation programmes offer the chance of more employment in rural areas, and help arrest the increase in urbanisation and the spread of city slums.

Wangari Maathai, as a prominent member of the Opposition in Kenya, has been repeatedly harassed, and in 1991 he was beaten and arrested. Many of those people working at the limit of what is tolerable to those in power, find themselves marginalised and persecuted. Others, however, have been sought out by authority, brought into government, as advisers or even ministers, sometimes to be brusquely ejected, when governments change or the implications of their work becomes intolerable to ruling and governing élites.

6. PERMACULTURE: BUILDING ON WHAT WE HAVE

BILL MOLLISON, RIGHT LIVELIHOOD AWARD WINNER 1981. Bill Mollison is the originator of permaculture, an integrated system of design, encompassing not only agriculture, horticulture, architecture and ecology, but also money management, land access strategies and legal systems for businesses and communities. The aim is to create systems that provide for their own needs, do not pollute and are sustainable. Conservation of soil, water and energy are central issues to permaculture, as are stability and diversity. Mollison's two early books, *Permaculture One: A Perennial Agriculture for Human Settlements* (Transworld Publishers 1978), and *Permaculture Two: Practical Design for Town and Country in Permanent Agriculture* (Tagari Publications, 1979), have sold over 100,000 copies. His new book, *Permaculture: A Designer's Handbook*, is available from the Permaculture Institute. The main focus of the Permaculture Institute is education. Since its inception in 1978, its certificated design courses have attracted more than 2,000 people, most of whom are now active in the practice or education of permaculture around the world. Other initiatives of the Institute include the formation of an Earthbank Society, which holds seminars on ethical investment and publishes on alternative economic and financial strategies.

TRADITIONAL CULTURES ARE not recuperable everywhere. And the survival of the growing global population could scarcely be guaranteed by even the most socially just distribution of resources, any more than it can, in the long run, by the present abuse of them. To wait for the regeneration of all the degraded ecosystems in the world would lead only to forms of Malthusianism which are already awakening in the minds of those who see the poor as expendable, rather than as vast reservoirs of popular creativity and resourcefulness.

The people of the growing cities must be fed, and by a decreasing number of people involved in agriculture; and while the possibilities of using urban land for food have not been adequately explored, there is at present an uneasy equilibrium between the unsustainable city, and increasingly unsustainable forms of food production.

Where sustainable farming practice cannot be resuscitated from within the living memory of its practitioners — as is the case in the West and in some profoundly colonised parts of the world — hope comes from an alliance of traditional knowledge and the 'design' of ecosystems; that is, a self-conscious restoration of what has been lost, by means of carefully crafted reconstruction guided by the same underlying principles that inspired traditional practice. Bill Mollison's permaculture is securely anchored in such practice, and is assisted by what he calls 'protracted thoughtful observation rather than thoughtless labour', looking at plants and animals in all their functions, rather than seeing any of them as a single product system. Of the difference between an Aboriginal and a ploughman, he says the latter 'would cut open his mother's breast to obtain milk, while the former takes only what is freely given, and with due reverence'.

Where older patterns of survival remain, as in the tropical forests, Mollison insists that these must be protected and enhanced. In the West, of course, the loss of such patterns occurred long ago. Where even the *memory* of such ways of living have been expunged, a judicious blend of art with nature can create a benign, rather than an exploitative symbiosis.

> Stabilisation and utilisation of the landscape is a moral issue, with global implications. The sight of poverty-stricken nomads following huge goat flocks is an end game in the environmental management strategy, as is a row of harvesting machines, a rabbiter with a pack of mongrel dogs and giant logging trucks. All are variations on the theme of biological extinction.
>
> It is our firm belief that if one cannot maintain or improve a system, one should leave it alone, thus minimising damage and preserving complexity. If we do not regulate our numbers and our appetites and the areas we occupy, nature will do so for us, by famine, erosion, poverty and disease. What we call political and economic systems stand or fall by our ability to preserve the natural environment. Closer regulation of available land, plus very cautious use of natural systems is our only sustainable future strategy. Perhaps we should control only those areas we can maintain, establish and harvest by small technologies, as a form of government upon ourselves and our appetites. This predicates that all human settlements should include total food provision, or else we risk the double jeopardy of sterile city and delinquent landscape, a fatal combination, where city, forest and farm alike are all neglected and lack even the basic resources for self-reliance.

There is a spare poetry in Mollison's insights. 'After poverty', he says, 'follows extinction, then desert, then salt and silence.' He offers a living demonstration that soils requiring a century to evolve under forest, can be recreated by humanity in just a few years. Some of his prescriptions are as startling as they are original. He advises suburban dwellers to shift their lawns onto their roofs for effective insulation, and to dig up their ornamental flowers to grow food. He recommends a clear fibre-glass pond or shallow aquarium as the best skylight in a house; and suggests houses with earth-walls, while trees or plants should be an integral part of the structure. This, of course, is common practice all over the South.

Mollison shows how desert ecosystems can be revived by modifying the microclimate in the immediate vicinity of each dwelling. Where Aboriginal practices have not been completely wiped out, ecologists and ethnobotanists should recover the information that lives on in the mind of older desert people — the use of plants for medicine and food, even though some 60 per cent of Aboriginal wild food plants are now extinct, and many others threatened. Mollison speaks of 'barefoot gardeners', an idea to go alongside a growing army of unshod professionals, among them doctors, economists, architects and planners.

Mollison is one of the rare Westerners to have grown up in a remote rural community, where life was governed by conditions not far removed from those that shape indigenous societies. In his native Tasmanian village, he learned the rich system of relationships between living things. It was a place as close as possible to self-reliance in the rich world.

We made our own boots, we had our own metal-works. We caught fish, grew food, made bread. Everybody had several jobs. I was lucky not to have had much formal education. I remember going to sea when I was four. I was tied to a strong post with rope, and I had a barracuda line in my hand. I could get a barracuda up to the rail, but I couldn't lift it on board. That was better than school. My father died when I was 14. I worked in his bakehouse for a couple of years, then at 16, I went off to sea, and stayed there till I was 28. In Tasmania, the winters are so severe that we generally lay up from mid-June. Then I always went to the high country, snaring, taking skins. Nine or ten thousand skins a winter, wallabies, kangaroos, possums. They were sold to the Russians. But you get sick of killing things. I made so much money. I never paid tax, I had no dealings with authority. The skin-buyers exchanged for cash. The money was left under a rock somewhere, and we left the skins hanging in a bundle from a tree. Nobody could say they'd seen the other person.

Then I was Field Officer with the Commonwealth Scientific and Industrial Research Organisation. You have to grow up in the bush to be able to stand it for any length of time. After six months on your own, you begin to disappear as an individual, you lose all sense of being human. When you come to a stream, you bend down to drink and see something in the water. You say 'What's that?' Then you realise, dimly, that it's a human being, and only after a little while do you realise it's you. Your sense of self disappears, you can't differentiate between yourself and a tree or the wind or the rocks; you become totally integrated into the natural world. It feels like a dream, neither good nor bad.

My job was specifically the behaviour of populations of animals in response to certain stress situations that we, to some extent, manipulated. The idea was to see what behaviour was produced by stress. There are thresholds of behaviours in rabbits and rodents, in which they run as a mass. It's called rabbit runs. It is a stress behaviour and it occurs when the population reaches a certain density. It is the same with human beings. There are definite thresholds of onsets and disappearances of behaviour . . . It may disseminate rabbits over thousands of miles, where they will pile up against fences, fill up streams, run across the bodies of others . . . It was a small step to move from that to the study of human societies. Right from the 1950s, I'd noticed that parts of the ecosystem I lived in were disappearing. Forests were being cleared and wood-chipped; scallop beds that had been fished for 200 years disappeared: dredgers ploughed them up and turned the whole seabed anaerobic. Whole beds of seaweed vanished after pollution spills.

People know what is happening, but they have to deny it. Mercury from the Hobart zinc works was contaminating fish. We chased the spillage from the zinc works, and we found all this mercury in sediments and in fish. We called a press conference. The university disavowed us and withdrew all research funding and support. The press attacked us, and all the fishermen and their wives attacked us, because what we had said meant the fish couldn't be sold because of the level of mercury it contained. The fishermen's wives went on TV and sat down and ate large dinners of fish to prove it was all right. We pondered on this, and we wondered how we could help people from rushing upon their own death. The answer is, You can't. They will shoot you rather than not rush upon their own death. This is because 'livelihood' — money — is seen as the only source of well-being, and without it, they can't pay for the carpet or the car. The log choppers will come and kill you, because their children's survival depends upon wood-chippings.

Eventually, the work we did became the basis for regenerative work, and for legislation; but the principle remains the same. We were protesting right from the 1950s, but whenever we did anything, we always set up a stronger suppression and denial. Police became armed. Next time we faced the police, we found they were dressed up like something from outer space. We would drive a spike into a tree, so when it went into the wood-chipping machine, the machine would fly to pieces. Next thing, there are armed guards with metal detectors. We found we were building a huge oppressive force, run jointly by the state and industry against their own people. Our phones were tapped, nice thick files were drawn up, later fed into computers and sent to the CIA.

I thought humanity is stupid, and also nasty. In 1972-73, I pulled out of society. I went into the bush and cut a two-acre space in the forest, and I planted a garden and built a barn and a wooden house. And I thought,

'That's it, bugger them, I can live as a castaway. I'll light a fire, wear skins, eat well, read.' I had put up with a lot of abuse; I stayed angry for two or three years. Then I thought, 'If people like me sit in the bush, the bastards have got an open goal. They can roll over everything. I'd better go back and fight.' But having made that decision, I said, 'I'll never harm them, never carry a weapon. I'll give them no excuse for carrying guns or using teargas. I'll go back to doing simple things, very basic.' Permaculture had been in my mind since the late 1950s. I thought I could construct an ecosystem. I always thought God was a bit of a dead loss, because everything was so random. If you organise it, you can make a better system than anything that exists . . . A recombinant ecology works better than any other. Go to a desert, get all the best things in existence, put them together, and you'll have something never seen in history — an immensely rich system functioning in thousands of ways.

God can't do as well. But don't forget, you're not God. You can't create life forms. So all you're doing is shuffling what is created into different configurations. Nobody did it before we did, I think. I came back with permaculture, and I was able to say to everybody that I was just a simple gardener. It was years before I read a review that said *Permaculture Two* was 'a seditious book'. People thought I was talking about gardens; few realised we were selling the softest form of total revolution. Self-reliance is seditious. When Sir Stamford Raffles went to Singapore, he went by way of Indonesia and saw how self-reliant people were with the palms that provided them with everything they needed. He said, 'These people are ungovernable.' There was nothing the government could give them that they wanted or needed. So what had to be done was clear. Cut the fucking palms down, so they became dependent, and hence governable. You can't govern independent people. They have no need of anything you can bring them.

Self-reliance goes with interdependence. Self-reliance is knowing you do what you are competent at. I'm competent at gardening and glass-blowing. That gives me a living, because I can trade it with others to provide myself with the things I can't do for myself. Self-sufficiency, on the other hand, means going off on your own, imagining you can do the whole thing for yourself — strip bark into paper, skin pigs . . . The society I grew up in was self-reliant. We had three blacksmiths, several carpenters and bootmakers, but we didn't mine the iron, we bought in pig-iron. We recognised we had to send out for some of the things we didn't make — cloth, for instance, apart from felted cloth, which they made, draperies, iron, spices, pepper. On the other hand, we did have places to boil salt, to make soap. Crockery; we made pottery; bricks and tiles.

It was a little port on the Straits where I grew up, between Tasmania and the mainland, the Bass Straits. We had our own idiom, very poetic, stories of apparitions and miracles. We travelled out from the Straits in small whaleboats, no longer than 20 feet. People sailed out, they didn't know where they'd been, so they called everything 'the other side'. You might be going to China, New Zealand, the Savage Islands. 'What did you see there?' 'Oh, there was cattle with huge horns and grass higher than their backs.' They'd probably been to South Africa. If there was hostility, they'd take to the boats: somebody would always stand by, up to their chest in water, ready to push off; they'd often go, lying down in the boats, bullets whistling through the sails . . . They'd bring back stories of being eaten by Maoris, seduced by Madagascans. They brought a Maori prince back once, and he married someone. The Straitsmen were escaped convicts, Irish and Jewish, they were Tasmanian Aboriginals and West Africans, Pacific Islanders and American Negroes who'd jumped ship . . . We're all married and related to each other, going from island to island, mutton-birding and stealing and telling lies to each other . . . That's how I grew up. Stories of people being abandoned on reefs and living on seals' milk. There was a great saga that went on between two men, Dobson and Rue; huge, strong, stupid Dobson, who used to knock down a chimney with his head, to show how strong he was; and Rue, who was small and vicious. He had been flogged. His back was a mass of scars. He had married at every port where there was a church. Off he'd go with his parrot, and he'd get the chaplain to marry him, even if the only woman was the daughter of the chaplain. They say he used to make them walk the plank. Dobson had a couple of very nice Aboriginal wives. Rue landed with Dobson on a reef one day to catch seals, and Dobson saw Rue go off, expecting that he would come back for the skins. But Rue simply went back to the island where they were based, took Dobson's wives and sailed away, knowing that the tide would come over the top of those rocks where he'd left Dobson. That's the end of fucking Dobson. He'd got the wives, that was all he wanted. But Dobson hung on. He made sealskin ropes and tied himself to the rock, so he could let himself get washed around in the high tide. And he sucked milk out of pregnant seals' nipples. After four or five days, a boat came and saw this strange man in sealskins being washed around. They put off a dinghy and lifted him in. Rue had got back to the East Straits, and there he is, lying with Dobson's wives and his own wives. And someone comes and says, 'Dobson he come!' And he says, 'Dobson is dead.' And Dobson, he come over the hill and say, 'Rue get down on your knees and say goodbye' . . . These conversations had taken place in the 1820s, but if you got a word wrong, everybody would say, 'No, he don't say that.'

All my life I lived with Aborigines. We'd harvest the sea birds, mutton-birds. It was a tradition in the Bass Straits. April, May, these birds lived down burrows. They lived with tiger-snakes down burrows, and when you put your hand down, it was Russian roulette. Tiger-snakes are a bright coloured species with hypodermic teeth, very powerful poison, the world's most powerful snake poison. They don't hiss, they bark . . . Anyway, down you'd go with the naked hand into these tunnels; if you touch a snake, you've got to react fast. Immediately you know whether you've got a bird or a snake. Birds always peck your hand, so you give them a finger, they fasten on to it. Then you draw them out, crack their neck, throw them on a spit. Then we'd pull them off and pluck them. That was our main winter food. Thick fat, they taste like whales or seals. Anything that eats krill has this oil, vitamin A. Three will kill you. If you want to kill somebody . . . The Queen of the Straits, she was expert at wiping out people. She used to kill them with mutton birds . . . Life was pretty light in the Straits. There were a few people you didn't go to sea with, because if you went to sea and were owed wages, you'd never come back. There were about half a dozen of them, but only stupid people would go to sea with them. We always reckoned anybody who did deserved to get bumped off.

As far as permaculture goes, I think I've put something in motion that no one can stop. It doesn't have a hierarchy, it doesn't have a centre. Nobody has to take orders. There are numerous projects; people are teaching others. If it's needed, it won't stop, and if it isn't needed, it ought to stop. For the moment, it goes on being more effective. One thing that heartens me, whenever you go to a meeting in Britain, you have these discussions, and people say, 'Well you can't change society.' And an old lady will always stand up and say, 'Rubbish. We did it in the war. We changed overnight. We took it up, planted our gardens with food.' If we want to, we can change. The people can do it. Government can't.

I'm pleased with what I've done. I've thought up a system which you can't attack. There's nowhere to attack it, and you can't stop it by shooting anyone. I'm finished with protest: keep on winning through practice. If we keep on doing that, they'll come in a decade and demolish the Narmada dam themselves. By practice you win. Protest is a waste of energy. But when you take the ground, you've got it for ever.

Human beings have always been left out of the energy equation. I am the only machine I know that can fuel itself. Given a few friends, I can look after myself and many others. This will do me as an alternative energy source. We have never been taught to have confidence in ourselves as our own salvation.

7. ACTUALLY EXISTING ALTERNATIVES

PLENTY USA, RIGHT LIVELIHOOD AWARD WINNER 1980. PLENTY USA, founded in 1974, is an international, non-profit, non-sectarian, relief, development, environment, education and human rights agency. It is a non-governmental organisation, associated with the Office of Public Information at the United Nations. PLENTY has been involved in a number of projects, both with Third World countries and in the poorest parts of the United States. From 1976-80, PLENTY employed more than 100 American volunteers in projects with the Mayan people of Guatemala, in primary health care, drinking-water systems, soya bean agriculture and communications technology. In 1978, the PLENTY Ambulance Service was established in the South Bronx in New York, providing free emergency medical care and training to the embattled residents of that ghetto area. Today PLENTY is involved in marketing Mayan textiles in the US for weaving co-operatives in Guatemala through its One World Trading Company, environmental protection and nuclear issues through its Natural Rights Center, Native American economic development, primarily at Pine Ridge Reservation in South Dakota.

MOST PEOPLE IN the west now accept the right of indigenous people to self-determination, if only because this right appears to require no sacrifice from the West. Somewhat fewer are those who believe that the social arrangements of indigenous societies have much to offer the West by way of example, or instruction in how to live. Even so, in the 1960s, many young Westerners did reach out for a way of living which explicitly took its inspiration from what were perceived as the values of less materialistic, more 'spiritually enlightened' cultures. PLENTY USA has its roots in the 1960s; but has been in a state of continuous evolution since then. It spanned the Vietnam war protests of the 1960s, consolidated its work both within the USA and the Third World in the 1970s, and has survived to link with the more clearly defined social movements of the 1980s and beyond. One of its most original characteristics has been its use of high technology allied to simple living. This has earned it the reputation of being a 'technological Amish' community.

In the late 1960s, about 300 people left the Haight-Ashbury area of San Francisco to look for a farm where they could live together and grow food. Almost a quarter of a century later, the search for a new value system has continued to evolve.

They settled a few thousand acres of poor farmland in Tennessee. It was an austere existence, but they reached a high level of self-reliance. Albert Bates, a founder member, says:

We lived well, on an income of one dollar a day per person. Newspaper reporters used to remark that these people were always smiling. And we did have a good time. But we felt it was not enough to be voluntary peasants in the United States. We felt we had to reach out, and transfer that ability to live well on a small amount to other people in the world who found it difficult to live at all.

Our broad-stroke agenda was the redistribution of wealth, primarily through structural adjustments and mechanisms that would remould relationships, rather than in a violently disruptive or injurious way. Secondly, we saw the control of growth madness as essential. We thought of ways to control the population explosion. One way we would contribute towards that was by holding down family size through natural methods. We also thought it proper to return to the family a sense of its own value and dignity. We wanted to give back the experience of childbirth as a sacrament to the family. Death also had to be taken out of the hospitals, and reintegrated within a harmonious relationship with nature. The third element in our agenda was the revaluation of the human dimension within the sacredness of the earth. We came out of a hippie philosophy that had looked at a lot of native American cultures. We didn't see ourselves as adversaries of the earth, and in that we distinguished ourselves from the mainstream.

We grew more than we could eat. We gave our surplus to a Mennonite Committee — potatoes, wheat, soy — to send to hurricane victims in Honduras. Then, in 1976, there was an earthquake in Guatemala, and we sent some of our people there. The most urgent need was for shelter, so we sent about 60 carpenters; and at one time, we had over 200 volunteers in the country. Later we learned that we had no real business sending all those Americans to Guatemala. Our approach was wrong. We should have waited for those people to say what they needed, and then asked whether we could help them.

Our approach is different now. We have found that we can use technology without it using us. One of the cottage industries we have developed is building geiger counters, which we do in an old horse-trailer at the back of the farm. It is quite an achievement, to run a pocket geiger counter off a simple 9-volt battery. Some of our people went to Byelorussia, to help communities measure radiation in the aftermath of Chernobyl.

The farm still exists after more than 20 years. It's been through a number of changes. Initially, it was completely communal. After 1983, it was decommunalised, and became a co-operative. People could come in, pay a certain amount of rent to live there — $100 per family per month. Then we added a school and stores. Rather than growing food collectively now, we have our own gardens. We have 80 weaving co-operatives in Guatemala making shirts, and the profits go back to them to help their development. That's the formula we work with — co-ops in various parts of the world, markets in the wealthier parts, and all the money goes back to them.

The numbers on the farm peaked in 1980 at around 1,500. By 1989, it had declined to 150; and in the last year it has gone up to around 300 again. Recently, about 40 of us have been saying we miss something, because when we were communal we had a certain amount of spirituality and sharing in decision-making. In fact, we shared the same cheque book. With 1,500 people that is a bit complicated. We felt we needed smaller extended families that could exercise their own economic power. The money we save for our old age can be invested in business within the community.

We belong to the National Historical Communal Societies Association, which has an interest in movements like the Shakers and Hutterites; and we're also part of the Utopian Societies Conference, which is concerned with fictitious Utopias, to see how they imagined it. It seems that if you can establish a democratic forum, if you have means for everyone to provide some input, that will affect the way things develop, then the organisation will tend to grow.

In the mid-1980s, we became more involved with the dollar system: we spent money in our store, paid for our kids to go to school, we became more assimilated into America. We've since stepped back from that a little. Of course, we started with people in their twenties, and they had children. Those children are now between 5 and 15, so the people now are in their forties and in their teens. The real question will appear in 15 years' time: what will those kids be doing? Of the oldest, some have left the farm, for work in medicine, the media and so on. About half remain, still working on the farm. Providing enough work within the community is an important issue. Some of us do work outside. I am an environmental attorney. There are 3 or 4 nurses in nearby hospitals. When we started, we had more than our share of PhDs, college degrees. I was then a graduate of Law School from New York. I became a flour miller for 7 years; and it was only after I suffered a back injury and had to take a desk job that I went back to practise environmental law. One of the skills that college-educated people in the United States lack is the ability to get along with each other. A lot of communities break up, because people cannot sustain long-term relationships. That is one of the ways in which we, in the West, are impoverished.

We have had more than 4,000 people pass through the farm. We've had 2,000 babies born there. We have become a focal point for the

Alternative School Network in the US. At one time, we were getting 20,000 visitors a year. We began to feel like Disneyland. It was more difficult to maintain chosen lifestyles as a voluntary Third World village in mid-America while under a constant barrage of tourism. Our chosen path now is to publish, to put out books and speakers to transmit information, rather than to be a centre for people to visit.

Most communal societies go through recognisable stages: at the beginning, they endure tremendous hardships, a reduction of resources. At that point, they are communal, share the common pot. Then as they grow wealthy from their pooled power, they tend to drop the communal aspect, and engage more with the outside world. Those that engage the most become assimilated by it. But developmental communalism means that you maintain enough of your original ideals and values to be able to experiment and change. You retain the democratic processes that help you to grow and evolve.

Although when we first met the Indian communities in Guatemala, we didn't understand what we were doing, nevertheless that was a profound learning experience for us. Before we met the Mayans, the work of PLENTY could be said to have been focused on the Third World. Our extended contact with the Mayans introduced us to the Fourth World. It changed us and our focus for ever. While the Third World has commonly been referred to as the 'underdeveloped' or 'developing' world, most Fourth World peoples would laugh at or resent such a description. In fact, Fourth World peoples represent long and continuous cultural links with ancient civilizations. Their world is quite developed, and despite the incredible culture shattering pressures inflicted by the so-called First World in its rampant quest for more land, cheap labour and natural resources, you can still find a sanity, grace and wisdom among Fourth World people that are rare in a world where progress and acquisition reign.

Though not all our work involves native peoples directly, our primary vision of what development should be about, and our role in it, stems largely from our experience of those people, and a real, shared spiritual understanding of the oneness of life and the sacred universe out of which our existence blooms.

8. HUMAN RIGHTS: A DYNAMIC PROCESS

THEO VAN BOVEN, RIGHT LIVELIHOOD AWARD WINNER 1985. Theo van Boven was for ten years until 1977 a lecturer in human rights at the University of Amsterdam, and from 1970 to 1975 the Netherlands' representative on the United Nations Commission on Human Rights. From 1977 to 1982, he was Director of the UN Division of Human Rights. Since then, he has been Professor of Law at the University of Limburg. In addition, van Boven has served on many councils and committees dealing with human rights, including the Council of the International Institute of Human Rights (France), and the European Human Rights Foundation (UK), of which he is the Chair.

THERE ARE OTHER ways of defending the cause of diversity, and the rights of indigenous peoples, minorities and dissidents. When he worked as Director of the UN Division of Human Rights, Theo van Boven worked constantly at the limits of what was possible within official structures. His opening statement to the 1982 session of the Commission on Human Rights was so forthright that he was asked to make deletions and amendments. His refusal to do so resulted in his contract not being renewed.

Theo van Boven was instrumental in carrying forward the debate on human rights, even when the Reagan era was making great efforts to subordinate human rights to the 'need to contain Communism'. Van Boven believes that the great international issues of our time can all be framed, argued and contested on the terrain of human rights: issues of war and peace, self-determination, colonialism, racism, apartheid, preservation and conservation of the environment, development, population, food, poverty, the establishment of a new economic order, a new social order and a new human order. Everything that has occurred in Eastern Europe and the former Soviet Union confirms this view.

Van Boven's definition of human rights is comprehensive and imaginative. His commitment to 'the right to development' was seminal in the United Nations' creation of its Human Development Index. This was published for the first time in 1990, and includes, in addition to orthodox measures such as the quantity of Gross National Product of a country, its levels of literacy and life expectancy. These supplementary indicators of human well-being give a more realistic picture than purely economic statistics.

Van Boven insists that not only the symptoms, but also the underlying causes of the violations of human rights be addressed. 'The interdependence between human rights, peace and development, means that freedom from fear and freedom from want belong as much to the concept of human rights as political freedoms.' (See Theo van Boven: *People Matter, Views on International Human Rights Policy* Meulenhoff, Amsterdam 1982.) He also makes the distinction between 'the realisation of economic objectives which may be achieved by repression and denial of human rights' and 'genuine development'. He is firmly against the virtues of 'quiet diplomacy', rather than publicity for abuses of human rights: confidentiality often serves as a screen for concealment of the truth. Nor are human rights a separate sphere from other categories of United Nations activity, but central to all of them: social inequality, racism, child labour, oppression of women, denial of the rights of indigenous peoples and migrant workers, the '350 million who are victims of a discrimination that has economic roots'.

The definition and defence of human rights are a *dynamic process*. It isn't only a question of freedoms to be preserved and protected, but also of the right to work for peaceful change.

> Unless we can effectively bridge the gap between the realms of human rights and economics, we risk the pursuit, on the one hand, of an international economic order which neglects the fundamental human development objective of all our endeavours, and on the other hand, of a shallow approach to human rights, which neglects the deeper, structural causes of injustice, of which gross violations of human rights are often only the symptoms.

While at the United Nations, van Boven was often negotiating with people on what ought to have been non-negotiable issues. A subtle interplay of forces sometimes conspired to undermine the work, for example, governments which permitted on the spot investigations of their human rights record, and which then exploited their own 'openness' to conceal subsequent violations. Van Boven believes that the 'third system' should be enhanced, the international networks, NGOs, linkings of people across the world, popular initiatives which will ensure that voices other than those of governments will be heard. 'Silence is the greatest threat to human rights.'

> The world rights situation is distressing, in spite of the dissolving of East-West tension. We are seeing a rise in religious fundamentalism, a recurrence of virulent nationalisms, as well as vast numbers of refugees and migrants who constitute servile minorities in other countries, intensifying poverty in the poorest countries, as well as excessive abuse of resources, leading to environmental destruction, and developments in science and technology that represent potential threats to livelihood and life. At the same time, new vulnerable groups are emerging — people living with HIV and AIDS, the victims of civil wars over drugs. There is, however, a far greater awareness of the connectedness of countries and cultures. Indeed, in the West, there are many popular responses to

perceived abuses. In 1991, for example, there were spontaneous movements in the West to safeguard the rights of Kurds in Iraq, the malnourished children of Albania, the children being killed on the streets of the cities of Brazil.

In spite of this, the protection of minorities through standard-setting implementation activities proved to be a near failure with the emergence of the nation-state and with the legitimation of the nation-state by the United Nations. The challenge of how to come to grips with the rights of minorities and indigenous peoples is one of the most urgent tasks. Although promotion and protection of human rights is one of the four declared purposes of the United Nations, only 0.7 per cent of the budget is allocated to it.

During the 1980s, many repressive military regimes were replaced by a version of democracy; but the violence inflicted under authoritarian rule, the reinforcement of structural inequalities, the integration of those countries into the international economic order and the growth of indebtedness have meant that the poorest remain as effectively disfranchised now as they were under the harshest regime. For human rights to be infringed by visible and known oppressors is one thing; for the creators of ragged insufficiency and perpetual hunger to be concealed by the workings of economic forces is quite another; and this makes the search for redress, in many ways, even harder than the struggle to overthrow tyrannical political rulers. Indeed, the continuity of policy between former authoritarian regimes and their democratic successors is almost complete. The only difference is that with democratisation, the advisers from the Western financial institutions arrive in the capital city more openly. They negotiate with governments in the full light of TV cameras, but the policies they advocate show no change: structural readjustment, the removal of subsidies from the necessities of the poor, more privatisation, renewed commitment to repayment of debt and the usurious interest charges. We can only wonder what will happen when these policies, under 'democratic' superintendence, fail. In some countries, there is already to be heard a renewed cry for 'a strong man', to restore order and discipline in the chaotic, impoverished, criminal cultures of poverty that have come in the wake of all the Western-inspired rectification plans: in the Philippines, there are many who look back on the Marcos years as a time of stability. I even heard Mrs Gandhi's Emergency in India described as 'a golden age'; while in Brazil many say openly that if there is to be unchanging poverty for the mass of the people, they would prefer the law of the military to the law of the jungle.

Extending the concept of human rights lies behind Rajni Kothari's *Re-thinking Human Rights*, published by Lokayan in New Delhi, India. (For further discussion of the work of Lokayan, see pp.160ff.) Rajni Kothari identifies 'the crystallisation of a mind-set in the elite which thinks of the "backward" as dispensable', as a major obstacle to a more imaginative perception of human rights.

> Interpretation of human rights has traditionally centred on violations by the state of constitutional rights, particularly those involving police brutality, unlawful arrests and 'Mafia' operations of ruling groups and parties; broadly, in the framework of life and liberties of the people. More indirect infringements of people's rights, and intrusions in the framework of civil society, the interference with environmental and life-support systems and diverse cultures and their ethnic identities, do not normally enter the arena of concerns, except where they take the form of state repression or terror. There has been a self-imposed restraint accepted by civil rights activists, that resists any call for longer-term struggles for social and political transformation, either *vis-à-vis* the social structure or *vis-à-vis* the state.

One of the questions raised by Lokayan is how far have the civil liberties of which the West is so proud been won at the expense of distant, unseen others, who die, out of sight of the TV cameras, not only through the obvious instruments of coercion, the attentions of death squads, drug lords, vigilantes and *justiceiros*, but also by those supreme generators of opaque 'impersonal' violence — economic forces: the children dying in the *barrios*, forest people killed by the unofficial mercenaries of the transnationals, the victims of malnutrition, whose abridged lifetime is spent in an often vain attempt to replace the energy they spend each day simply trying to survive. Kothari says:

> The industrialist whose factory effluents pollute a river, the village landlord who keeps a landless labourer in bondage, the contractor who recruits the rural poor for construction projects in the capital and pays them starvation wages, the municipal authorities of a city who fail to provide slum-dwellers with water, all these people — chosen at random — can be held responsible for the same end which results from a 'violent action', namely dead and maimed victims.

The Consumers' Association of Penang (see pp.161ff.) makes the point even more explicitly, in relation to the human rights of children:

> Children who pick cotton balls in Egypt, shear sheep in Peru, pick tea leaves in Sri Lanka and tap rubber in Malaysian plantations, make carpets in Iran, Pakistan and India, are merely the weakest and least conspicuous link in a long economic chain that can easily be followed all the way to the stock exchanges in New York, London, Amsterdam and Tokyo.

Resisting Conformity: The Survivors Of Torture

INGE KEMP GENEFKE, RIGHT LIVELIHOOD AWARD WINNER 1988. In response to Amnesty International's appeal in 1973 to the medical profession to help fight torture, Dr Inge Kemp Genefke formed the first Amnesty International medical group in Denmark. Its pioneering investigations into torture and its consequences for its victims led to the establishment of more medical groups, and by 1982, there were 29 such groups with over 4,000 doctor members. The need for treatment and rehabilitation of torture survivors led in 1982 to the establishment of the International Rehabilitation and Research Centre for Torture Victims (RCT) in Copenhagen, with Dr Kemp Genefke as Medical Director. RCT now has over 30 medical and administrative staff. RCT has organised international seminars in Denmark, in the Philippines, and Kenya. Its research programme has contributed enormously to understanding the treatment of torture victims. To help spread information, in 1987 RCT established its International Documentation Centre, to include papers, reports, press cuttings and audio-visual material about every aspect of torture and its consequences, much of which is not registered anywhere else. A group of Uruguayan physicians, supported by RCT, created a national medico-ethical commission of doctors and lawyers to investigate allegations that more than 60 doctors have participated in torture in Uruguayan camps and prisons, and to impose punishment on those convicted. Dr Genefke is concerned with the issue of doctors as torturers, and in 1986, RCT and the Danish Medical Association organised the first international meeting on the subject since the Nuremberg trials.

DR GENEFKE'S WORK is also a celebration of human diversity. For torture, too, is an extension of the desire to eliminate difference, to extinguish dissent, to impose kinds of uniformity which the human spirit finds intolerable.

Torture in the modern world, as Peter Vesti, psychiatrist at RCT, says, has little to do with extracting information. Sophisticated methods of spying and surveillance have made the use of torture for eliciting information utterly superfluous. The intention of torture is to break down personality, to cripple the psyche: to immobilise the individual whom those in power wish to silence. Inge Kemp-Genefke calls it 'the killing of a soul'.

The objective of torture is to stifle resistance. Its purpose is rarely to kill, but rather to permit the mistreated individuals to be released into society, so that they may serve as a warning and example to other would-be ideological deviants and recalcitrants. 'Their role is to act as a kind of living dead, to inspire terror.' Nor is torture a residual activity in the world. Amnesty International estimates that it is systematically used in over 60 countries, and that it exists in 30 more. Dr Genefke says that few political leaders admit they use torture.

> Iraq is one of the few to do so. Some years ago, after examining people from Iraq, I went to the Embassy, and said, 'Here is the evidence, it is horrible.' And they said, 'Yes, we do it. We have an enemy that has to be dealt with. What would you do?' That is the only time I heard it admitted so serenely.
>
> But most dictatorships, even the most brutal, like to show a respectable face to the world. So that is one weapon we have against them. And then, you can't just start torturing in a country. You need what economists call the infrastructure. You need to train torturers. There are schools for torturers, international networks. Survivors tell of being taken to places where there are demonstrations of torture. They hear them speaking various languages. As a doctor, a neurologist, I can see that people have been treated in similar ways: there has been systematic instruction on how to do it.

Dr Genefke and her colleagues at RCT have observed in recent years the emergence of more sophisticated forms and techniques of torture. Its objective is now perhaps not so much brutal physical scarrings as more subtle, and in many ways more 'effective' psychological woundings, damage inflicted upon the integrity and sense of self-worth of the person. In the process of breaking people, driving them to the limits of endurance without actually killing them, the torturers could never function without the help of doctors; a complicity which makes of torture a grisly profession. One of the principal current concerns of RCT is to outlaw all such medical practitioners, whose presence at the scene of torture is indispensable, for it is their role to advise whether or not the recipient is 'fit' for yet more torture, and to issue death certificates when the victims succumb.

Torture is, of course, an ancient practice, and it is unlikely that it can ever be totally eliminated. 'They were very good at it, even at the time of the Inquisition. They were clever and knew what to do.' It is simply that the refinements made available by contemporary technology give its perpetrators hopes of impunity.

There are many similarities in the testimony of survivors. Most say that the abuse they have been subjected to makes them feel humiliated, unworthy, even guilty.

> In torture methodology, they use simple objects; like nails to put out the eyes, or small knives, or cigarettes or excrement. That way, every time you are out in the normal world, you will see nails, knives and cigarettes everywhere, and on the unconscious plane, you are back again in the torture chamber. We know that simple things give rise to attacks of

anxiety — seeing a policeman, of course, or the sound of children crying; the screech of brakes, the light being turned on suddenly. But here at least we can intervene effectively.

One of the most rewarding aspects of the work of RCT, as indeed of other centres of rehabilitation that have been or are being set up in such known sites of torture as Turkey, the Philippines and Pakistan, is that the healing of damaged individuals has a high success rate. If the survivor has been deliberately addicted to drug abuse, however, it can be more difficult. In the majority of cases, the treatment works, because the people were never sick in the first place. Quite the opposite in fact — they were often some of the most vigorous and well-functioning members of their society. The steps towards the restoration of health are usually straightforward; first, the individual emerges from the internalised sense of worthlessness. Then he or she expresses anger against those who abused them. Finally, there is the achievement of a sense of balance, a retrieval of a feeling of self-value and esteem. Indeed, the psychiatrists say that there is a far higher success rate than is the case with the more familiar forms of psychiatric illness, which often prove far more intractable. It is, perhaps, worth reflecting whether what is known about the restoration of self-worth in the individual might not also be useful in dealing with those whose cultural development has been impaired.

The breaking of individuals, the crushing of dissent, the eradication of opposition, brainwashing and 'correction' of deviants, show little sign of diminution, according to Amnesty International. While most torture survivors treated in Copenhagen came from South America in the 1970s, recently, more have come from the Middle East, including Iraq, Iran and Turkey, many of them Kurds.

We know something about the making of torturers. The authorities take young people, mostly from a conservative milieu and from rural areas, and then they put them through an extremely harsh training, where they are humiliated, beaten and ill-treated for some months. They are made to do stupid things, they are never allowed a night's sleep, and so on. They are dehumanised; and then they are told, 'Now you are the best trained soldiers in our army.' After this, they are billeted close to a torture centre, and they are taken to where people are being brutalised. If they can stand it, they are sent to learn more and more about it.

When we set up the centre, we were advised to do so by specialists who had worked with concentration camp survivors. We have learned a lot since then. In fact, I'm amazed at how much we can help. I always thought doctors could give some consolation, alleviate the pain, but we can in fact go a long way towards healing. But you can never understand.

This is what they say to us, 'You can never know the hell we have been through. Words cannot describe the horror.' I don't think we will ever understand the world of the torturers. The survivors dream, and they sometimes see us in their dreams. One survivor said to me, 'And you were there, and the soldiers came and took you away too; and I said to myself, "Now she will know what torture is."'

When I went to Turkey, we had meetings and congresses at Izmir, Istanbul, and Ankara, and they were always crowded. Whenever I was saying these things, the people were so silent and attentive, you could hear the breath of the people. You could tell there were many who had had direct experience of what we were talking about. The military were often present, out of uniform. I would say, 'Now we'll have half an hour of questions.' Those sessions always went on for at least two hours. And you could tell people knew what they were talking about. By the way they ask questions, you can tell they have been tortured.

Denmark has traditionally been a haven for political refugees and victims of persecution. In the last few years, however, with rising unemployment and a feeling of insecurity, racism has been on the rise, as elsewhere in Europe.

The majority of people in Denmark are not, of course, racist, but small fascist groups are manipulating people. We made a film on refugees in Denmark, following them through the system. There is a scene on a bus, where Anna, one of the refugees is sitting in the bus with her son. A Dane says to her, 'Stand up. Stand up for a real Dane.' People have been beaten and destroyed and scorned and shouted at. We do our best to restore them, and then when they go out onto the city streets, they are back in the torture chamber again . . . I want to say to people that by spitting at refugees, you are helping Iraq's president and all the other tyrants in the world, you are allying yourself with the forces of oppression.

The decay of the absolute creed imposed upon the people of Eastern Europe means that, at least in those places, the atrocities committed against individuals in its name will now be a thing of the past. Even so, into that vacuum pour older nationalistic fervours, xenophobia and racism. And indeed, where the market economy has swept in to displace the cumbrous mechanisms of state planning and control, this, also, demands its tribute of human sacrifice. For the belief that the West is not a promoter of inflexible ideology is also false; or perhaps it would be more true to say that the ideology is not elaborated in theory. What is inflexible in the West is its practice: it does not restrict thought or speech, but that which cannot be turned into profit rapidly disappears from view in its cosmos.

In fact, what is regarded as a neutral process of 'normal' transformation, as 'modernising' and 'developing' the countries of the South, is also a form of violent reworking of the sensibility of human beings, a reshaping of them so that they conform with a universalised Western model of 'homo economicus'. This involves the dismantling of subsistence and peasant sensibilities, the breaking and refashioning of the psyche of small farmers, nomads, pastoralists and tribals. It is nothing less than a restructuring of humanity in the image of industrial society. It requires the inferiorising of other cultures, the destruction of self-esteem, a devaluing of the local and familiar everywhere; and this is less remote an experience than we like to think from those more rigorous and systematic breakers of souls in the prisons of Baghdad, Teheran, Karachi, Ankara or Manila. That a similar transformation occurred in Europe not so long ago seems to have been lost to the memory of those whose more recent experience of the remoulding of humanity in the interests of being turned into 'consumers' seems to have effaced everything else.

The idea that the dissolution of socialism means the end of attempts to coerce human beings into conformity with revealed truths could not be more mistaken. The cohesion of all societies required a shared system of belief, an ideological underpinning. That the West is governed by reason, that its science and technology are free of value-judgements, that its culture is universal and therefore above the ideological fray, is far from truth. The West may well elaborate its beliefs in the realm of reason, but they are conceived in faith, constructed upon mythic structures that are actually far more baleful than the myths of forest or river people now driven to the edge of extinction. The Judaeo-Christian-Islamic (and of course, Marxist) belief that humanity is apart from and above nature, and that the conquest of nature is therefore both a legitimate and desirable objective, has long been acknowledged as the source of the present crisis in the global environment. Indeed, it has been the working out of this belief that has risen to its murderous and potentially omnicidal apogee in the industrial era. Although Western industrial society now claims to have changed its values, and to be concerned with conservation and environmental restoration, it cannot separate these things from the further growth and expansion of its own system: it looks to the very source of the damage to set it to rights. It is in danger of making yet another split: delegating to the green and environmental movements the task of 'cleaning up the environment', while permitting its economic system to continue 'the creation of wealth' — another division of labour which helps the West to dissimulate its real intentions, even from itself. In the meantime, its colonising power is unabated. It still sends forth its missionising agents, those whose versions of development lead to violent coercions against any who seek another path. That the West does not see itself as motivated by ideology at all, but as guided by universal principles, is what makes it so dangerous. Those who are secure at the heart of imperial projects are rarely best placed to judge the effects of their work; and it is always a temptation for the powerful to mistake their power for truth, to see in it a sign of divine blessing; especially when their eager converts show such eagerness to support their judgement. Where they do not, less ambiguous forms of compliance are sometimes employed.

HIGH CHIEF IBEDUL GIBBONS, on behalf of the people of Palau, RIGHT LIVELIHOOD AWARD WINNER 1983.

SELF-DETERMINATION for ethnic groups, countries or nations, is one of the most fundamental freedoms. The spread of political monocultures is no less damaging than any other extinction of diversity. This means struggle, not only against the violent suppression of cultural identity, but also against the manipulation by powerful countries of ostensibly democratic processes, in order for the powerful to achieve outcomes which suit their strategies and purposes.

Palau comprises the first islands east of the Philippines. There are 300 islands, with no more than 15,000 people. Few have known greater obstacles on their path to self-determination in the 20th century. German before 1914, Japanese between the wars, Palau became part of the United States Trust Territories of Pacific Islands in 1947. The trusteeship was established by the United Nations, 'to promote the development of the inhabitants of the Trust Territory towards self-government or independence'.

An anti-nuclear constitution was prepared for the proposed Republic of Palau in 1979. This prohibited the 'testing, storage or disposal within the territorial jurisdiction of Palau of harmful substances, such as nuclear, chemical, gas or biochemical weapons, of nuclear plants and waste, without the express approval of 75 per cent of the voters in a referendum'. The United States objected to this from the outset, as being 'incompatible with its defence responsibilities for the area'. Behind this lay the uncertainty of the future of the vast Clark and Subic Bay bases in the Philippines.

In the first referendum in July 1979, 92 per cent of voters opted for the constitution. Under intensifying pressure, further referenda were held in the years that followed. The US offered Palau a compact of free association (such as that with the Marshall Islands), whereby the US retains responsibility for security and defence. In spite of an enhanced aid package, the pro-US vote, although increased, failed to reach the necessary majority. In any case, the people of Palau knew what had happened to the radiation victims and landowners of the Kwajalein range in the Marshall Islands. The compact would permit the US to take as much land as it required for military installations.

Bribery, intimidation and confusion yielded to more violent episodes: one president was murdered, another committed suicide. There were firebombings of the homes of well-known opponents of the compact. The influence of the US has been so overwhelming that its aid has created a dependent society that relies on imported goods, to the detriment of its own abundant indigenous resources. Within a few years, Palau had become a transparent miniaturisation of 'development' patterns that are normally more opaque: once a peaceable self-reliant way of living, it had been contaminated by violence, corruption and all the evils of domination short of military occupation.

The Compact of Free Association would bind Palau closely to the US for 50 years, although financial support would end after 15 years. It could never be terminated by Palau. Exclusive military rights to the US could never be abrogated without US approval. Palau would have to hand over to the US any land required for military purposes. At the same time, US citizens could migrate to Palau, set up homes and businesses quite freely.

The latest plebiscite in Palau was in February 1990, when the Compact received the lowest voter support to date. It reconfirms the resistance to coercive methods to achieve a 'democratic' result desired by the US; and is an assertion of autonomy and independence, although the price paid by the people of Palau is high. Their resolution to preserve a democratically-agreed constitution has required great tenacity and strength of purpose in the presence of such a vastly superior force. The struggle was more recently taken forward by women elders, who had reinstated a court case that seeks to have the Compact of Free Association declared unconstitutional.

The alternatives facing Palau are: US Commonwealth status (like the North Marianas Islands); the Compact of Free Association; or complete independence. There is a fear that if the Compact is not accepted, the US will impose total recolonisation of Palau, with a 'residential representative' of the US commanding wide powers. The possibility of complete independence remains, but the advantages are not clear-cut. For one thing, Palau has already become a scene of gangsterism, both local and imported. There is a danger that it might become prey to mafiosi, and at the same time the islands would lose the protection of the American courts. There is also the fear of all dependent societies — that the complete loss of US help would plunge the people into poverty. There has been a loss of confidence in the possibilities of self-reliant renewal.

If the UN Trusteeship Council approves the termination of the existing status of Palau, this would still have to be approved by the Security Council. If the US had coerced Palau more directly, China and the former USSR would have imposed a veto.

The people of Palau have received support from the outside world — the

International Commission of Jurists, and the American Civil Liberties Union. Jakob von Uexkull of the Right Livelihood Foundation was an observer at some of the referenda. Palau did succeed in blocking a major US foreign policy initiative for over a decade. The US could not accept the freely chosen constitution of Palau because it would have set a precedent that would interfere with what the US regards as its global defence commitments, and its role in what its allies have once more begun openly to refer to as its function as 'the world's policeman'.

At the UN Trusteeship Council Meeting in May 1990, it was recommended that the US should delete the military provisions, in view of the absurdity of the series of failed plebiscites, and in conformity with the Charter of the United Nations, with General Assembly Resolution 1514(XV) of 14 December 1960, and with the declared United Nations International Decade for the Eradication of Colonialism. In any case, with the disappearance of Soviet power and the end of the cold war, the urgency of the US presence in the area is much reduced. This shows that the disturbance and violence that have come, not only to Palau, but more especially to the Marshall Islands (also linked by a Compact of Association to the US), whose population has been irradiated, evacuated, disrupted and violated by years of nuclear testing, have all been to no purpose. Indeed, it was disclosed in May 1990 that the Marshall Islands were maintained by the US as a test site of a particular kind. After testing bombs and weapons, the US Department of Energy undertook long-term human and environmental testing, so that the US would understand the long-term effects of radiation, should the US need to use such weapons in any military conflict.

There are few things more poignant than the wreckage of yesterday's strategic imperatives of the powerful. The disturbance of the Pacific Islanders now seem a supremely redundant and costly human sacrifice; and they are unlikely to be the last in spite of the new world order, as all the victims of development would probably testify, had they a voice in the world's busy monoglot media.

PART 2: MAKING VISIBLE

After the protection and enhancement of diversity, making visible is, perhaps, the most significant contribution of those who are trying to define another worldview; although for many, these are meaningless hierarchies. For instance, Dr Genefke is both seeking to preserve dissent and the rights of minorities, and at the same time is making visible torture, its effects and consequences.

Making visible operates on many levels. It means naming and counting the elided costs of economic accounting systems that simply 'externalise' what they cannot measure. It involves making visible the value and beauty of marginalised cultures. It means making visible the effects, for instance, of radiation and other unseen contaminants. It includes making visible the unpaid labour of women and children. It also means acknowledging the creativity, inventiveness and powers of those millions of people who live and survive outside formal economic systems. It demands recognition for social justice, for the acknowledgement of popular and traditional ways of seeing the world, and of their potential role in future strategies for planetary survival.

9. THE URBAN POOR: AN INVISIBLE RESOURCE

JOHN F.C. TURNER. RIGHT LIVELIHOOD AWARD WINNER 1988. John Turner has spent over 40 years working with the practice and developing the theory and tools for self-managed home and neighbourhood building in Peru, the United States and the United Kingdom. He worked in Peru from 1957 to 1965, mainly on the advocacy and design of community action and self-help programmes in villages and urban squatter settlements. He later lectured at the Joint Centre for Urban Studies of the Massachusetts Institute of Technology, and at the Development Planning Unit, University College, London. Since 1983, he has devoted himself to his non-profit consultancy, which he established in 1978. His publications have had a great deal of influence on housing policies worldwide. *Uncontrolled Urban Settlement: Problems and Policies* was published in 1966, *Freedom to Build, Dweller Control of the Housing Process* by Macmillan in 1972; *Housing by People, Towards Autonomy in Building Environments* by Marion Boyars in 1976. From 1983 to 1986, Turner was co-ordinator of Habitat International Coalition's Habitat (HIC) Project for the United Nations International Year of Shelter for the Homeless, 1987. The HIC Project carried out a global survey of recent and current local initiatives for home and neighbourhood improvement. From over 200 Third World cases identified, 20 were selected for in-depth documentation, and were published as *A Third World Case Book*, ed. Bertha Turner, (BCB, April 1988).

IN THE FACES of the migrants to the cities of the South can be read an epic story of rural dislocation, environmental ruin and extreme social injustice. Within the next two decades, the urban population of the world is expected to exceed that of the countryside. Although there is now evidence that some earlier UN predictions of bloated city populations will not be realised, and despite the greater fluidity that exists between town and country than is sometimes understood by the idea of 'urbanisation', there will still be growing pressure, both on unwieldy urban agglomerations and on the exploited rural areas that must feed them.

At ten o'clock in the morning, the dim gothic interior of São Paulo's Catedral dé Se is full. The people are not praying, but sleeping, a ragged humanity, slumped in the hard pews and covered with coarse blankets; a frieze of rough statuary. Here, at least, they are safe from the predators who roam the Praça de Se outside. A cathedral of impoverished dreamers, cold and silent, a *Totenschiff* with its drifting cargo of refugees from economic and developmental violence.

Urbanisation in the South today is, in many respects, unlike the experience of the early industrial era in Britain. Then a severe discipline, required by the factory system, was imposed upon a raw rural sensibility. Now, the same process is accompanied by an orgiastic consumerism, an absence of controls, which means that resistance to social disruption and exploitation is harder to organise.

The life of migrants is penetrated by an iconography of privatised dreams, which also calls into existence strange new divisions of labour. Economic development to the poor woman from Mato Grosso means paid employment, cleaning the floor in the porno movie house, where the men masturbate in mechanistic accompaniment to images of brutal sex. The vendors on the viaduct of Sta Ifigenia stand guard over the offal of industrial society, as though entrusted with its greatest treasures — T-shirts emblazoned with obscenities, value-added, nutrition-subtracted foodstuffs, magazines with titles like *Girls Who Dig Girls* and *Anal Sex*, tarot readings, barbie dolls and war toys.

The square outside the cathedral is part market-place, part fairground. It has the aspect of a rural meeting place. Gypsy women from the North in lime-green or scarlet flounces, read the hands of credulous passers-by; sellers of traditional medicines, barks, herbs and roots, offer relief from syphilis, ulcers, cancer and worms; a man attracts a crowd by breaking glass bottles with his bare feet. The ornamental fountain serves as bathing place for the homeless, and the faded washing of the poor is laid out on the green-painted benches. At night, in the Rua Marquesa de Itu, the young transvestites, gaudy as tropical birds, cluster around the purring Opels and Cadillacs, and climb in behind the smoked-glass windows.

There are a million unemployed in São Paulo. Last year, there were more than 2,500 murders. New death squads have appeared, eliminating the young small-time crooks, children really, who prey on poor neighbourhoods. These, and feuds between rival drug gangs, leave a bloody cargo of human wreckage for the municipal ambulances to clear from the streets. In one parish after a recent weekend, there were 43 funerals — more than half of the dead had been murdered; the others, young children, were the victims of that other violence: malnutrition and curable disease. The city is overcrowded, scarred by alcoholism, drugs, crime, the breakdown of families. In addition, São Paulo, like the other growing cities of the South, spread circles of desolation around themselves, as they draw ever more resources and people from the spoiled hinterland.

And yet, people always say that this is better than where they have come from. Their lives, scarred by migration and upheaval, are also suffused with hope, creativity and formidable energy.

According to Jorge Hardoy and David Satterthwaite at the International Institute for Environment and Development in London, there are now 1.3 billion people in urban centres in the Third World; at least 600 million of them in life- and health-threatening homes and neighbourhoods. It is common for between 30 and 60 per cent of the population of big cities to live in illegal settlements or tenements.

City governments still regularly clear squatters from pavements, from private and public land in cities as diverse as Bombay, Seoul and São Paulo. But many now recognise that those who migrate to the urban centres have taken a step that cannot easily be reversed. It is acknowledged that even the flimsiest, most makeshift shelters of newcomers will, over time, be transformed into decent neighbourhoods and communities, provided that people are given security of tenure of the land, and the opportunity to build for themselves. The slums may appear to the tidy-minded to be unsightly and random collections of people who blight the city landscape and drain its resources. In fact, the people create work for themselves in the urban economy, performing valuable services — domestic work, laundry, selling fruit, vegetables and snacks, offering transport and other amenities to the very people who are the most vociferous about their encroachments.

If governments are now coming to understand that the people themselves are the most effective architects, planners and builders, especially the women, to whom much of the labour of creating a home falls, this is due in considerable measure to the pioneering work of the late Hassan Fathy, Egyptian architect and author in 1973 of *Architecture for the Poor* (University of Chicago Press, and Right Livelihood Award winner in 1980). This work has been amplified and carried forward by John Turner.

Turner insists that neither the state nor the market can deliver adequate housing to the majority of the city poor. The market requires too great a capital investment, which is not available for such uncertain returns, and the state not only rarely has the resources, but also takes away the freedom of the people to construct for themselves. Nowhere are these shortcomings more apparent than in the *cortiços* (tenements) of São Paulo, where, in one infamous apartment block, more than 10,000 people occupy apartments that have been illegally sub-divided. All over the South, 'low cost housing has been appropriated by the only people who can afford it, the middle class.'

In Manila, in the Philippines, only about 15 per cent of the people can pay for typical market-provided housing. The Freedom to Build Corporation in Manila is directly inspired by John Turner. The Horacio de la Costa project at Novaliches, on the periphery of the city, provides householders with loans of up to 80,000 pesos at 6 per cent interest. For this, they receive a basic unit of grey breeze-block construction on plots of 55 square metres. Each structure is simply the most rudimentary shell. As people's income rises, and their work prospects improve, they add to, embellish and extend the simple building, according to their tastes and means. The back wall can be easily opened up, and there is room for a second storey to be added. Some people have already installed new doors and windows, even though the development at Novaliches is not yet finished; others have built a terrace, created a garden, erected a grille and railings. Most of the people here had come from insanitary, insecure slums. It is a place of great vitality, tangible hope.

Even in areas where people first settle in the cities, or where invasions of land are organised, the transformation in the space of a few years can be dramatic. 'They should not be called invasions,' said the organisers of one community in São Paulo, 'because that makes it sound like criminal activity. We call them occupations.' John Turner says:

> That the mass of the urban poor are able to seek and find improvement through home ownership (or de facto possession), when they are still very poor by modern standards, is certainly the main reason for their optimism. If they were trapped in the inner cities, like so many of the North American poor, they too would be burning instead of building.

When the inhabitants of an area have security, can control the major decisions, can make their own contributions to design, construction and management of housing, both the process of participation and the environment which this produces, stimulate social and individual well-being. When they have no control over and no responsibility for key decisions in their own housing, dwelling environments may well become a barrier to personal fulfilment and a burden on the economy. A 'good' environment is not necessarily of a high material standard: a cheap shelter may release money for the family's more urgent priorities, especially when the children are young. The functional relationship between inhabitant and habitat is what counts; location close to work may well be more important than high standards of amenity.

Many of John Turner's insights have been reached through an imaginative understanding of the social and psychological journey of the urban dweller. Turner's experience was gained in Peru, at a time when half the city of Lima did not even appear on any map, and 50 per cent of the adult population had been born in the provinces.

> When people move to the city, traditional sources of security — the family, subsistence farming — are undermined, and must be substituted by the job market; and home ownership, no matter how basic, offers an alternative form of economic and social security.
>
> Successful urban planning depends upon the alignment of government action with the priorities of the forces of popular settlement. Official housing policies have often 'telescoped' the organic growth of cities as embodied in people's own efforts at self-improvement. The imposition of modern minimum standards on popular urban housing is an assault upon the traditional function of housing as a source of social and economic security and mobility.

John Turner is an advocate of the maxim that, 'appropriate technology is technology that people can appropriate.' People have been ground between the millstones of state control and market forces: from unworkability in Eastern Europe to unsustainability in the West. In Eastern Europe, the state undermined all popular initiatives; in the West, the community base is so eroded that it hardly exists. In the South, the initiative is still there, although constantly under attack; but at least there, people can do things for themselves, seize land, create spaces where there is scope for their own self-determination and control.

More recently, Turner has sought to bring back to the North some of the insights gained in the South. He seeks to reintegrate the functions of neighbourhood, so that living, working and leisure are less dispersed and fragmented. 'In the most highly maldeveloped societies — to which the rest aspire — most people live alone or with one other.' (In Britain, 25 per cent of households consist of a single person; a proportion that is expected to rise to one in three early in the next century.)

> The great majority commute to employments which are themselves increasingly remote from the production of goods and services. Typically, work is eliminated from neighbourhoods in urban-industrial societies, either by restrictive zoning or by the elimination of local manufacturing or trading networks. Divorced from home and work life, creative, recreative and cultural activities are restricted to leisure time. Industrialised, institutionalised and professionalised patterns of settlement and building types waste space and land, time and life, energy and materials — our irreducible inventory of irreplaceable resources. Most surviving neighbourhoods that work and struggle to maintain and regenerate themselves, their own economies and cultures, are materially poor. Hope for the future lies in the fact that so many of the poor in poor countries manage to do so much with so little. While the rich do so little with so much, there can be no future.

Not for the first time, the poor may be seen as offering both hope and instruction; not through their poverty, but through their energetic strivings for a secure and modest sufficiency. It is a lesson which the rich are bound to resist; for just as the shining imagery of the West is projected across the world, detached from the human, social and environmental costs it involves, so, in exchange, what comes back to the West are the scenes of desolation, backwardness and poverty of the South, shorn of any of the humanising influences of community and custom, especially of the work of women, which makes it more bearable than those bare images alone could possibly suggest. This highly tendentious two-way flow of partial information serves as a constant reminder to the privileged of the fate that awaits them, should they be so foolish as to jeopardise their good fortune by questioning too closely the wisdom of the existing arrangements. The noses of the poor press constantly against the windows of the TV screens of the West. It is extraordinary how *images* can serve to block perception; and the creativity and hopefulness of the poor remain invisible to the troubled, though largely unresponsive rich.

ELA BHATT, Self-Employed Women's Association. RIGHT LIVELIHOOD AWARD WINNER 1984. Ela Bhatt is a former lawyer and social worker, who in 1968 was the chief of the women's section of the Textile Labour Association of Ahmedabad. In this position, she became directly aware of the conditions suffered by poor self-employed women, in the city, and elsewhere in South Asia. In order to address the poverty and lack of control over their working conditions, Ela Bhatt set up the Self-Employed Women's Association in 1972. Within three years, SEWA had 7,000 members, and was registered as a trade union. By 1988, there were 100,000 members in six Indian states. Through organisation and solidarity, SEWA members have new negotiating power with their employers. They established their own bank in 1975. This now has over 22,000 accounts, and has rescued thousands of women from money-lenders, pawnbrokers and middlemen on whom their labour was dependent. The average repayment rate on loans is 94 per cent (see Kalim Rose, *Where Women are Leaders: The Self-Employed Women's Association*, 1992, Sage Publications India; and Zed Books, London, 1992) Ela Bhatt has taken the struggle for justice and recognition on behalf of self-employed women into the national and international arenas. SEWA is campaigning for a convention on Home-based Workers' Recognition and Protection for the United Nations' International Labour Office.

EVEN BEFORE THEY seek shelter, the priority of the city poor is work. For 20 years, Ela Bhatt's SEWA has been a focus for the poorest women to organise themselves. It has strengthened and succoured groups of workers previously believed to be beyond the scope of trade union, or indeed, any other social organisation.

The women are mostly self-employed. This means that they have created work for themselves at the lowest level of reward. Great profits have been made, mainly by men, out of their 'invisible' labour. They have been described as 'marginal', 'peripheral', part of the 'informal' economy. They are *chindi*-workers (quilters), vegetable vendors, home-based workers, *bidi*-makers, block-printers, headloaders, sellers of second-hand clothes, makers of *papad* and *agarbatti*, cane or handicraft workers, recyclers of paper, metal, rags or plastic. If they have remained invisible to the eyes of economists and planners, their presence has been all too clear to middlemen and wholesalers, who have taken advantage of their isolation to pay them at pitifully low rates. One of the greatest inhibitions upon their ability to upgrade their work and skills has been the non-availability of credit, which has led to dependency on money-lenders. The formation of the SEWA bank has transformed the lives of many women. The level of default is lower than in commercial banks.

SEWA found that many traditional skills had been lost or degraded through 'development'. About 20,000 women in Ahmedabad had become dependent on paper-picking for a living, which requires no skill and brings poor rewards. SEWA is concerned to consolidate and enhance skills, and to facilitate the marketing of products through co-operatives. Applying skills collectively has achieved what could never have been accomplished by individuals alone. A new and flexible form of trade unionism has emerged, which empowers, makes connections and raises consciousness through *doing*.

SEWA identified three levels of exploitation: the immediate exploiter — the cruel policeman, the rapacious employer, the vicious contractor. Supporting these is a second level of injustice — government agencies and legal structures: the Labour Department, for instance, corrupted by employers, helps these to avoid labour laws. The municipality criminalises poor vendors: there is no space for vendors, therefore they are illegal, no matter how vital their function in provisioning the city. Finally, there is injustice at the highest level, institutionalised in laws and policies, and buttressed by international networks of wealth and power.

The philosophy of SEWA is that members will work outwards, from a perception of the local constraints on their lives, and come to understand little by little, the complexity of the wider oppressive forces, nationally and globally. Many women in the city know that they have been driven there by technological change, evicted from settled patterns of living by 'development.' For instance, a vendor borrows 50 rupees a day to buy vegetables, and pays back 55 rupees in the evening. This woman may have been forced to leave land that had been degraded by river-effluents or salination: memories of her former agricultural function live on in her vegetable dealing. A farm labourer, in the season when there was no work, used to weave cloth. She has been displaced by the availability of cheaper mill-produced cloth, and has become a rag picker, in a ghostly gesture to her spoilt purpose. Bamboo workers find they can no longer buy bamboo, because it has all been sold to paper-mills. The forest-dweller who harvested grass, seeds and honey, is now banned from the forests. Many other craft skills of seasonal agricultural workers have been lost because of dwindling markets.

While a proportion of men migrate to Ahmedabad and find work in the formal economy, women often remain in the village; and this is the reason for SEWA's expansion into rural areas in the past five years. In some places, up to 80 per cent of villagers are in debt. Women who used traditional techniques to make day-to-day utility items have been ousted by mass-produced industrial products. The disemployment of weavers, potters, cobblers, has led SEWA to think about the survival of traditional crafts. This can be achieved only by upgrading skills, gaining direct access to raw materials, making and selling goods through bulk orders or directly to consumers. In India, 'labour saving' means 'human wasting'. A form of development which creates wealth by mechanising production can only add to an already vast reservoir of unemployed and underemployed; and it is to counter the effects of this that SEWA has extended its activities.

SEWA has also initiated a wide range of socially supportive services for women — health care, child care, water and sanitation programmes, housing projects, protection against violence and sexual harassment, legal aid. Exploitative employers have been pursued in the courts, and there have been campaigns to regularise child labour (its abolition would damage families in which children often contribute essential income), and to rehabilitate the victims of communal violence. The great majority of the members of SEWA are Untouchables, or from other Backward Castes, Muslims and tribal women. Their common plight has proves a formidable solvent of communal and caste differences; the more so since the last two years have seen an upsurge in communal conflict all over India, following the rise of the fundamentalist Bharatiya Janata Party.

The self-employed sector comprises 90 per cent of manufacture in India. Although SEWA was originally a dissident offspring of the Textile Labour Union, it has become a unique and seminal force, serving as model and inspiration to those seeking to organise the excluded. In 1987, the National Commission of Self-Employed Women was set up, and the report it produced was accepted by the government. In 1989, the V.P. Singh administration included Ela Bhatt in the Planning Commission. In spite of this, the linking of the struggles of poor workers, especially women, to the wider framework of trade unionism, remains to be accomplished. There is still much work for SEWA to do; it remains a dynamic, living movement.

WINEFREDA GEONZON, Free Legal Assistance Volunteers Association. RIGHT LIVELIHOOD AWARD WINNER 1984. Winefreda Geonzon, who died in 1990, was a Filipina lawyer, who in 1978 became the Legal Aid Director of the Integrated Bar of the Philippines in Cebu, which brought her into contact with the many injustices and abuses of the legal system which occurred during the martial law years of the Marcos regime. People, including young children, were jailed without charges or trial; imprisoned beyond their term; tortured and brutalised; or simply forgotten in prison. In response, Geonzon set up the Free Legal

Assistance Volunteers Association (Free LAVA), as a free legal aid office for victims of violations of human rights, poor prisoners who could not afford to hire a lawyer, and people whose cases had implications for social justice. As its reputation grew, Free LAVA involved growing numbers of lawyers, students and community groups in its work. A Documentation and Research Group gathered legal evidence for abused or wrongly imprisoned people, a Legal Services Group undertook their representation, a Civic Assistance Team sought to administer to their basic needs in prison and provide for their rehabilitation. By 1987, 26 community groups were involved in Free LAVA's work.

ALTHOUGH MARTIAL LAW was lifted in 1981, and the Marcoses deposed after the display of Corazon Aquino's people power in 1986, there has been no improvement in the plight of the poorest. Quite the contrary. The persistence of civil conflict provides a cloak for official and semi-official violence against the poor and against those fighting for social justice. Indeed, after Aquino's Total War policy against the insurgents from 1987, there was a worsening of human rights violations in the country. There are now over one million internal refugees in the Philippines, displaced as a consequence of military action or 'pacification' programmes.

The poor are criminalised. The jails of Cebu City are full: people accused principally of 'economic crimes', driven to despair by loss of livelihood, unemployment, social violence. For many of them, justice remains a travesty. The police regularly raid the poor areas, round up young men at random, and accuse them of unsolved crimes. It is easy for the poor to be thrown into prison and forgotten, children as well as adults. In the city jail, I saw ten-year-old twins, who had been accused of theft. Minors who can be bailed to their parents are allowed home, but those with no responsible adult to care for them must stay in jail: the deprived suffer, and the most deprived suffer most.

Cebu is a spreading ramshackle city, and has the air of an unfinished place, with buildings in rough concrete and breeze blocks, rusty metal roofs, pot-holed roads, festoons of cables across the streets. It seems the buildings are there simply to bear the logos of transnational companies — Mitsubishi, Sanyo, Sharp, Coca-Cola, Marlboro, Nabisco. The banks are windowless fortresses guarded by armed security workers. The shops are full of imported junk — Pee Wee crunchies, squid rings, corn- and potato-based snacks, Mutant Teenage Ninja Turtles merchandise, electronic keyboards, kitsch holy pictures, plastic flowers, fast food, Washington Red apples and California oranges (in a country which has some of the most succulent fruits in the world, mangosteens, custard apples, rambutans, mangoes), powdered hair-dye, soft toys, cameras, junk medicines. The church of Santo Nino in the downtown areas was the first Christian church in the Philippines. Destroyed by fire, the effigy of the saint miraculously survived the flames. Outside the church, along the stone weathered to a spectral grey-white, a long line of human misery presses itself against the walls, immobile as carved buttresses — crippled children, malformed adults, the blind, sick and defeated, hands outstretched in supplication. Inside, the scalloped altar piece, with barley-sugar columns and effigies of saints, chandeliers and plaster mouldings, delicate fretted woodwork, dwarf and diminish the people, from whom the low hum of prayer is stirred by the humid draught from straw fans. In Cebu, the contemporary cargo-cult of consumerism exists side by side with the ossified religion of the former conquerors. On Mactan Island is the statue of Lapu-Lapu, who killed Magellan in 1521; but Magellan's cross remains near the pier, commemorating the spot where King Humabon of Cebu, with his queen, daughters and 800 subjects were baptised.

Duljo is a wretched slum area reclaimed from the sea, which has more than its share of residents in prison. The houses are of bamboo nailed to batons, with metal roofs rusting in the rain; narrow mirey alleys, with pigs on a leash in tiny yards. This is the area close to the docks, warehouses for grain, timber and sugar; fish market, metal workshops, battery-rechargers, recyclers of rubber tyres which are made into floats for fishing, cabinet makers, carvers of holy statues, shellcraft workers; there are horse-drawn *caleças* and cycle rickshaws for hire. The unemployed young men stand idly in the rain. Danilo was in prison for eight years for a murder he didn't commit, and is still serving his sentence, although on parole. He and his wife work selling food they cook on a wayside stall. George, too, was in prison for murder, and even though the complainant has withdrawn the accusation against him, the case has still to be heard. He works whenever there is a ship to be unloaded, and is paid 50 centavos for each sack of grain he lifts. Each sack weighs 50 kilos; he weighs 49. The roads are crowded with women selling fish, firewood, charcoal or coconut husks for fuel; there are cycle- and radio-repair shops, men at sewing machines, flower sellers, lighter-repair stalls, vendors of lottery tickets. Some people are roasting a pig on a spit for a wedding; it rotates over a fire protected from the rain by a length of polythene. The Flores de Mayo festival is being celebrated in a little church: girls in pink and yellow, with silvered cardboard wings, carry bunches of crimson tea roses. Some boys sit under the canopy of a cycle rickshaw to shelter from the rain; they grin, as though unaware of their fate as tomorrow's sweated labour or jail fodder.

The city jail is a concrete structure with round watchtower, high walls surmounted by barbed wire. On the edge of Cebu City, it occupies the site of the former airport. The bare cells with cement walls are a series of iron cages, a forest of bars. Each was designed for 35 men, but currently contains 70 or 80. There are buckets for slopping out, and juveniles are not separated from adults. There are people here accused of murder ten years ago, who have never come to trial. Others have seen the judges in their case promoted, die or emigrate; or their papers have been lost, which has plunged them into official non-existence, another form of living death. Over the cells there is a huge effigy of Christ crucified.

Among the prisoners was Julius Gacayan, who is 20. He was arrested when he was 16 for stealing a motorbike with two friends. They both blamed him, and he was taken into custody. On his way to court, he slipped away and ran into the hills, where his relatives have a farm. The police could not pursue him, because the area was controlled by the New People's Army. Because of this, he was assumed to be a supporter of the insurgency. Later, he was picked up by vigilantes of the Citizens' Army. One of their members had been killed, and they accused Julius of the murder.

As a result, Julius's father has had to leave Cebu for Manila. The forces of the Citizens' Army threatened his life, and have declared the whole family a menace to the community. This means that the family is now ostracised by their neighbours. Their hut was burned down. The mother comes to jail to visit her son. She touches his face with her fingertips; it is as though she is saying goodbye to a condemned man. Julius buries his face in his hands. He says he knew nothing about politics. They have never been subversives. All he did was commit an act of youthful foolishness.

Paolo, who is 46, is accused of rape. He was originally charged with non-payment of a debt. Released, he was apprehended the following day and accused of 'acts of lasciviousness'. Not told who the complainant was, he later learned that she was a member of the family to whom the debt was owed. His case was filed away in the archive because of administrative error, and he has not come to court. That was in 1984. His family has stopped visiting him.

The provincial jail, in contrast to the city jail in the centre of Cebu, is more humanely run. At least there, juveniles are separated from adults. There are about 30 young people in a cell apart from the main body of the prison. Many come from Consolacion, a settlement some 15 kilometres away, where many squatters were relocated about ten years ago. Ruela Patigaon is 20. He has been in prison three years, accused of homicide. The lawyer dealing with his case has died and has not been replaced. Arnel Rosalita is a slight boy, whose 15th birthday it is. The others sing 'Happy Birthday to You' in English. He is a second-year high school student, who stabbed to death a 19-year-old. It was, he says, in self-defence; when attacked by the older boy, he seized a knife from a nearby food stall and struck out with it. A small 15-year-old is accused of rape and murder. The boy is undersized, incapable of rape, but he was with an older man who ran away. As accomplice, he must bear the whole charge. He has no father, and lives with his grandmother in the mountains. Three boys, Rodolfo Blanco, 15, Marcillo Granada, 13, and Jerry Caneta, nine, are accused of robbery. They have been here four months. When a Free LAVA worker telephoned the court to find out when the case was coming to court, nothing was known. The case had been filed and forgotten. Roy Sotto is 20. His mother left the family to find work in Manila as a maidservant. Roy has been accused of drug pushing, but says that the police planted ten sticks of marijuana on him.

Free LAVA has a threefold approach to the work: crime prevention, free legal advice and assistance and rehabilitation of offenders, including employment loans. There is also a programme of recommending prisoners for release, pardon and parole. Many of the workers at Free LAVA have themselves been wrongfully imprisoned, including Nonoy, who spent eight years in jail accused of murder. Among the young people in the provincial jail, LAVA has started a scouting troop, run by Tony Auditor, himself a former prisoner; and as part of the prevention programme, scout troops operate in the community. Winefreda Geonzon believed that constructive community work is the most helpful way of preventing young people from coming to the attention of the police. At the summer scout camp in the hills overlooking Cebu, many of the mothers came to see their children assemble to receive their colours and awards. Their pride in their sons and their affection for Winefreda were very moving.

Later, I went with her to visit the homes of some of the families she has worked with. Just behind the Capitol, the US-style government building, with dome and classical façade, runs the Guadalupe River, which divides the North of Cebu from the South. On the steep banks of the river bed, the people have built their homes. After months of drought, the river has been reduced to a muddy trickle. There is a wide expanse of dry bed, where young people have set up a baseball post. People sit out in the cool of early evening. Palm trees grow out of the riverbank, and creepers and shrubs have sprouted, now that the drought has just broken. The houses are of rattan, bamboo and nipa, cardboard and wood. The waste water trickles out of pipes, and spills in a spread of moss and algae onto the rip-rap of concrete and stone walls that have been raised up to prevent flooding. Those who have built up the bank beneath their house will be safe when the heavy rain comes; others will see their houses swept away, as occurs almost every year. Teofila says her house was carried away downstream by last year's floodwaters. The neighbours helped her and her husband to drag it back, and now they have made breeze-block foundations to strengthen it. He drives a jeepney, for which he pays the owner 225 pesos a day. He starts work at six in the morning, and finishes late at night, for a profit of only 60-70 pesos a day, well below the minimum wage. Many of the men here work as security guards at banks, hotels or private companies, for a salary of around 3,000 pesos a month. The women wash for 150 pesos a month from each family they wash for. They do their washing in the muddy waters of the Guadalupe. They dig a pit in the sand, close to where the river flows; and the water is filtered through the sand, so that when it reaches the pit, it is perfectly clean. The washing dries in the strong disinfecting sunlight, and smells clean and sweet. It is unlikely, says Teofila, that the owners of the washing ever think about the places where their linen is cleaned. Drinking water has to be purchased from the owner of a brick house on top of the river bank, five centavos for four litres. Some women work on shellcraft, which is a major industry in Cebu. Formerly, they worked in a factory, where they acquired the skills, and then they set up on their own account, with a loan from Free LAVA. They buy shells, an electric drill, and wicker baskets which they adorn with festoons of coloured shells; these are sold to a stall-holder for 44 pesos; he sells them for about 100 pesos. Others go for export to Japan through a middleman, who visits the area every few weeks to collect the finished work. The women say that all they ask of life is to be left alone to improve their lives and the prospects for the next generation. Modest enough ambitions, but scarcely realisable when their children's role is to fulfil that of criminal or hoodlum, in order to justify the vast expenditure that goes on police, paramilitary groups, vigilantes, the armed forces and corrupt politicians.

Winefreda Geonzon was born in the hills North of Cebu. During the Japanese occupation, when she was 15 months old, her father was out in the fields, and he met with a group of Japanese soldiers. As he turned to avoid them, they shot him. Winefreda's mother was left with seven children, the youngest only three months old. They had a small piece of land, but it was rocky ground on the side of a hill, impossible to cultivate since they had no money for seed. The children worked in other people's fields at harvest time, while their mother stitched for a garment maker. Winefreda would go to the seashore, catch fish for the family, and gather shells for sale to shellcraft workers. She worked on farms for payment in corn, worked in the corn-mills, separating grain from chaff. Later, she became a teacher, which continued for nine years, and then a stenographer, while she studied law. In response to the human rights abuses of the Marcoses, she felt she was called to work with the victimised and unrepresented. Her faith and courage protected her; and she continued to work until a few days before her death from liver cancer in July 1990.

In spite of the squalors of city life, few people wish to return to their home-place. One of the most degraded urban settings in the world must be the Dantesque landscape of Manila's 'Smoky Mountain', a vast garbage heap which has been colonised by around 5,000 families, in defiance of the sulphurous fumes and smoke still rising from its smouldering core. That those living here should express their satisfaction with it gives some idea of the violence and poverty which they have fled. To see the huts constructed on levelled terraces in the flank of Smoky Mountain in the drenching summer rain, when the slurry and mud effaces the margins of the road, and even the rusty jagged metal of the go-downs and huts seem to melt in rust-coloured liquid, is, at first sight, an appalling spectacle. A generation of children has already been born here, in a junk yard culture of throwaway goods. But the people cheerfully explain that they are waiting for the waste carts to arrive with the daily cargo of Manila's garbage. If they work through the night on the detritus, recycling metal, paper, plastic, wood, rags, they will earn up to 150 pesos, which is more than the minimum wage. In the city, an income is the first necessity. And in due course, when they have levelled the land, planted trees and shrubs around the houses, the land will become valuable, even desirable. The people have a vision of the future that is not accessible to those who can see only the present horrors.

10. DEFENDING THE BIOSPHERE

THE CHIPKO MOVEMENT. RIGHT LIVELIHOOD AWARD WINNER 1987. The forests of India are a critical resource for the subsistence of rural peoples throughout the country; but especially in hill and mountain areas, both because of the food, fuel and fodder they provide, and also because of their role in stabilising soil and water resources. As these forests have been increasingly felled for commerce and industry, Indian villagers have protected their livelihoods through the Gandhian method of *satyagraha*, non-violent resistance. In the 1970s and 80s, this resistance to forest destruction spread throughout India, and became organised and known as the Chipko Movement. The Movement is the result of hundreds of decentralised and locally autonomous initiatives. Its leaders and activists are primarily village women, those who are most closely affected by the lose of their local resources. Men are involved too, however, and some of these have helped spread information about the aims and purposes of Chipko in the wider world, including Sunderlal Bahaguna, Gandhian activist and philosopher, who walked 5,000 kilometres across the Himalayas in 1981-83; Chandi Prasad Bhatt, one of the earliest Chipko activists, who fostered locally based industries based on the conservation and sustainable use of forest wealth; Ghanashyam Raturi, the Chipko poet, whose sounds echo through the Himalaya of Uttar Pradesh.

NOWHERE IS THE RELATIONSHIP between the growing city and the degraded rural hinterland more painful than in Delhi, some 200 kilometres from the foothills of the Himalayas. Connaught Place, centre of the Lutyens imperial capital, has conjured forth a vast population, many of them from the hills, an army of hustlers, survivors, salespeople, servants and self-employed. These exiles must somehow find the money to send home to those whose economic security has been undermined by environmental breakdown, deforestation and damage to the fragile hills.

Their need to survive has led them into new forms of labour, much of it created by tourist pollution. In Connaught Place, there are fortune-tellers, palm-readers (I.C. Clear), astrologers, head-masseurs, ear-cleaners, shoe-shine boys; vendors of cloth, sandalwood, jewels and carpets, bangles and handicrafts, gold and ivory; *bhel-puri* and *bhajis*, *channa* and *agarbatti*, drugs, aphrodisiacs, sex and money at unofficial rates of exchange. There are those who ask if you want to do business, any other business, like at the end of a committee meeting. They will take you to brothels where girls may be had for Rs10 or Rs1000, where boys will make themselves agreeable; they will escort you round Delhi, show you where you can buy silver filigree work, find rare coloured birds from Kerala, precious stones, Mughal miniatures. And everywhere, unemployed graduates beg foreigners to help them find a passage from India, to anywhere, to obtain a visa, to find a job. They will go anywhere in the world — drive a taxi, work in a factory, become a waiter, a janitor, shine shoes. Only not here. A throng of young men, for whom education has spoiled the home village, and who can conceive of no desirable future for themselves, not merely in their own village, but even in their own country. They long to be elsewhere, away, abroad. Even in India, which is supposed to be a symbol of tradition and changelessness, many people, especially the 'educated' — that is those schooled to an alien culture — have found their attachment to the local and familiar brutally severed. The sense of rootedness and belonging has been wounded in these boys from the hills. Everything, it seems, that comes from the hills is transformed: the forests become timber, the streams become water resources, the men become boys.

Here, perhaps, is another reason why the making visible and regeneration of traditional cultures is of the first importance to those concerned with alternative patterns of development.

The whole economy of the Indo-Gangetic plain has been threatened by deforestation. Although even in the colonial period, forests had been felled in the Western Himalayas for railway sleepers, intensified felling occurred after independence, and road construction in the 1960s opened the area to tourism and pilgrims. Men have always been the beneficiaries of intrusions of the outside economy — roads connect them to dependency, the cash which buys terylene shirts, transistors, alcohol and cigarettes, roads lead them to the excitement and promises of jobs in the plains. It is the women who stay. The initiative and enterprise of men appear differently from the women's perspective. For they must remain, must go on living off the impaired resource base, must find enough to feed the children, walk lengthening distances to find fuel. It is this courage and tenacity that have led to the major role for women in Chipko.

Development has dispossessed people of their ancient ability to manage and harvest the environment — water and land resources, fodder and food, honey, fruits, animal products, building materials, medicinal herbs, raw materials for local crafts. As a result, it has become clear that what have been regarded as minimum basic needs — food, clothing and shelter — depend for their realisation upon a healthy resource base. The struggle of the forest people was originally over safeguarding access to the resources of their habitat; what they learned through that struggle was that once a critical limit of degradation has been crossed, the politics of distribution became irrelevant for the survival of the people.

At Rishikesh, a town whose whole economy seems to be founded on the spiritual tourism of ashrams, the Ganges reaches the plains for the first time: ultramarine, a clear ribbon of sky between banks of glittering white sand.

The road north to Narendranagar rises quickly. Gangs of tribal construction workers are widening the highway, so that the equipment for the planned Tehri dam can reach the site. Workers chip away at the crumbling hillsides, and build walls to prevent major landslips. Even so, minor falls occur all the time; a cascade of stones blocks the road in a cloud of reddish dust.

The tops of the hills are fringed with oak, sour wild mango, bhimal, Persian lilac, a margin of fragile green around sharp peaks that cut like blades into the tender blue of the sky. Where the sun strikes the terraces of cultivation carved into the hills, they shine, an emerald stairway of spring wheat and millet. Beyond the foothills are the Himalayas themselves, shades of glassy rose and blue.

The values borne by Chipko represent both continuity and renewal of an ancient culture, in which everything, trees, rivers, even stones, are conceived of as a living entity. Each individual forms part of all other life and non-life, one with the earth; a concept that requires respect for all that surrounds us, since self merges with the rest of creation.

Sunderlal Bahaguna says that of all the colonised countries in the world, India was the only one to seek inspiration in its own past.

The peoples of North America, Mexico, could not withstand the invasion by materialistic industrial culture. Indian culture was nurtured in the forests. That is where the sages, the *rishis* lived. The old education system sent the young to the ashrams of these sages at eight years old. In the story of Krishna and Sudhaman, the sons of rich and poor families lived together. They worked in the fields together, sat under trees and discussed problems with their teachers in the form of question and answer. They came to the conclusion that there is life in all creation, and that human beings are not necessarily superior to other forms of life. Western civilisation tells us that nature is a commodity, and that society is only human beings. They are masters of nature. The thinking that made us the masters of nature has now made us the butchers of nature. Rishis had a worshipful attitude to all forms of life. Trees, rivers were worshipped, wild boar, fish. The mouse is the horse of Ganesh, and Lakshmi, goddess of wealth, rides on an owl. Austerity was honoured and respected more than kings, because one who lives austerely will take less from nature. The roots of Chipko lie in these characteristics of Indian culture.

People in the West imagine the ecological movement was born in the West. It was not university professors, nor political leaders who gave birth to it, but village women, because this message is inbred in their hearts. They had no formal education, but they worshipped the tulsi plant, the sacred symbol of the flora. My mother was illiterate, but after taking her bath, she always watered the tulsi plant.

The forests had always been owned by the community which depended upon them. The first time they came under government control was in 1805. Because of the wars in Europe, all the oaks of England had vanished, and trade needed ships. The East India Company was in search of strong wood for ships. So the teak forests of Malabar were taken over for the supply of timber. The communities revolted; as a result, the first Forest Officer in India was neither botanist nor forester, but a police officer. The demand for timber increased for construction of the railways after the Indian revolution. There were many uprisings over control of the forests. There was a revolt in the Himalaya region in the early 20th century, and that became part of the independence movement. Where I lived, in Tehri-Garhwal, the movement took inspiration from Gandhi, and there it established a parallel government. All the rulers were arrested, the army was sent, and it fired on the people in May 1930. Seventeen were killed.

Much of the early work after independence was done by Mira Behn, the English woman who was a disciple of Gandhi. She established an ashram at Rishikesh. There were floods of the Ganges. She decided to go and find out where the floods were coming from. She went into the hills on horseback, and realised that it was caused by deforestation, and the change in forest-cover of the Himalayas. Monocultural commercialisation had already begun with chir pine, a species that would yield timber and nothing else. Mira Behn wrote *There Is Something Wrong in the Himalayas* in 1949. Mixed forests had been converted into pine. Nobody listened. I had joined the Gandhian movement when I was 13, and I became interested. I was later to go round the villages of Himalaya, spreading the message of Gandhi. That was the time of the Chinese invasion; everybody was upset. We said, 'Chinese aggression we can overcome, but floods we are sending from the Himalayas are a different kind of invasion.'

In the sixties, we had organised an anti-liquor movement. Liquor shops were spreading, and women were bearing the burden of their men's drinking. So we had the basis of a movement of women. Then the forest was on our mind. We thought the problem was of contractors indiscriminately cutting trees. So on the anniversary of the 1930 massacre, there was a great gathering in that place, and the people made a pledge to protect the forests, revive the old relationship between forest and people. We said the contractor system should be abolished, and the people should have the raw materials for their own forest industries. This became the basis for Chipko, and at the same time, we started small units of forest-based industries, turpentine from resin, wood-based activities. We walked over the hills, using songs to take the message to the people. There is a song which says, 'If you see a eucalyptus tree, pull it out, because it spoils the others; it takes too much water, and is a friend of the capitalist.' I walked 2,500 kilometres at that time.

In 1975, the government of Uttar Pradesh agreed to end the contractor system. They told us to form forest labour co-operatives. This we did. But we found it makes no difference — whether we or the contractors felled trees, they were still cut down. By 1977, we concluded there should be a ban on all felling.

When the authorities saw it as simply an economic struggle, they could understand that, but as soon as it became ecological, they couldn't. They became more hostile. It made very little difference to them whether the raw material should go to local industry or to industry outside the region. But when we demanded a 10-year ban, that meant loss of revenue, and was a blow to their whole theory of commercial forest management. It was proposed that felling cease and tapping be suspended for ten years. The central government agreed, but the state government of Uttar Pradesh was not ready for that. We became more militant, went on symbolic fasts in places where forests were being auctioned. In 1977, the women turned axemen away with their demonstrations. Then they tied sacred thread round trees marked for felling; they tied raki ribbons round them (that is the ribbon sisters tie around the wrists of their brothers) as symbols that they would protect them with their lives.

The Advani forest was saved by the women in 1977. Those who took part then evoke the days and nights they spent, guarding the trees. When the labourers came to fell them, the women addressed them, saying, 'Brother, don't do this.' When the women hugged the trees and cried out, some of the labourers were afraid. They fled, crying, '*Devi cher gayi*!' because they saw the women with streaming hair and angry faces, and they thought they were incarnations of the spirit of the trees. The women talk of 'environmental sin', to be dealt with, not by violence, but by awareness, in the way that religion seeks to make the sinner conscious of his or her wrongdoing.

Sunderlal Bahaguna of Chipko says the establishment has two principal weapons, which are *fear* and *greed*.

Our main task was to make people fearless and greedless; in other words, selfless. These are the alternative weapons. Because in any struggle, violent or non-violent, you need weapons. This was the speciality of Gandhi, to invent new weapons. If you fight fear with fear, you will only create more terror. Even if you win, you will need a bigger army to maintain your victory. That we have seen with the experience of

Communism. Similarly, if you make people more greedy, by promising them rewards, there will be no limit to it; even if you achieve your objective, people will ask for more and more. To fight devilish weapons you need divine weapons. If my adversary becomes fearless, he is elevated from inside, and becomes noble.

The Forest Officer came to the place where the people were meeting, the Advani Forest, and he caught the headman of the village, and said to him, 'You had assured us that the logging operations would go ahead. What has happened?' And the headman said, 'Oh sir, now the whole thing has changed. Things are no longer in my hands. Today if I tell you to fell the trees, I will not even get food in my own house. The women are against it, and they have organised themselves.' 'But after all, you are the headman of the village.' He said, 'The leader of the whole thing is my wife.' And that lady presided over the meeting on the dais. The Forest Officer told them what he had learned in college. 'This felling is only weeding.' The women were not convinced. He was angry. He said, 'You are foolish village women. You know what the forests bear? Resin, timber and foreign exchange.

> '*Kya hai jangal ke upkar?*
> *Lissa, lakri aur vyapar.*'

And the women immediately stood up and said, 'Yes we are thankful to you.' Then they said,

> '*Kya hai jangal ke upkar?*
> *Mitti, pani aur vyar.*'

'What do the forests bear? Soil, water and pure air.' The basis of life. This comes from the hearts of the women.

Of course, big national and international organisations came to suppress what we had done. The bureaucracy, scientists, the Ford Foundation came and tried to popularise another faction of Chipko, those who were in favour of providing raw material to industry and controlled felling. The World Bank had a big scheme for plantation forestry. They called us rebels, and sent armed force to that area. But the women were not intimidated. Now the consciousness of these things has spread all over the country, and it is not so easy for the despoilers of the forests to have it their own way.

Originally, the struggle had been against the take-over of the forests by the colonial authorities. Later, it became an issue of a fair return to the people for the produce of the forest. But that was overtaken by the question of sustainable forestry — protection rather than production. The dilemma of the Himalayas exemplifies in microcosm the issues of sustainable harvesting and equitable distribution which affect the whole planet: without the former, there will be nothing to distribute.

> Government afforestation programmes consisted of conifers, eucalyptus and poplars. Many of these just withered and died. Local people know what grows, and since we have been involved in regeneration, there is a far higher rate of survival. We plant walnut, soapnut, bakin, toon, China Pear, maple, orange and lemon, bhimal, cedar, poplar, willow. A hundred years ago, these hills were more than self-sufficient. They used to export honey, herbs, wood, dairy products; 16 or 17 items were listed by the gazetteers. Now, the only export is the people. But in the hills, the traditions and resources of the people are still there. We have faith in our system and in our ability to restore it.

The Chipko Movement succeeded in compelling a 15-year ban on commercial green felling in Uttar Pradesh, and in putting a halt to clear-felling in the Western Ghats and the Vindhayas.

> We must evaluate benefits and costs as they affect people's lives, not in narrow financial terms based on market factors. What is required is an *ecological audit*, which is not the same thing as an 'environmental impact assessment'.

One of the difficulties is the popular perception that 'ecological concern' is a separate issue from that of 'development'. The ecological movement is frequently misrepresented as being interested only in non-material and subjective factors, such as aesthetics, whereas development is seen as rooted within material realities. This false polarisation only serves to conceal the real conflict, which is between ecologically balanced development (which is very difficult to define), and unsustainable, destructive economic growth (which is what we see everywhere).

Chipko has also been active against other attacks on the resource base: limestone quarrying, for instance, in the Doon Valley in Uttar Pradesh, which had damaged the underground aquifers. More recently, Sunderlal Bahuguna undertook a hunger strike against the proposed Tehri Dam. He grew up in what will be the submergence area, and he has now settled in one of the villages of the site of the dam. This project was conceived as long ago as the 1940s: an earth and rock-filled dam 260.5 metres high, near the confluence of the Bhagirathi and Bhilangana rivers. It is an area subject to earthquakes (such as that which occurred in Tehri-Garhwal in November 1991). The rocks on which the dam is to be constructed are deformed, and unlikely to bear the weight of the vast volume of water of the impounded lake. If Tehri is ever finished, it would be one of the highest dams in the world, and, says Bahuguna, invite a disaster of epic proportions.

Chipko embodies a tension which is present in many of the new social and environmental movements, and one which once characterised the old labour movement: is reform of existing industrial society possible, or is a more radical change necessary? Because the conflict within the labour movement was decided definitively in favour of reform — and the reverberations of the collapse of the Soviet Union only emphasise this — it is by no means therefore a foregone conclusion that the fate of the Green movement is determined in advance. The question addressed by the Greens now is whether a transition to a more equitable and renewing society can be made without violent discontinuities. Which are the elements with which the alternative movement can engage creatively? Is it conceivable that present-day concentrations of power would acquiesce in their own dissolution in the interests of a survival wider than that of their own privilege?

This 'fault-line' also runs through the Green movement in Europe, in the discussions between so-called realists and fundamentalists. Before the defeat of the Greens in the German elections of 1990, Petra Kelly felt that as the Green party had gained ground, it had tended to lose some of its earlier passion and commitment. Did this mean that the arguments had already been won, that other parties had accepted the agenda determined by the Greens, or did this mean that access to power had effectively dissolved some of the earlier radicalism? (For further discussion of these issues, see pp.173ff.)

HELENA NORBERG-HODGE and the LADAKH ECOLOGICAL DEVELOPMENT GROUP (LEDEG), RIGHT LIVELIHOOD AWARD WINNERS 1986. The Ladakh project was set up in 1978, to counter the baleful effects of Western development on this small high-altitude desert area on the western edge of the Tibetan plateau. The area had been virtually closed to outside influences until the mid-1970s, and Helena Norberg-Hodge has been able to monitor forms of cultural contamination that have occurred since that time. LEDEG has two primary emphases: technology and education. It has undertaken wide-ranging work on appropriate technologies, and the educational effort has focused upon the celebration and enhancement of traditional Ladakhi life and culture. Her book, *Ancient Futures*, was published by Rider Books in 1992.

HELENA NORBERG-HODGE has been a rare witness to the effects upon distinctive values and ways of life of the region since it was opened up to industrial society through tourism 15 years ago. Part of her work has been to make visible not only the damaging effects of a more powerful and alien culture but also the strengths and values that humanity needs from traditional, renewable ways of living.

Ladakh is a Buddhist enclave in Jammu and Kashmir, in the Himalayan rainshadow. It is 11,500 feet above sea level, and the traditional culture is based upon raising sheep and goats, yaks and cows, and the cultivation of barley and wheat on small plots watered by glacial meltwater. The population is only 125,000. Norberg-Hodge went to Ladakh in the early 1970s with a film crew. She was so moved by what she saw that she remained there, learned the language, and later set up LEDEG. She has seen the erosion of self-reliance: locally produced shelter and clothing have been displaced by dependency-creating imports. Barley growing and animal husbandry have yielded to the import of rice from Punjab. Jeans and polyester replace local fabrics. Cement becomes a substitute for the adobe bricks of traditional construction. Among the social consequences are the appearance of crime, alcoholism, and, for the first time, communal conflict between Buddhists and Muslims.

In Leh, capital of Ladakh, the Centre for Ecological Development has concentrated on technology that can be manufactured and maintained locally, and that is benign, both environmentally and culturally. Only minor modifications to existing technology represent powerful tools for regeneration: for instance, the adaptation of ordinary waterwheels used for grinding grain to produce electricity for lighting. Because the area has only 100mm of rain a year, and skies are frequently cloudless, solar heating, ovens and food driers are effective. Ladakh adobe walls are perfect for Trombe walls. (These have vents at regular intervals along the floor and below the ceiling. The external south-facing wall is painted black and covered with glass. The air warmed between the glass and the wall circulates by convection through the vents.) Traditional story-telling, songs and plays are used to help restore local tradition, and with it, self-esteem.

Ladakh can follow the Hopis, Eskimos and Samoans and be decimated, or they can build on the wisdom of their own past to become a model of controlled, ecological development.

When I first came to Ladakh, the life I saw came as a revelation. Until that time, I'd accepted changes in societies as part of some evolutionary process. I had accepted the Western model of human nature — that we are aggressive and selfish, and that culture plays no significant part in shaping human beings. But peace and co-operation were the basis of Ladakhi culture. I saw my own culture in a different light. Of course, whenever you say this, you are accused of being romantic and nostalgic. The same thing happened to Margaret Mead much earlier, in Samoa. She had said that her experience of this culture was that it was peaceable and co-operative. After she died, a male anthropologist came out with an attack on her as an individual and upon her arguments, saying that she had been a young impressionable woman, influenced by her professor in America, and that she had come with preconceived notions, and had not been able to speak the language. They can't say the same thing about me, because I am a linguist and I soon learned Ladakhi. I experienced the difference personally. I remember, one evening, at dusk, I was out alone, and I became aware of a group of men coming towards me from the opposite direction. And I felt completely *safe*, which is not how a woman feels in industrial society.

Initially, I stayed there for two years. Then I came home, because my mother was dying of cancer. She was very young. I realised that this was a disease of industrial society. I had been very close to her; and it made me the more determined to change things.

The West has created an economic and technological monoculture, which is now being imposed everywhere. I have seen the way that it has affected Ladakhi society from the beginning. After the tourists came with their wealth, I began to be treated as superior by the people. They had learned to think of themselves as inferior. It has created two cultures — 'modernised' Ladakhis and the traditional culture. Traditional farmers have an expansive sense of self: the boundaries of the ego are not narrow. There is little separation, no sharp individuation. They merge more readily with others and with the environment. When you see what happens to young Ladakhis under Western influence, we are talking about *the making of a different kind of human being*. It is a form of re-education which trains the young to become part of the international money economy. It attacks the wholeness of the Ladakhis. They were never traditionally separated into age-groups. Growing up, children see and interact with people of all ages. Both sexes take part in child-rearing. With mixed ages, one child can hold out a hand to a smaller one and teach her to walk. When children are all of the same age-group, there is none to help one another, none to serve as an inspiration to the younger ones. All you can do with your own age-group is compete. As a child, a young boy will have father and grandfather as part of the nurturing experience. The tenderness of men is not blocked, but has an outlet for its expression.

It is no exaggeration to say that Ladakhis are pulled away from indigenous knowledge as soon as they enter school. The first thing that school does is to eliminate agriculture as a viable occupation for the vast majority. We are exporting this model of driving people out of agriculture into urban life. The very few who do go on to study agriculture go to agricultural college, to study out of books written by people who have never been to Ladakh. Every human being on the planet who is studying agriculture is learning from a reduced pool of knowledge, highly standardised, and removed from specific ecosystems. In Ladakh, for instance, experts in animal husbandry said that local animals are not productive enough: we should introduce Jersey cows. They said this business of going up into the high pastures has no place in the modern world. In the high pastures, the yak is one of the most important animals in the world. The yak prefers to stay at 5,000 metres, that is around 16,000 feet. It has a lot of hair, doesn't like to get hot. It is supremely adapted to those conditions. It wanders, covering vast distances in desert mountains, gathering what grows wild, and converting it to energy and food for the human population. So when you bring in Jersey cows, they can't even get up to those elevations; which means that you've flung away those resources. The Jersey cow has to be stall-fed, so you have to cultivate fodder, which starts competing with the land needed for human food. Fodder is now very scarce, and more expensive than barley, which is what the people eat. Then they have to build special shelters for the cows. Under these artificial conditions, the Jersey cow does actually produce more milk than the yak, but it is questionable whether it is more nutritious than the milk of the female yak. It is certainly more expensive.

The Ladakhis are, like all traditional peoples, very careful in expressing themselves about reality. They will have thought about it, deeply, and when they speak from experience, they name it with far more humility than we would. If what they speak about has a narrower range than a Westerner, it has a depth that you rarely find in the West. We will talk about Iran or China or the moon with great certitude, but without any direct experience. In Ladakhi, we have 25 ways of saying, 'to be', all depending upon your relationship with what you are describing. The feedback mechanism of reality makes you more humble, because you are aware of the changes, the contradictions, the paradoxes in the way you affect reality, and in the way it affects you. They will have observed the world minutely. A Ladakhi child will have learned from her mother that on this side of the valley there is a little more sun, and on that side a little less because it is shaded by the mountain, and as the sun moves through the sky, the landscape is alive and changing. She will learn that the conditions for growing things will change within a hundred metres.

The Western culture is now so pervasive that in order to resist it we have to engage in all sorts of paradoxes. You need a Westernised person to fight that monoculture. The others can't do it. They can't speak the language, for one thing. Their occupation and education locks them into agriculture. It doesn't mean that they are narrow-minded or that their world is small. But they cannot struggle against the outside influences unless they become part of those influences. Western culture, because of the specialisations we are forced into, operates at an intellectual level, separated from reality. And to dance back and forth between the intellectual and experiential levels is very difficult.

The problem is that the outside influences are themselves a form of violence upon indigenous culture. When there is violence in response to them, the Western universalisers say triumphantly, 'See, this is human nature, and it is violent and aggressive.' Last year, there were protests in Ladakh by Buddhist farmers against the dominant Muslim traders, although the traders had co-existed peacefully with the subsistence culture for 300 years.

Helena Norberg-Hodge sees decentralisation as the best hope for any movement towards practical and sustainable development.

Ladakh was a self-reliant, small culture. Decentralisation is a great generator of diversity, and diversity is far more efficient than so-called economies of scale. Any small farmer will tell you that if you ignore the fact that conditions are slightly different a little further down the hill, you have wasted the potential to produce food efficiently. At the moment, what we are doing is saying, 'Let's forget about growing things on land that is a bit hilly, a bit uneven. Let's just concentrate on the so-called breadbaskets and rice-bowls, and have these enormous flat areas, where we can use our machines and high inputs.' But small-scale agriculture is more efficient, there is more diversity in crops, it safeguards food security in the face of pests that can wipe out monocultures overnight. At present, fewer and fewer people are in agriculture. Policy ought to be to stabilise or increase the numbers in agriculture in a small-scale, ecological way. Then you wouldn't have the wasteful extravagances involved in the transport of basic necessities over vast areas. If you produce for need locally, you get fresher produce. The only people who would suffer are the middlemen. Once you remove people from food production, they forfeit control over their lives.

What is it that disgraces the traditional herbal remedies of the *amchis* (healers) in Ladakh, the familiar foods, the immemorial artefacts? What is it, all over the world, that drains the native landscapes of vitality, that makes of the home-place appear at the same time bleak and stifling, and sets humanity in movement, a long frieze of migration, on foot, with donkeys, camels, carts, battered cars, trains, aircraft, everywhere going from country to town, from village to city, from town to metropolis, from South to North; always following the source of their dispossession?

Perhaps it requires the insight of someone from the South, whose own society is living through a transforming moment, to remind us of what many in the North have forgotten. Claude Alvares, in *Homo Faber*, (Allied Publishers,

Bombay 1979; and Zed Books, London: *Decolonising History: Technology and Culture in India, China and the West*), illuminates the promises and deceptions of industrialisation, when he writes of Britain in the early industrial period:

> Poverty in one sphere was exchanged for poverty in others that seemed less vital at first: entertainment, education and social activity. And it is the lack of these forms of experience that has created the urgency of the consumer society. New needs sprang up because of the changed life-styles: the old methods of satisfying human need were destroyed or rendered obsolete . . . New needs arose because of the new pattern of living itself. Society has relied heavily upon the economic system to right this situation. Man has had to be encapsulated increasingly in his own creations to make his urban life-style workable . . . After the industrial revolution, the demands of culture came gradually to be fulfilled through an extension of the productive system over non-economic areas of life. In this sense, British society proved to be, not merely the workshop of the world, but also a laboratory in which far-reaching results first appeared.

When the economy colonises every area of our experience, and this artefact is exported to formerly self-reliant cultures, it is, perhaps, only to be expected that the experience will be one of violent disturbance and loss of meaning.

11. COUNTING THE REAL COSTS: THE WESTERN MODEL, MIRAGES AND MIRACLES

The belief is widely held, especially in the West, that the Western model of development remains a valid prescription not only for the newly liberated countries of Eastern Europe but for the Third World as well. This is seen in the unvarying prescriptions offered by the Western financial institutions to all those countries that fall under their superintendence, no matter what the local conditions or needs. In support of this thesis, the dramatic success of the newly industrialised countries of the Pacific rim are always cited as shining examples. If Taiwan, South Korea and Singapore can succeed, then what is to prevent the Philippines, India, or even Mali or Chad, from taking the same path?

Walden Bello, now Director of Food First (see pp.145ff.), has been looking critically at the Asian 'miracle' economies, with a view to their replicability in the world. It soon becomes clear that there has been very little in the way of critical appraisal, apart from some modest research into the exploitation of labour. He believes there are good reasons for this.

> Everybody bought in to the idea that they had made the transition from underdevelopment, perhaps by questionable methods, but certainly that they had achieved high growth rates. Nothing succeeds like success. And progressive economists had also allowed their critical faculty to lapse because they found it useful to cite Taiwan or South Korea as examples to rebut the orthodoxy that free market liberalisation was the only way forward in Asia, South America and Africa. The fact is that one of the causes of the success of the newly industrialised countries was heavy government intervention, and this was useful to counter the World Bank, IMF and United States' pressure to cut government intervention and subsidy. This meant that progressive economists forgot their function and failed to point out what damage this rapid industrialisation was inflicting upon the people. Consistently high growth rates, as well as the paradigm of free market versus state intervention, prevented a critical view. And this is the context in which what has happened should be understood.
>
> Were those economies really successes? Were they replicable? Were they desirable? In terms of success, it was one-dimensional: they had high growth-rates. They were scarcely replicable, because they were products

of an era in which the United States was the main proponent of a free trade liberal economy worldwide. That has now gone, and will not be repeated, because the US has become very protectionist. These countries had gone for growth at a time when the US market was fairly liberal, and they had attached themselves to the US market. That export-oriented growth of Taiwan and South Korea is not going to be repeated; not least because its ideological function has been rendered superfluous. As for desirability, the answer is no, because the single-minded pursuit of GNP has entailed very high social costs. In addition to this, the environment has been ravaged in those countries. Taiwan is now a toxic island. And then, indigenous agriculture has been destroyed by being subordinated to needs of export-led industrialisation. Agricultural population is now lower than 20 per cent. What is more, there is also a problem of legitimacy, because the success was dependent upon repression of labour. So labour now sees the issue as the need to redistribute wealth from past growth, which means democratisation. This becomes an obstacle to further growth. And these economies have not the base from which to make the leap into further growth: they are technological colonies of Japan. There has been little technology transfer. They depend upon efficient organisation of cheap labour; and in that respect, they see themselves caught between cheaper labour economies — Indonesia, Thailand — and the high-tech economies of the US and Japan. They are likely, therefore, in the 1990s, to see lower growth rates and worsening social justice. Their problem is whether they will be hurled back into the Third World by the crisis they will face. By denying democracy, they were able to purchase maybe three decades of high-speed growth, but now the costs are beginning to catch up with them; and there is no way round the whole question of democratic development. The internal tensions are likely to grow stronger.

What is also happening is that the advantages of cheap labour economies are, to some extent, being negated by more efficient automation in the rich world: in electronics, wiring done in labour-intensive processes in the Philippines or Taiwan is now being automated. The same is true with car production: clever use of high-tech processes, with some labour-intensive functions, negates the advantage of cheap labour in the Third World. In addition, the Japanese labour force is increasingly participatory, involved in decision-making and innovation. American corporations transferring to the Third World still want a mechanistic, robotic work force; and this will soon no longer be competitive. And of course, South Korea has one of the most highly centralised and coerced work forces in the world. It is militaristic management; there is no room for autonomy on the shop floor. Countries that have highly-motivated work-forces would be more likely to be successful. There is, however, little prospect of this at the moment, because there are so many factors, both local and international, that are against the emergence of newly industrialising countries. New development strategies would have to be of a radically different kind; they would be opposed to current models of industrial transition according to neo-classical economics.

Walden Bello believes that new 'radical models of growth' must evolve. There is a tension between those who think of growth as inherently malign and those who look to sustainable growth. Bello thinks that the tendency to romanticise traditional lifestyles and to seek inspiration in their version of sustainability is not going to be helpful either to the West or the developing societies.

The people of the Third World do want improvements in health, in income, they do want greater decision-making power over their lives. They want to be free of the rules of tradition, and don't want to be enslaved by community, no matter how egalitarian. People do want individual space. That doesn't mean the universal cult of the motor car. I know that traditional lifestyles have had communitarian and collective aspects that are good, but they have also had the subjugation of women and lack of individual development. I think advances in living standards, political freedoms and cultural enrichment are desirable for people in the Third World. I think, for example, the VCR and the personal computer are liberating tools: the personal computer was vital in my work when we were trying to bring down the Marcos dictatorship. Maybe what is wrong is the ownership of a VCR and a computer by every individual. We could have socialised community use of advanced items; what is wrong is the corporate multiplication of needs . . . Certainly, the destruction of indigenous communities is horrible. But that doesn't mean that we condemn everything that comes with the oppressive system, because more than anything else at this time, we need the end of mechanistic ideologies, and the last thing we would want is the imposition of a new ideology that says everything about the past should be preserved. One of the positive legacies of Marx — and I'm not a Marxist — is that methodically and ethically, it teaches you that there are both good and bad things within any given system.

The encounter with a repressive and oppressive system does not mean that your way of defence is to *go back*. The way is to move to a more liberating future that takes some aspects of that encounter and transmutes them into an emancipatory potential. The growth versus environment debate is, in many ways, I think, a false debate. You can have a sane growth that respects the ecological equilibrium. You can be both practical and respectful of community and environment at the same time. We need to go beyond such false dichotomies that would say all growth is bad, and environment good, all communities are great and any movement towards more complex societies is bad. These are totalising thinkings: if I were to propose Western anti-growth notions to Third World communities, they would laugh at me.

If Walden Bello says the experience of the newly industrialised countries is not replicable, and their qualified success is precarious, Martin Khor, of the Consumers' Association of Penang (see pp.157ff.), evokes the position of the majority of Third World countries as one of abject dependency. It is clear that there is, as yet, no example of equitable, sustainable and ecologically sensitive development in the world; but that renders the search all the more urgent. When Martin Khor refers to traditional societies, this is not in order to recommend that the West emulate their life-styles, but simply to point out that they embody certain principles and values which may be usefully accommodated in any hopeful alternative to present patterns of development.

Martin Khor believes there is a direct parallel between the relationship of dependency of children upon adults, and the inferiorised relationship of many Third World countries which remained subordinated to neo-colonial tutelage of the West.

Many Third World countries had their growth and development misshapen during the colonial period. This has continued through the time of formal decolonisation; in fact, it operates with increasing viciousness today, and with perhaps even more devastating effect, because at least under colonialism people realised that they were colonised. Therefore they had the identity of colonised people struggling for freedom. But when you continue to be colonised without realising it because the culture of being colonised is deep within you, then the colonised have no consciousness of their position. This means that there is little impulse towards any idea of liberation.

That consciousness is less because we have political independence. But in the world economic order, we find more and more resources being channelled from the Third World, physical, financial, cultural, and even more intensively than in the colonial period. The wealth filtered away is not only through interest paid on debt, but through losses due to the decline in terms of trade, royalties paid on patents, capital flight. It may be as much as \$2-300 billion a year; the true figure is very difficult to determine. This is economic colonialism. But if you don't know you're being exploited because this seems to be the just, fair, objective workings of the market-place, then this is how the colonial culture seeps into you.

The conflict between capitalism and socialism remained always a quarrel within industrialism. That is not to say it hasn't been a very real conflict. But apart from that, there is another problem. We have come to define capitalism as big capitalism, monopoly capitalism, whereby a few big companies get bigger and bigger, controlling more and more of the world's resources. On the other hand, we have defined socialism as big socialism, whereby few people control large sectors of the economy; what we might call monopoly socialism.

Now although the transnationals are coming to the Third World, dominating a significant part of the economy, you also have many examples of small capitalism and small socialism co-existing to some extent. If we want to look to the ideology of the future, we shouldn't be saying, 'Is capitalism better?' or 'Is socialism better?', nor that capitalism has proved itself by the collapse of socialism, and the road forward is now to embrace the free market for everybody. The question is, what kind of market, what kind of enterprise, what size? For it may be that the way forward for the Third World, and perhaps even for the rest of the world, is a combination of small-scale capitalism and small-scale socialism — the family firm in industry and services, the family farm in agriculture; and co-operative industries and service enterprises and farming co-ops. Very often this is called the 'informal sector', which is a very doubtful expression. In many Third World countries, the so-called 'informal sector' is 60-70 per cent of the economy. We have a term in Asia, 'the people's economy', an economic unit relying basically upon the family's labour, and which doesn't purchase other people's labour, or if it does, they are people known to you, direct social relationships, and there is no exploitation. In periods of economic depression, when the world market is cut off from you, you find a flowering and expansion of the people's economy. I think we are entering such a phase now, with the world market shrinking, people go back to the family firm and farm. Now, in classical economics, you would call them the petty mode of production, with two variants: one petty subsistence mode of production, in which the family is self-reliant in producing its own food, making its own clothes, building its own house and so on; and the second is the petty commodity mode of production, in which you do produce for the market. We could have a combination of both, communities producing for each other, perhaps even producing for other countries. But this would mean trade in goods on an equal basis, and basic goods required by both communities or countries. This would be a model for South-South economic relations, and ultimately, even North-South. This is already a reality in many Third World countries; one in which local resources are used, with technologies that are appropriate to the cultures, the resources and the human beings operating them. The advantage of the small-scale approach is that it celebrates diversity, and uses the ingenuity of people, and returns to them the joy of working together.

It isn't that the people who run the existing system are evil: they are rational economic animals within a totally irrational system. It is the chronic insecurity that drives even the big companies to ever larger markets in order to produce more, to lower their cost of production so they make more profit. And when this competitive drive between companies is set in a social context where there is immense inequality in the distribution of wealth, income and therefore purchasing power, then the entrepreneur says, 'Where is the market?' He does not say, 'Who are the human beings, what are their needs and how can I answer them?' He will see that the market is with the 20 per cent of the population who control 80 per cent of the purchasing power of the country. And you can extrapolate this to the world as a whole. So he will produce for those with purchasing power. But since that 20 per cent have already satisfied their basic needs, he will have to create supplementary needs, to make those people feel insecure unless they buy a pen for $1,000, when one that costs two or three dollars is perfectly adequate for its function. Unless a man has 30 pairs of shoes — one for jogging, one for hiking, one for squash, one for badminton, one for partying, one for the board meeting — he feels inadequate. This is the Imelda Marcos syndrome, but it does fuel the system. We have to ensure that people feel unhappy with their appearance unless they use perfumes, make-up or get plastic surgery . . . This has a major impact upon culture, and leads to the fact that when I respond to you, it is my appearance that responds to yours, rather than your reality to my reality. And this culture of promotion is a by-product of the economic system, cultural transformations arise out of the needs of the economy, and human beings are dragged along in its wake.

It may be that the dissatisfactions felt in the West with the social costs of development there — crime, violence, loneliness, family breakdown — will lead to the growth of a new counter-culture of the Green movement; and the people there may look to the Third World — as happened, to some extent, in the 1960s — in search of wholeness and humanity. And then the people of the Third World will say, 'Hey, these people themselves are not happy, and have lost confidence in their own values.' There might be hope in such a possibility, but it's a big fight, because the two forces confronting each other are the Green force and the corporate force; and the latter is demanding more freedoms and more liberalisation and more territory into which to expand.

Vandana Shiva made an interesting speech last year, entitled Decolonising the North. Perhaps it is only the Third World that will be able to decolonise the North by showing the North what they have lost, and indicating a hopeful future. I think that the present system already belongs to a bygone age. The future lies in those societies that still exist in the Third World, indigenous, local, traditional. It may be that the vast mountain of debt that has continued to fuel the system will lead to its collapse, and the return to self-reliance may be forced upon the world, a coming back to more modest ways of living may be a consequence of pressure rather than of choice. In that sense, it may be that economic breakdown saves the environment; or it could be that environmental collapse caused by accelerating growth will eventually lead to economic collapse: the industrial system may be ruined for ecological reasons rather than economic ones. These are the two possible scenarios, I don't know which is preferable. But in an age of crisis and multiple breakdowns, people will need hope, and that is our task. We have the force of ideas, but we don't have the physical might and the pervasive presence that the big companies have. We appear to be lunatics, because we are sane in an insane system.

JOSE LUTZENBERGER, RIGHT LIVELIHOOD AWARD WINNER 1988. A Brazilian agronomist and engineer who worked for 15 years for the chemical company BASF, but left in 1972 to start a vigorous and successful campaign against the over-use of agrochemicals. In the 10 years after 1978 the use of such chemicals in his home state of Rio Grande del Sul fell by more than 70 per cent, which largely reflects his work with local farmers and their association on 'regenerative agriculture' — the process of increasing the fertility of the soil through food production rather than the reverse. He has also been an effective critic of the many World Bank projects in Brazil, and was an important influence in crating a new environmental awareness in the Bank. He became Minister for the Environment in the Collor government in 1989. Lutzenberger shows how the systematic application of scientific and technical knowledge to environmental problems can help to address the global ecological crisis.

THE DYNAMIC THAT drives and draws people the world over into urban industrial life appears irresistible. The one-way, irreversible journey from biosphere to technosphere has a compelling power, which defies understanding in the terms in which such processes are usually expressed. Lutzenberger believes that this is because modern industrial society is unaware of the extent to which it has become a religion, a proselytising, messianic religion at that. We are dealing here with perceptions that cannot be reached by reason. The basic dogma of this religion is that we have the key to secular forms of salvation, and that key is technology; and this can transform our world into a paradise. The nature of industrial society remains hidden to itself, and while this remains so, it will continue to inflict untold — because unperceived — suffering on others.

It seeks to compel the whole world into this way of thinking. It cannot conceive that the Indian in the forest could be happy. Even monstrous substitute religions like Nazism or Stalinism demanded of their subject peoples certain sacrifices — frugality and self-denial — in the interest of their higher truths. But modern industrialism demands of its votaries total self-indulgence, orgiastic excess, prodigality and waste. Therein lies its powerful appeal. Those who can waste the most then become the most worthy citizens, because they contribute most to GNP. Of course, as with all religions, there are sacrifices: but these are invisible, for they are passed on elsewhere, conjured out of sight, so that this form of development looks like pure unalloyed gain.

We live in a 100 per cent technological society, in which most people are technologically illiterate. If a culture has a technology that is open and transparent, then all its members can understand functions that are not their own. In a society where the collective technology is comprehensible, nobody mistakes the gallows for the plough. But we are in a situation where people can no longer distinguish between the gallows and the plough: they cannot tell the difference between an instrument of domination and instrument of liberation.

We need a political critique of technology. The essential difference is between *science* and *technology*. Science is understood by few. Whenever people say science, they usually mean technology. Who, studying only medicine or agriculture or engineering, ever quietly opens a book on the history of science? If they did, they would see the emergence, dominance, dissolution and decay of old and new paradigms. Belief in one is constantly yielding to the belief in that which supplants it. If they looked at it in its entirety, they would perceive those elements that are purely *ideological* in the whole story.

Everything is always ideological. But ideologies have to be built on the natural sciences, they must have their roots in the natural world. Purely political ideologies just hang in the air, like modern economic ideologies, like Marxism, for which nature does not exist. Modern economics believes that raw materials exist in unlimited quantities, and that the world has an infinite capacity to absorb all waste — a unidirectional flow from one infinity to another. I always ask, 'What is the basic postulate? Where do you think that belief will lead to? What is the act of faith underpinning it?' That is a political critique of technology.

Our anthropocentric world view, inherited from its Judaeo-Christian origin, leads to a cramped ethic. Those religions saw relationships only between humanity and God. For Marxists, there isn't even God: there are only human relationships, which makes for an even more narrow ethic. For Buddhists, Hindus and all indigenous people, those we call 'primitive', their ethic embraces the whole universe, in which everything is sacred. They don't have to make divisions between the sacred and the profane.

Many of our biologists have become necrologists. They prefer dead things, or rather, living things that have been killed in order to study them. A biologist ought to be what the British used to refer to as a *naturalist*; a dialogue with nature, wise, disciplined and suffused with love, awe and understanding. When we use the words science and technology interchangeably, and then claim that science is 'value-free', then naturally, those who make atom bombs can say 'What I am doing is value-free.' Science is not value-free. It is a value in itself. It is a religious activity, in the sense that it has to do with ethics. When science prostitutes itself, it is no longer science. Then it is not value-free, it is valueless.

Science is reverence in the presence of the divine beauty of the universe. That is not technology. Technology, however, is also emotional. It uses the knowledge that scientists have gained from nature in order to impose its will upon it. Technology does not want to preserve and maintain the world, but to change it.

A scientist and a technologist stand before a great mountain, perhaps the Sugar Loaf in Rio de Janeiro. The scientist wants to know how the mountain evolved. That takes her into the realm of geology, cosmology, the solar system, the origins of the universe. And then, when she sees the rich and vital life that bedecks it — the woods, lichens, flowers, cacti and all that is on that marvellous wall of rock, she sees the great panorama of organic development, and is lost in wonder. The technocrat looks on the same scene and asks himself, 'What can I do with it? Are there extractable ores? Can I maybe level the mountain, fill in the bay, and make millions out of it as real estate?' He, too, is deeply emotional, but it is an aggressive emotion. The scientist is contemplative.

Since Lutzenberger became a member of the inner cabinet of the Brazilian government, he has concentrated on access to policy-makers at the highest level, in the hope that this would prove the most effective means of spreading the ideas and values he holds to. Direct personal contact with politicians, industrialists and economists may, he believes, have its effect. Indeed, many founders and initiators of the alternative movements have become advisers to, or even members of, governments in the past five years. Some, like the German Greens, gained parliamentary representation; others have won international recognition for their work. Many are keenly aware of the tension between the desire to maintain their own integrity, and the need to modify the values of the powerful defenders of the status quo. Most advocate a non-adversarial approach: there is no point in turning into enemies those with whom we disagree. It is a question of convergence, of common pathways. There is, as Robert Jungk, of the International Futures Library in Salzburg (see p.206), observes, considerable unease among those officially managing the present crises. They are well aware of the dangers confronting the world. It is more helpful to offer them succour and co-operation than to antagonise them.

The themes of colonialism and neo-colonialism recur frequently in the discourse of those in the alternative movements. Lutzenberger is eloquent on the consequences of centuries of colonialism in Brazil. Unlike the USA, Brazil was not colonised by people who had turned their back on Europe. It was settled by exiles of the Portuguese nobility. The land was divided into *capitanias* by those who hoped to get rich and return to Portugal. In the USA, on the other hand, a vibrant peasant culture evolved among people for whom there was no going back. Although the culture of the indigenous people of the USA was destroyed in a most brutal fashion, the culture that took root there was far healthier than anything that occurred in Brazil.

Because it was a land-based culture, the cities of North America were never beautiful. Brazilian cities were more like those of Southern Europe — look at what Manfred Max-Neef writes about Tiradentes. But the *caboclo* of Brazil is not a peasant, he is a permanent fugitive from the landlord. The land that was divided up between the descendants of the original settlers were tracts of millions of hectares with no settled borders. Here, the landlord is not a big peasant, nor the peasant a small landlord. Landlords hired day labourers, who had no scope for independent existence. Sometimes, the caboclo managed to escape, or in his free time, he could make small plantations on the steep slopes, grow manioc, sweet potato. In the USA, by contrast, the farmers moved to the plains, and the land was rich. In Brazil, the small farmers got only the hardest land, and they never received property deeds. Although such land was of no use to the landlords, they never gave the caboclo property rights. They didn't want independent people.

Peasants want to grow food and make a good life. Peasant culture leads to a diversified landscape, even though the original landscape may disappear. There will be a variety of production — tomatoes, fruit, vegetables, goats, sheep, handicrafts. Where there is a healthy peasant culture, there is social justice. When landlords own all the land, they don't care about food production — they can import it from anywhere. They care only about making money. And that means monocultures —

whatever will grow under local natural and market conditions — coffee, sugar, cattle, coconuts. They ensure that the population remains as poor as possible, because of the need for cheap labour in the plantations. In the North-East of Brazil, labourers are forbidden to grow a single banana, they cannot own a goat. They get the price of a share of what they produce, but they may grow nothing they can use, no mangoes, no guavas. They must buy food from the landlords' shops, and they remain forever indebted.

The one exception was in the South of Brazil where, in 1822, Donna Leopoldina brought German immigrants into the country. The big landlords hadn't taken the South, because it was still disputed territory. Of Rio Grande do Sul, 40 per cent of the land was forest, the rest pampas or prairie. Immigrants pushed into the forest, and they received something the caboclo had never had — deeds. Every immigrant was given 25 hectares of land and the rights to it. In fact, these migrants were city people, they were lumpenproletariat. But they dug themselves in and became Brazilian farmers — one of the epic stories of history. They grew corn, cassava, sweet potato, manioc, adapted to local conditions, ecologically reasonable. They did slash and burn in some places, but left 30 per cent of the state still covered with forest. Sustainable agriculture — the only peasant culture in Brazil. Within 50 years, most of the lowlands were occupied.

Later, Italian peasants came. The Germans had taken the valleys, so they took the hillsides. They really were of peasant origin, with a tradition of vine-growing. They made stone buildings, where the Germans had built with wood. Italian houses were constructed on slopes, always with a cellar for wine. Still a beautiful peasant culture; all illiterate, but with their settlements they brought priests and teachers, and, like the Germans, developed clubs, hospitals, orchestras.

In 1935, when I was a child, these cultures still flourished. Italian and German were official languages. It was a productive, sustainable way of life. In 1939, during the dictatorship of Getulio Vargas, it was systematically destroyed. Vargas was a Germanophile, a fascist and admirer of Hitler. In 1939, however, he closed the German language schools, ordered priests to cease preaching in German and Italian. Why?

He was a big landowner, with hundreds of thousands of hectares. Like all the landlords in the 1930, the *fazendeiros* in the South were becoming poorer, while the peasants were becoming more prosperous. Vargas didn't like the growing power of the small farmers. And by the 1930s, mass communications had led to every corner shop having a radio. People would gather round to listen in every town and village. Landlords in other parts of Brazil feared that their day labourers might discover that there was no misery or starvation in the South. They might learn that there were ways of being free within Brazil itself, and they might then respond accordingly. So the culture that was such a threat had to be destroyed.

This destruction was, in many ways, the forerunner of forms of 'development' that are wrecking huge areas of our country today. Now the excuses are even more thin. They say the Amazon is being destroyed because people must be fed. What hypocrisy! They clear the forest, then sow grass-seed by plane to create extensive cattle ranches. The productivity of these ranches is a scandal. They produce 30-40 kilos, at most 50, of meat per hectare per year. A single brazil-nut tree, three or four to a hectare, can produce 500-600 kilos of valuable nutrients. Existing forests can nourish far more people than anything that replaces them. The caboclos say, 'When the cattle come, we have to go, because the cattle are bringers of hunger.'

Lutzenberger insists that the prescription that, 'more development is necessary in order to create the wealth that will pay to cure the damage that unbridled development has caused' is calculated to compound the ills it claims to cure.

The same is true of those who say that poverty is at the root of most of the environmental degradation we have today. But it is the other way round: most of the poverty we see in the world is the result of the destruction of traditional cultures, of the rape of their resources in the name of 'progress', of the uprooting of people who are left with no choice but to mourn their losses in the festering slums or violate the last remaining wildernesses.

12. MAKING VISIBLE: THE RADIATION THREAT

ROSALIE BERTELL, RIGHT LIVELIHOOD AWARD WINNER 1986. Dr Rosalie Bertell received her doctorate in Biometrics in 1966, and has worked in the field of environmental health since 1970. She is now President of the International Institute of Concern for Public Health in Toronto, Canada, and is one of the founding Commissioners of the International Medical Commission based in Geneva, which works with health professionals to implement the concept of health as a human right. Bertell is also Editor-in-Chief of International Perspectives in Public Health, and author of *No Immediate Danger: Prognosis for a Radioactive Earth* (The Women's Press, London, 1985.) Bertell has served as senior cancer research scientist at Rosewell Park Memorial Institute, in Buffalo, New York; consultant to the US Nuclear Regulatory Commission and the US Environmental Agency; and participated in joint research projects with the Japanese Scientists Association and the Institute for Energy and Environmental Research in Heidelberg, Germany. Her major research projects include the Tri-State Leukaemia Survey, which assessed hereditary and environmental factors which increase the leukaemia rate; death rate of infants with low birth weight downwind from normally operating power plants in Wisconsin; a birth defect study of the Navajo Indians exposed to nuclear testing in Nevada, and uranium mining; an assessment of cancer risk and probable genetic damage to offspring of Japanese nuclear workers and a risk analysis commissioned by the German parliament, for nine accident scenarios at the Kalkar nuclear breeder reactor in Germany.)

MAKING VISIBLE INVOLVES not merely bringing into the economic accounting system the suppressed costs of the labour of women, nor the externalised damage done by economistic ideology, but also the unseen damage inflicted upon human beings victimised in the name of military or technological development. Through the International Institute of Concern for Public Health, Rosalie Bertell has monitored the testimony of radiation victims all over the world, and has consistently resisted the denials and indifference of governments and official organisations concerned with the radiation industry. She has criticised standards set by the International Commission on Radiological Protection.

There must be a different model of decision-making, which will give the victims a voice, and which will reveal the *political* nature of what are presented as *technical* decisions and trade-offs. In No Immediate Danger, Bertell had stated: 'There is no safe level of exposure to ionising radiation; therefore a permissible level is set. This is a trade-off of health for some 'benefit': the worker receives a livelihood, society gets military 'protection' and electrical power is generated.

She estimated that the victims of the nuclear age, including both military and commercial industries, were at that time (the early 1980s) around 13 million. Today, given better research estimates, they are closer to 30 million.

One place where the work of Rosalie Bertell has given courage to and strengthened the resistance of people to the dumping of radioactive waste is at Bukit Merah, near Ipoh, Malaysia. There, she prepared scientific evidence on behalf of the residents who, with Friends of the Earth Malaysia (see p.40), have organised against the polluting and dumping by the Asian Rare Earth Company, a collaboration between the Mitsubishi Corporation and B.E.H. Mineral, a Malaysian corporation. This enterprise is a classic example of practices which are now prohibited in Japan being exported to a country prepared to welcome even the most malign technologies as evidence of its advanced 'development' strategy. Alliances between national governments and transnational companies present a uniquely powerful challenge to citizens' groups. (Such collusions are often supported by the workers in the enterprises. So great is their dependency upon the income from the only source of work they have, that livelihood takes precedence over life itself. Indeed, this tragic dilemma is at the heart of what is wrong with existing patterns of development. Where unemployment and poverty are the only visible alternative to damaging technology, where even the lives of those we love are in jeopardy, our 'choices' that lead us to defend jobs at all costs is the most poignantly eloquent comment on the true nature of the freedoms we enjoy.)

Asian Rare Earth processes monazite to produce yttrium, a rare earth used in the electronics industry. It also creates lead sulphate and thorium hydroxide, a radioactive waste with a half-life of billions of years. At Bukit Merah, the people knew nothing of the nature of the plant until it had been operating for several years after it was set up in 1982. When they became aware of the dangers, they took out a court injunction, and the works closed down for a year. The company was given permission to reopen in October 1987, after a temporary waste storage building had been constructed. It was issued with a certificate of safety by the Atomic Energy Board of Malaysia. The Anti-Radioactivity Committee formed by the community took the company to court a second time, for damaging the health of the people. A verdict after the prolonged hearing was still awaited in 1991.

It emerged that the company had been dumping the waste promiscuously around Ipoh, in leaky drums around streams and settlements. Surveys showed that the children of Bukit Merah have dangerously high levels of lead in their blood. But it was not until three years ago that children began to develop brain tumours and leukaemia. There have also been abnormal numbers of miscarriages and birth defects. In spite of the evidence of Rosalie

Bertell and her colleagues, the authorities deny the danger, saying that radioactivity from the plant is lower than the 'background radiation' of tin-mining, which has been traditionally a major economic activity in Ipoh. Many of the tin mines have now closed, but the old workings still scar the landscape. Ipoh, which is the second city of Malaysia, with a population around 600,000, is surrounded by hills, and a constant haze hangs above it. The limestone hills within the city have been ravaged by the cement industry, so that many of these stand, exposed and crumbling, like broken teeth.

Chong Kim Choy is the chair of the Anti-Radioactivity Committee. He tells how the people of Bukit Merah came here 30 years ago from the countryside. They built their own houses, and they work as craftspeople, shoemakers, small traders. Many have improved and extended their dwellings over the years. Chong tells how his four daughters have already moved away with their children; indeed, about one-third of the people have already left the area. Hew Yoon Tat is a vendor who sells pork. He has been interned under the Internal Security Act, which has been used to suppress dissent in Malaysia. 'In the beginning, there were demonstrations of up to 20,000 people, but when the government started to use the ISA, they became afraid.' Lok Yan Ngo says that the action group is now caught between the fear of government repression, and fear for their children's future. The parents of those children who have fallen sick or died have reached a state of desperation beyond anger.

The general manager of Asian Rare Earth admitted that Japan has ceased to import and process monazite because of the danger of radioactive pollution. 'It shows that Japan thinks the life of people in other countries is worth less than Japanese lives', said a mother of one of the sick children. 'What is worse is that our government seems to share that view.' Those who argue that economic domination is less malign than other forms of imperial conquest might perhaps look at the wasted bodies and frail faces of the children of Bukit Merah. Without strong and committed support from outside the country, the resistance of the people would have been far less effective.

Rosalie Bertell now fears that environmental awareness may lead to a 'recuperation of our work', and that superficial, image-conscious 'solutions' might be offered in place of the more difficult work that remains to be accomplished. In fact, some Western leaders have even promoted uranium industries and nuclear power as 'environmentally clean', as a means of countering the greenhouse effect. As a Commissioner on the International Commission of Health Professionals (ICHP), Rosalie Bertell is able to present radioactive pollution as a human rights issue at the United Nations.

'There has been irreversible damage, and every day it continues.' Rosalie Bertell sees the constant growth and expansion of militarism and its faith in the nuclear armoury, as a form of addiction; and the mass of the people are the 'passive co-operators'. Like gambling, or any other form of addiction, militarism is riddled with wild excess, lying, rationalisation and secrecy. It is a bitter irony that the very mechanisms justified as necessary for our 'defence' should be the very agents of undermining the most effective defence which the human body has against disease. The effects of radiation lower the immune defences of every exposed person. Nuclear defence, therefore, is the supreme example of iatrogenic activity — it causes and exacerbates the ills it purports to cure.

Radiation is also one of the most tragic examples of externalised costs: in this case, they are passed on to future generations, through insoluble problems of the damaged gene-pool of humanity, and the persistence of noxious waste in the environment for an indefinite future. The idea that the future will somehow take care of itself offers comforting illusions about the omnipotence of our technology, and of the redemptive capacity of our science. It encourages us to believe we can escape the consequences of our own actions; which all tends to infantilise us, by making us more dependent upon the dubious sagacity of experts.

But of course, we have changed bad behaviour and iniquitous practices in the past — slavery, for instance — so there is no reason why we shouldn't change our behaviour in this respect also. People change by *being able to imagine an alternative future*. The crisis is structural. We are at the limits of what is possible within the present structure, and we need to reorganise. This is why respect for dissent is important, Through the diversity this represents, we shall make the creative breakthroughs. Disagreement and dissent lead to true integrity. We should celebrate multiplicity, variety.

Like any other addiction, we look to the source of the wrong in our search for a cure. The best thing is to *stop* the militarism to which we are addicted. Dealing with the environmental and social consequences of that addiction is more difficult. It may take 100 years to build up an alternative behaviour, but if we don't stop, future generations will not even have the chance to try. I would like to see every person, especially every woman, take responsibility for her own life, because I don't think change will occur unless we do. I would like to see every sector of society imagine a different future, and put serious time and effort into it. The biggest obstacle to change is people's own negative self-image. It would involve a shift to a non-dominance view of creation; a stress on *being* in a process rather than *having* finished products; a spirit of service, a feeling of being part of the earth, and the evolution of the human species into an awareness of the global community. We must get rid of the road-blocks that hinder the coming together of the human species into a co-operative, integral, social whole. Among those road-blocks are the International Commission on Radiological Protection, and the United Nations Security Council, which rewards nuclear addiction with superpower status. The UN requires the ability to disarm the bully on the block, rather than to reward him with honour and respect. While the 'passive co-operators' of addiction don't have the self-confidence to act, nothing happens. Once they say they'll no longer co-operate, once they say, 'This is nonsense,' then things can change very quickly. Look at the Berlin Wall: the magic that kept it up for so long was co-operation.

The best way out is to find a clear, powerful issue, around which people can mobilise. An analogy with the past might be the eight-hour-day in the trade union movement. The early industrial period was a time of extremely hazardous occupations — the machinery, the furnaces, the dangerous materials, all of which were a threat to the life and health of the workers. Eventually, they woke up to the fact that the efficiency and profit of industry were based on a trade-off of their life and health. So they started to rebel, and they invented the strike. It was very chaotic and disorderly; every group seemed to have its own analysis, its own philosophy, its own social dimension. But what made it all gel into a true political force for change was the eight-hour-day. It is a beautiful idea, because it cuts across ethnic differences, sexual difference, even work-type — it doesn't matter if you're in a steel mill, a pit, a hospital. It doesn't make you have to choose between analyses and philosophies. It's simple, it's based on survival. But the unions which accomplished this earned the power to sit at the table with employers and enter into the decision-making process.

In the environmental movement, we are not yet sitting at the table. We still need that one simple issue. The hazards which used to be concentrated in the work-space are now being dispersed, dumped in the water, buried in the ground, sent up the stacks; so the threat is now the living-space. So it is a very good analogy. It suggests we won't get any place until we organise. What we still need is the clear single issue on which we can organise; something that will make the people get up and say, 'No, this is crazy, we're not going to stand for it.' It might be toxic waste, sickness in children. We are almost there, but not quite. This is the source of the present tension. When it goes, it will move fast.

I think the days of the trade unions are finished. Their issues should be incorporated into law, and their expertise should pass to the citizen groups. The labour unions devised wonderful things, like arbitration, worker-health laws, pre-hiring physical examination, workers' compensation. All this was very creative. It was a layer of complexity without which there would have been no advance in the industrial age. If industrialism had gone on as in the beginning, it would have destroyed the workers. What we need is a comparable complexity in the area of environmental issues.

I've been working at Blind River, Ontario, which is a one-industry town. The industry is uranium-refining. What you find is that the workers' health is good, but they're sending the waste up the stacks and dumping it in water. The workers have fought to clean up the work-place, but where is it going? So the community looks at the workers, and says, 'The workers aren't sick, so why should we be sick?' Recently, we dealt with an accident that helps to make visible the effects on the community. Their filter blew out, and they were releasing raw uranium yellow-cake out of the stack for 32 hours. It went over the Indian Reserve, Missassaga Indian land. So we can pick that up, and show the depression in the white blood count of the children who were playing during the accident and not warned. The community took the brunt of the accident, whereas the workers were probably OK in the plant.

In the early industrial era, those with money knew they could buy a house remote from the sources of pollution. They could pay for the best medical care. Now, no one can buy exemption from the pervasive toxins in the environment. There is nowhere to hide from the consequences of our actions; that it is so frequently the aim of the powerful to conceal those consequences shows the level of their fear and irrationality.

The intermediate goal of money will no longer procure the final end. This throws into chaos traditional hierarchies and privilege. Not all the rich yet realise it. What we are at is not the end of the world, but at the limit of our old structures and received mental categories. Once you hit upon the fact that we can change our heads, and devise a new model of being in the world, then we can go. Our construct of the world is what has to move — it is a self-imposed limitation. Much of it is sexist, because men had carved out the economic and political structures as the way to survive — the idea that if you have money and power, you can buy everything else. It is a moment of chaos and of opportunity. I think that life is stronger than death, and the little daisy still comes through the cement sidewalk. I think life will come through, if we have time.

The vision has to be there, too. I think the big issue, the vision, is health, survival, healthy children, water, food, meaningful work. The power to change comes out of the vision. But we have to make change possible; and that means we have to get out of the way this male concept of how to do it. That is a barrier, and a big one, because they are so sure of themselves. One thing that scares me is when the people of the West say, 'Well we got the world into this mess, we have to get them out of it.'

I want to say, 'No, get out of here. Stay out of the way. The people who were not in a mess in the first place have the best likelihood of getting us out of it.' The two areas that need the most work are both in the First World — the unmasking of the military, and the manipulation of information.

The International Institute of Concern for Public Health has initiated health surveys, which have been devised by local communities, together with health professionals, in order to do their own local health assessment.

The survey covers things like residential history, life-style, past medical history, occupational exposures, hobbies and activities; we also cover reproductive experience and the health of children. Then this information, in the collection of which the community has taken part, is put into the computer, and we can make up health profiles for the community. These can be broken down into sub-community profiles, to show differences in various parts of the city, the health of workers as against non-workers, those in one industry as against those living down wind from a plant, those whose water supply is city water as against those who use a well. You can also profile the health of one city against another, and then meet with the people to discuss which aspect of health most concerns them. One community was concerned with suicides in the young: young people were sniffing gasoline, destroying their brains. This came out of despair at any kind of a future. Then you can initiate a public health programme and evaluate its effectiveness. For example, if they highlight respiratory disease as a major anxiety, you look at a polluting factory in the neighbourhood, do a clinical analysis of the respiratory disease. Then when releases from the factory have been modified, you can actually show whether there has been an improvement in the community's health. So you are not taking the experts' word for anything, but providing a tool for the community, using which they can get the answer to their most urgent questions. You are also changing the focus of epidemiology, to prove that something either improves or decreases the quality of life for everybody, on a local basis, anywhere. I call it creating a new level of medical care. If somebody comes to you with polio, you do everything you can to improve the condition of that person, so you don't neglect the body of knowledge that is designed for all polio cases. However, that person might need something else, might also have heart disease or whatever. So you have a localised public health scheme, as well as the sophisticated epidemiological stuff that nobody can do because it is too expensive, or whatever.

There are gross public health problems, like the dumping of mercury into water, whereby you get Minamata disease. You could stop that instantly, by not dumping the mercury. But there are very few poison models where you have a specific health end-point. In fact, most of the pollutants we now use are an intensification and concentration of pollutants we've always had; therefore you don't get a different and new end-point, but you find an escalation of the effect, in that the number of people affected is far higher, or the intensity of the illness much greater. For example, radiation is a naturally occurring pollutant, which takes its toll of health. If you increase radiation in the environment, you're going to get more of the same thing, but you're not going to get Minamata disease, as you do when you put mercury into the drinking water. Then you have to deal with the legal system which says that you have to prove that this person's disease is *more* probably caused by the exposure than not, which means that you can get legal compensation only if you more than double the rate of naturally occurring disease. So if you increase the cancer rate by 40 per cent, that is not doubling. So although it is more probable than not for each individual that it was not caused naturally, you cannot get legal recourse. That is why I am calling for proportional compensation, so if you can say the rate has increased by 40 per cent, the polluting industry should pay 40 per cent of everybody's compensation.

Dr Bertell was originally a mathematician, and she worked for a major corporation. She later went for five years to a Carmelite retreat. The community was completely self-reliant. There, she learned the possibilities of co-operative sufficiency. She says there are something like 3,000 religious communities in the United States, all of them living and successful models of a more harmonious and modest way of living, a vast unrecognised resource, which suggests that the sources of future hope are closer to hand than we realise. Such communities resemble traditional Third World communities, which many people lament the passing of, and which are believed to be an impossible ideal for rich Western society. Those hopeful alternatives, with their 'joyful austerity', already exist, here and now. The terror of loss which inhibits those who live in fearful dependency on the existing ways of answering need, is actually groundless.

On the other hand, the pressures against those working for change are getting stronger. We should regard this as a sign of success. The sweeping changes that are already in train in the world make those in power desperate, angry and demanding. Even they feel that time is on the side of those who want change. There is no need to antagonise them.

Speaking of human suffering, Rosalie Bertell says:

The crucifixion has been badly presented. It is really a very *kind* way of God's letting us see the worst part of our behaviour. It is God's way of not *forcing* us, but of putting our actions right in front of us, and saying, 'Look, this is what you do.' The suffering of the Third World *ought* to be teaching us what we are doing, it ought to be reflecting our behaviour back to us. It is very visible today. We are killing people in the Third World for our self-maintenance, just as we killed Jesus. We are randomly killing people with technology and pollution. We are taking the bread of the poor and building military machines with it. We are killing people with dollar wars and economic deprivation. This is murder. If we can't see it, if we are too busy looking only at the beautiful things in creation, we are missing something.

DR ALICE STEWART, RIGHT LIVELIHOOD AWARD WINNER 1986. Originally a clinical physician, Dr Alice Stewart became the youngest woman to be elected a Fellow of the Royal College of Physicians in 1946. In the same year, she joined the Unit of Social Medicine in Oxford. In 1955, she and her colleagues noticed the rapid increase in leukaemia among children, which seemed likely to have environmental causes, and the idea for the Oxford Childhood Cancer Survey was born. One of the key early findings of this survey was that children who died of leukaemia or cancer had been X-rayed *in utero* twice as often as healthy children. This controversial finding eventually led to the ending of X-rays for pregnant women, and confirmed Stewart's interest in and focus on the effects of low-level radiation. The Oxford Survey was extended to adult cancer sufferers, and further data were collected which supported the original conclusions, which were finally accepted by the International Commission on Radiological Protection (ICRP).Meanwhile, Alice Stewart had become involved in a study of the nuclear industry at Hanford USA, which found that for a large group of workers there was evidence of a cancer risk comparable to that of pre-natal X-rays at supposedly safe dose levels. This ran counter to ICRP recommendations, themselves based on the data from atom bomb survivors, which underpin the world's largest study of the cancer effects of radiation. Stewart's findings created further controversy and denials. This led her to turn her attention to the A-bomb Casualty Commission data themselves. Her findings here were equally controversial, and implied that all radiation protection committees have been grossly underestimating the number of cancers caused by background radiation and other low-dose circumstances. This conclusion has not yet been accepted by ICRP. Stewart's commitment to work that is deeply unpopular with the nuclear establishment has cost her academic preferment and research funds.

ALICE STEWART'S WORK on the effects of low-level radiation was met with a barrage of denial, later faint praise, and finally, grudging acceptance. This demonstrates just how difficult it is to gain recognition for that which is not immediately visible. A woman saying deeply unpopular things in a male stronghold is given a unique insight into the way discrimination operates. At 85, however, Alice Stewart is still working with undiminished energy and excitement.

She expected hostility and resistance. When it was found that children exposed to X-rays *in utero* had an increased risk of dying of childhood cancers, Dr Stewart says, 'There was bound to be resistance, particularly from the medical establishment, and after all, the use of X-rays had proved such a useful aid to diagnosis.'

The subsequent work on low-level radiation with Thomas Mancuso at Hanford, Washington, showed that the low-dose effect on children was also observable in occupational exposure of adults, employees in the nuclear industry.

> I went to the United States in 1974, to take part in what the Department of Energy imagined would be a reassuring study into the effects of low-level radiation on plants and animals, and of course, the team came up with its findings on the threat to human beings. All research into low-level radiation was stopped, and the funds withdrawn. If I had not brought back a copy of the Hanford data to Britain, they would have been destroyed. All we had said was that one per cent of the workers in the industry had an occupational disease. We didn't realise that the radiation industry wouldn't see it like that at all. To them, it meant they would have to pay out vast sums in compensation.

Dr Stewart predicts a great increase in the number of cancers if present levels of 'safety' are maintained; and the problem of nuclear waste remains insoluble.

> It wasn't until radiation cooled down to present levels that the earth's surface became habitable. You cannot bring this issue home to people until long after it is irreversible. It doesn't have the same dramatic and visible impact that other disasters might.
>
> When the nuclear industry started, it was known to be dangerous. There had been a group of radium luminisers in the thirties who had licked their paint-brushes, and nearly all of them died of the effects of radiation. In the beginning, the authorities were sincere when they set the levels of safety according to the state of their knowledge. It was only when the nuclear industry became so closely meshed with the weapons industry that it became affected by secrecy and corruption.

The A-bomb survivor studies set the current standards for radiation exposure. Dr Stewart and her colleagues discovered flaws in the conclusions drawn from the studies. By mistakenly viewing the most disease-resistant A-bomb survivors as though they were typical of the entire population, analysts seriously underestimated the harmful effects of radioactivity. After five years (and no surveys were conducted on Hiroshima or Nagasaki until the first post-war census in Japan in 1951), the studies showed that the non-cancer death rate was slightly lower than normal, and showed no sign of being related to the dose of radioactivity received. It was concluded from this that nothing happened at a low dose; cancer had affected only those who had had a high dose. From these conclusions the risks to workers in the nuclear industry were extrapolated. Dr Stewart demonstrated that the survivors were far from being a 'normal' population: the fact that they had survived at all indicated that they were likely to be a healthier than average group. Their 'normal' death rate ought to have been lower than average. There had been a 'silent crippling'. Many had suffered damage to the bone-marrow; their apparent non-cancer death might well have come from their falling victim to opportunistic diseases because of a weakened immune system.

This meant that all the standards set on the basis of the A-bomb studies were suspect. The approval by the US National Academy of Science of standards based on the premise that the effects of the bomb were negligible after five years was irresponsible. As a result of extrapolating from high-dose to low-dose effects, we have underestimated the risks from low-level radiation. Thus may be gloomy news for the nuclear industry, but it is good news for those seeking the causes of cancer.

Low-level radiation is a carcinogen. Many people now accept that it is causing some cancers. Indeed, it may be causing a majority of them. It is possible that radiation is not the worst carcinogen, but it is certainly the most ubiquitous. The background dose of radioactivity is so uniformly low that the only danger to plants and animals comes from the molecular changes which occasionally alter the behaviour of daughter cells. These mutations are the basic cause of cancer, but this risk is too small (and the latency too long) for the extra deaths to have much effect on reproductive efficiency. But human-made additions to background radiation have disturbed this planetary equilibrium and shown that radioactivity has tissue-destructive as well as mutational effects. They have also made it possible to estimate the cancer induction risk, provided there is a correct assessment of the radiation dose and all interference factors.

> Of course, our work has not always been uniformly right. But we have represented certain ideas which, had they been stifled, would have left the world poorer. If you say unpopular things, you pay professionally. That is only to be expected. When I came back from the US, the Windscale enquiry was about to start. I thought, as good citizens, we had a duty to tell the people what we had found. I thought the industry would welcome our findings, as genuinely concerned about the consequences of their activities. But instead, I found I was public enemy number one. We were

ostracised. No one wanted to know. I suppose it is natural that people want to hide things. We tend to lock things away in cellars and attics and shut the door. But one day, that door will force its way open.

Social medicine is a vital area of concern. So many of the health problems of the contemporary world are invisible; and since women's work has been invisible, it is particularly appropriate that those hidden dangers should be a preoccupation of women. We have identified a threat to well-being, and offered up our work to those whose job it is to formulate policy. Although I've never been partisan, as a woman I've been on the side of life, of minimising all avoidable injury to human beings.

MORDECHAI VANUNU, RIGHT LIVELIHOOD AWARD WINNER 1987. Mordechai Vanunu was born in Morocco, and moved to Israel with his family in 1963. After three years' military service, he began a physics degree at Tel Aviv University, but had to abandon this for economic reasons. He became a technician at the Dimona nuclear plant in 1976. In 1979, he began studies at Ben Gurion University, Be'er Sheva, in philosophy and geography, graduating in 1984. He became a lecturer in philosophy. He had become increasingly politically active, calling for equal rights for Palestinians within the state, and the inclusion of Palestinians in negotiations for an independent Palestinian state. He also advocated religious freedom, and separation of religion from the state. He opposed the Israeli invasion of Lebanon in 1982. In 1985, he was part of a mass lay-off at Dimona. In 1986, Vanunu talked to the UK *Sunday Times* about the Dimona plant, revealing that Israel's nuclear capability was far greater than suspected, that Israel probably has a stockpile of 100-200 nuclear weapons, can make thermonuclear devices of greater power than atomic bombs and that Israel also collaborated routinely with South Africa on nuclear matters. Soon after the *Sunday Times* article, Vanunu went missing. A few weeks later it transpired that he had been lured to Rome by Israel's Secret Service, kidnapped and taken to Israel where he has been in gaol ever since. His trial for espionage and treason opened on 30 August 1987 under conditions of the most intense secrecy, and he was sentenced to 18 years' imprisonment in March 1988.

Vanunu's revelations were exhaustively checked by the *Sunday Times* before their publication, and they have not been seriously challenged. The seriousness of this nuclear capability in perhaps the most unstable area of the world is an issue that has received little attention from the international media.

PART 3: POPULAR EMPOWERMENT

Popular empowerment is the third major theme in the attempt to formulate an alternative world view. This version of power is something far removed from the sense of 'purchasing power', which is the promise of the dominant world system; and it goes far beyond a political empowerment which entitles its beneficiaries to pull a lever or cross a piece of paper once every few years. Empowerment in this context means a dynamic and continuous engagement of people in the shape and direction of their society in such ways that they can feel and expeirence their influence upon it.

A number of elements are necessary for new forms of popular participation.

13. SMALL IS STILL BEAUTIFUL

LEOPOLD KOHR, RIGHT LIVELIHOOD AWARD WINNER 1983. Leopold Kohr, born in 1901, was educated at the universities of Innsbruck, Paris, Vienna and the London School of Economics. After a career as correspondent in the Spanish Civil War, he entered academic life, at Rutgers University in the US, at the University of Puerto Rico and at University College of Wales, Aberystwyth. He was the originator, and for 25 years, the solitary advocate, of the concept of the human scale, and the idea of a return to life in small communities, both of which were later popularised by his friend Fritz Schumacher in his *Small is Beautiful*. Kohr has consistently advocated the effectiveness of the small autonomous unit in the solution of human problems. His ideas have been elaborated in many books, including *The Breakdown of Nations* (Routledge & Kegan Paul 1957); *Development without Aid* (1973) and *The Overdeveloped Nations*, both published by Christopher Davies, Swansea.

EMPOWERMENT OF PEOPLE is possible only within small, comprehensible communities; and many of the advocates of feasible, emancipatory alternatives are grounded in a passionate attachment to the local: Jose Lutzenberger's love of his native Rio Grande do Sul is one example, Bill Mollison's affection for his Tasmanian background is another. Leopold Kohr's native village near Salzburg, and the range and variety of its people, informs his diagnosis that *size* is the most dysfunctional factor in human communities. In his *Breakdown of Nations*, he recommends 'not the Balkanisation, but the Scandinavisation' of Europe into smaller states — Burgundy, Lombardy, Bavaria, Catalonia, Wales, Navarre: these are traditional regions which still exist as identifiable and potentially autonomous countries. Like unwieldy nation-states, the existence of a global market is another monument to the giantism Kohr detests. He talks of the 'harmony produced by balanced *diversity*'; and expresses a particular fondness for Lichtenstein, Andorra and the Swiss cantons as manageable units which command a sense of belonging in their people, and which are small enough to facilitate real participation.

Kohr emphasises that smallness is not the answer to all human ills ('Even in the most humane and modest society, 100 per cent of the people will still die'), but that reduction in scale leads to a corresponding reduction in the intensity of tyranny, wars, atrocities, abuses of human rights. The unavoidable afflictions of sickness, dissolution and death can be minimised, not aggravated, by smaller concentrations of humanity. Although Aristotle's dictum that, 'The best limit of the population of a state is the largest number which suffices for the purposes of life, and can be taken in at a single view,' may not be universally realisable, Leopold Kohr estimates that ten million is the extreme upper limit of a population able to take part in and feel strong allegiance to a single social and political entity.

Schumacher acknowledged his debt to Leopold Kohr; indeed, the maxim 'small is beautiful' had originally been, in Kohr's version, 'small is glorious'. It began as a joke during a breakfast conversation in Canada one morning in 1939, merely a throwaway remark; although, as Kohr says, he became convinced of his own argument. 'I was', he declares with characteristic humour, 'my own first convert. Although the idea is serious, you can see it was born with a birth defect, conceived in a spirit of levity.' He says that smallness is a form of nature: everything grows just until it reaches the dimensions that serve its function. 'Only human beings have the notion that if a small thing is good, a larger one is better. In politics, sociology, and economics, we believe that the laws of nature are suspended.'

Kohr's distaste for the European Economic Community derives, not from a fear that the nation-states will lose 'sovereignty', but that the total will more effectively eclipse and smother the local. 'Should we fear the reality of German re-unification?' he asks. 'Of course we should, but not because they are Germans, but because any concentration of power is a threat.' Indeed, the geographical areas that comprise Germany have been at war for far fewer years than almost any other part of Europe during the past nine centuries. Kohr points out the ironic symmetry in Western Europe celebrating the break-up of the Soviet Empire, at the very point where its own identities are being submerged in a wider entity.

War, tyranny and violence derive from the very existence of excessive, centralised power. The thought of throwing the explosive that we hold in our hand comes, not from our philosophical attitude, but from the fact that we are holding it.

At a certain order of magnitude, power can do nothing but express itself; and at a critical level, it invites submission from the vast majority of the people within the country that wields it.

Most nation-states that have invaded, conquered and annexed others have done so in the name of 'unity'. Let us have more separation, division, disaggregation. Similarly, in economics, the same counter-productive tendencies are exhibited by size. We need more and more goods to cope with the very problems created by their proliferation. The quality of more numerous goods, and their ability to satisfy our wants, seem to have declined in proportion to their increased availability.

Leopold Kohr has been called the 'father of the Greens', but he feels that many of the programmes drawn up in Green manifestos are side issues which cannot be resolved until the central issue is addressed. Reductions in size will take care of much of the rest.

It is all very well to cry 'down with atomic energy', and to demonstrate outside nuclear plants, but that is probably the only form of energy capable of serving the overblown entities it must provide with power. Agitate, rather, for the recreation of Wessex or Andalusia or Navarre. Advocate windmills, but not to serve existing masses of land and people. The local is retrievable.

Indeed, the generation of power is a metaphor for everything that is wrong with size; and the ambiguity of the phrase is significant. The scale of the technology generates more and more political power for its owners and controllers.

Of course, the reconstruction of the over-mighty nation states in smaller units would be possible. It can be done, certainly, but if you ask me, 'Will it be done?' then I have to say, 'No, I do not think so.' Nor should we mistake the virulent nationalisms arising in Eastern Europe and the Soviet Union as an example of what I mean: these are the deformities of years of repression and denial, a consequence of local identities crushed in the interest of a centralised, chimerical socialist unity.

There was Antiquity, and then the Middle Ages, and after that the Modern Period. People are aware that we are entering a new era. At present, I call it the Age of Senility, because we are kept alive only by means of a life-support system that uses ever more resources, and prolongs life artificially in its addiction to size.

MIKE COOLEY, RIGHT LIVELIHOOD AWARD WINNER 1981. Mike Cooley worked as senior design engineer in the aerospace industry. In the early 1970s, he was one of the pioneers of the celebrated Lucas Workers' Corporate Plan, whereby the employees, threatened with redundancy, organised across factory and union boundaries to draw up their plans for socially useful production. Although rejected by the company, which sacked Cooley in 1980, it led to the establishment of the Centre for Alternative Industrial and Technological Systems at the North-East Polytechnic in London. Cooley became Director of the Technology Division of the Greater London Enterprise Board, and he organised the London Technology Networks, linking community groups, universities and polytechnics in the development of ecologically and socially desirable products. Cooley has been involved in a number of independent but related projects, including the London Innovation Trust, the Technology Exchange, Twin Trading (which stimulates fair and mutually supportive trading between industrial and non-industrial countries), and the ESPRIT project 1217, which is in the process of designing and building a Human-Centred Advanced Manufacturing System, in which human skills are enhanced rather than diminished and subordinated to machines. Mike Cooley's book, *Architect or Bee?: The Human Price of Technology*, was self-published in 1980; and extended, updated and reissued by Chatto and Windus in 1987.)

THE REGENERATION OF the local is directly linked to people's sense of their own creativity and the value of their own experience. This is as true of the West as it is of forest dwellers. One of the consequences of highly centralised production processes is that they become distant from the point of purchase and consumption. The most telling critique of mass industrial society is, perhaps, that many people in the

> advanced industrial societies have lost the sense of how things have made, and how they work; have been dispossessed of the skills and abilities involved in the manufacture of daily necessities. Goods become available only by means of the money that appears to conjure them out of thin air. This absence of direct experience of production, in turn, makes us more open to the false claims of publicists and advertisers, and it leads to a loss of faith in our own powers and possibilities.

Resistance to these tendencies was one of the major impulses behind the movement by the workers of the Lucas Aerospace Company in Britain, when they were threatened with mass unemployment a decade ago. They did not want to see the dissolution of hard-won skills, and the extinction of intricate patterns of working together, simply because there was no apparent market demand for them. They sought to overcome that most damaging of all the multiple divisions within capitalist society, that of 'producers' from 'consumers', by setting out to devise a new range of products, which they and those they loved might conceivably need. They came up with a wide range of socially useful ideas, all immensely practical, and within their own competence to produce — medical equipment and appliances, portable life-saving devices to be carried in ambulances, which would prevent heart patients from dying before they reached hospital, do-it-yourself dialysis machines, carts for spina bifida patients, forms of transport that could be adapted to both road and rail. Although Lucas rejected the plan, many of these items have now been developed and taken up by other companies. The inventiveness and ability of people which are neglected are, according to Mike Cooley, another waste of precious resources, of a piece with the squandered natural treasures of the earth. 'People have become de-skilled, and in the West, many have seen the making of useful things taken out of their hands, with a consequent loss of control over their lives.' Mike Cooley now sees that the work of the brain is now also being objectivised in machinery, just as happened with manual labour at an earlier stage of industrial 'development'. He is now concerned with what he calls an 'anthropocentric technology', one that will enhance the skills of people rather than diminish them.

Existing technology tends to undermine people's powers and faith in them. Technocratic jargon shames tacit knowledge, silences spontaneity and inventiveness. It eclipses the knowledge that resides in fingers, in intuition and experience. Some big employers now realise that it is counter-productive to repress the abilities of their workers too much. General Motors, for instance, found that their employees had become too passive. They had invested so much in fixed capital that this had left little space for any initiative on the part of the workers. With the money invested in fixed capital, they could have afforded to take over Toyota!

This is confirmed by the experience of a number of US-Japanese joint ventures. The GM-Toyota combined project in Freemont, California, faltered because GM could not yield production decision-making power to labour, because this was such an alien tradition to GM. Mike Cooley says:

The Japanese had invested in human beings, and whatever one may feel about the way they go about it, the US has historically seen its work-force as a liability, not an asset.

New technology can be used to extend and empower people. new distributed systems can be applied to create information highways. Computers don't have to isolate people, turn them into the passive recipients of entertainment or centrally managed information, but can bring them together to pool resources, to share and disseminate radical, even subversive ideas, to develop strategies for change, to imagine different futures.

In the past two years, Mike Cooley has been working on a report for the EC on European Competitiveness in the 21st Century. It concludes that competitiveness might, in the future, be articulated more to the saving of energy, ecological values and socially useful products. It also suggests ways in which accelerated migration from the periphery of the EEC (that is, the movement of people on a large scale from Portugal, Greece, Denmark, Scotland, towards the centre — Germany, France, South-East England, Northern Italy) might be halted. The areas of population loss are those which also have rich cultural traditions. Distributed systems can help to bring the margins closer to the centre, and act as a means for enhancing the local, for celebrating diversity, rather than promote the homogenising tendency inherent in the idea of a single European market. They can assist in retrieving a capacity for local action, and can deliver people from the monoliths of state and market.

Much of our ingenuity has been deployed to develop labour-relieving machines that multiply our strength and decrease human effort. That was a highly desirable pursuit when human beings had to perform such destructive and back-breaking labour in the early industrial period. But that historical process may now have become counter-productive, in the sense that we are inventing machines to replace areas of competence which it is inappropriate for human beings to shed, and which may disadvantage us in other ways.

Cooley is preoccupied with what he calls 'Delinquent Genius'; that is, the way in which we devote our astonishing ingenuity to absurd or malign ends.

For instance, the cult of the artificial, whereby we simulate natural things and are lost in admiration for the substitutes we've wrought. You can now buy robot-dogs; different grades of dog, with variable bark, or, if you prefer, a simple growl. They provide you with the companionship that people seek in dogs, but with none of the inconvenience or mess. They don't require feeding and you don't have to take them for walks. Then there is the 'virtual funeral', which nobody has to attend in person, but which brings people together on a series of multiple screens, in presence of the casket. That costs $32,000. There is also a geriatric robot, which is designed to look after the elderly. Its advertisers say that it doesn't hover in the background waiting for you to die, in order to seize your goods. It won't rob you. It is programmed to ask you about your children, to tell your favourite stories over and over again. It never gets bored.

There are, apparently, growing numbers of people in the USA who believe that they are computers: it has become a recognised form of psychiatric illness. They cannot take instruction unless given information in machine-code, and they have lost the capacity for initiative. One psychiatrist reported that, trying to put a patient at his ease, he invited him to take a chair. Instead of being reassured, the patient became close to hysteria, asking, 'Which chair? Which chair?'

The great virtue of humanity is that we are unlike machines. What machines can do well is in terms of predictability, repeatability, mathematical quantification. Those functions should mesh with the creativity of people, the imagination and spontaneity, which are unique to human beings.

In the Lucas Workers' Combine, we asked people to imagine what they would like the 21st century to bring; and then we worked backwards, looking at the obstacles to be overcome if we were to achieve their vision, and asking what steps would be required to come as close as possible to its realisation. One worker said, 'There is nothing wrong with building castles in the air, as long as you construct secure stairways to reach them.'

We should be talking about *energy*, too, in the widest sense of the word:

soft energies, savings to be made through more durable products, but also human energy, in every sense of the term. The possibility of substituting human power for other forms of energy should not be discounted. After all, we do seem ready to give up activities at one level, only in order to recreate them artificially at another. Look at the people using bicycles for exercise in their home, when they could be cycling to work. Similarly, the transportation of centrally manufactured goods all over Europe, indeed, all over the world, is obviously an absurd waste of energy. We should be looking at changes from economies of scale to economies of scope; that is, smaller quantities of products made and distributed locally.

It is perhaps a mistake to conceive of science and technology as universals. They ought to be seen as part of a culture, an expression of different societies. There are local sciences and technologies, in the same way that language or literature are culturally specific; organically linked to the available materials, the local needs.

I was never so completely absorbed by engineering that I could ever have become totally immersed in industry. I've always taken ideas from poetry and literature. Writers often prefigure things, even if in an incomplete or intuitive way. When I wrote about the information society in *Architect or Bee?*, I said that it was really a data society: data had superseded information, which in turn, was replacing a knowledge that had already ousted wisdom. I was told that there was something similar in T.S. Eliot, who wrote, 'What wisdom have we lost in knowledge, what knowledge in information!'

We confuse *socialised knowledge* with general knowledge. What is *known* in libraries, stores of information, data bases, places of higher learning, dispersed among experts, is simply not accessible to most people. Knowledge is not embodied, but objectivised. We are living in a present-tense technology, one that wipes out past and future. We are witnessing clearances of the mind, just as we once saw the Highlands cleared for sheep, the forests for timber, the cities for railways or roads. They replaced muscles with machinery, and now minds can be substituted by artificial intelligence. But only if we allow it to happen. This is why the celebration and re-awakening of people's critical and creative capacities are vital. Human inventiveness never dies, although it may be put to sleep by existing technology.

Mike Cooley's faith in the creativity of people finds sympathetic assent in the work of many others in the alternative movements. It may be that mainstream distrust of popular initiatives is an over-reaction against Marxist faith in the redemptive power of the working class. Simply because no race, class or caste of human beings has been vouchsafed a mission of transcendence, this does not mean that working people, the poor, the formally uninstructed are without a capacity for visionary innovation. Indeed, there is a danger that the redemptive role once borne by the proletariat may now devolve upon indigenous and tribal peoples; this would be a pity, for it would obscure the truly instructive example which they can offer the world in the meaning of hope and renewal.

14. REGENERATING LOCAL COMMUNITIES

AMORY AND HUNTER LOVINS, RIGHT LIVELIHOOD AWARD WINNERS 1983. Hunter and Amory Lovins work together as analysts, lecturers and consultants on energy, resource and security policy in over 15 countries. Hunter Lovins has degrees in law, and political studies and is a member of the California Bar. For six years, he was Assistant Director of the California Conservation Project. Amory Lovins is a consultant experimental physicist, educated at Harvard and Oxford, who has published a dozen books, held various academic chairs, and served on the US Department of Energy's senior Advisory Board. His best known book is Soft Energy Paths: Towards a Durable Peace (Harper Colophon, New York, 1979.) In 1982, the Lovinses founded the Rocky Mountain Institute (RMI), of which they are currently President and Vice-President respectively. RMI now has a staff of 30, and is an independent, non-profit research and education foundation, seeking to foster the efficient and sustainable use of resources as a path to global security.

EMPOWERMENT IS INSEPARABLE from decentralisation and regeneration of local autonomy, in both North and South. The Lovinses have been concerned to demonstrate the possibilities of regenerating local communities, showing how 'plugging the leaks' of wealth flowing from small towns and settlements can reverse long-term patterns of decline, which people had come to accept fatalistically. This is certainly effective in the area of energy. In many communities, up to 20 per cent of income is spent on energy. More than 80 per cent of this expenditure leaves the locality where it is spent. Energy efficiency programmes can stanch this outflow; and the money saved can be used as a base for reinforcing community reconstruction. (Alice Tepper Marlin, Right Livelihood Award 1990, of the Council on Economic Priorities in New York, estimates that if the United States had spent as much from August to December 1990 on improving energy efficiency as was spent on mobilising for the Gulf War, the US could have eliminated its oil imports from that area.)

By buying locally wherever possible, by marketing local products, by using local skills, great savings can be made on energy used in transport. Decades of decline can be halted and reversed by this means. *The Energy Casebook*, published by the Rocky Mountain Institute in 1989, records many practical projects, where popular enthusiasm and commitment have been mobilised in the interests of saving on costly forms of energy. In Osage, Ohio, for example, $750 per household per annum was saved by energy efficiency, revitalisation of local agriculture and provision of cheaper local health care. By supporting existing businesses, dependency on distant suppliers can be reduced, with all the wasteful energy costs involved. Since 1973, efficiency has become a far greater source of 'new' energy in the US economy than all expansion of fossil fuels; since 1979, the US has 'generated' more than seven times as much energy from savings as from all net expansions of energy supplies combined. Of these expansions, more were from renewable sources than from non-renewables.

Among the examples of renewable local energy practices cited by the Lovinses are hydropower (which provides 13 per cent of US electricity), which for many communities, on a small-scale and thoughtfully designed on appropriate sites, makes good sense, provided that these would not disrupt the environment or local economies; solar power (by combining good solar design with efficiency, it is now possible to build homes in just about any climatic zone, which need almost no additional energy, yet which remain comfortable all year round.) Since the energy crisis of the 1970s, some 800,000 solar collectors have been sold in the US. Geothermal energy is used in some areas of California and Colorado, and most of the big American windfarms are also in California. Wood provides almost twice as much *delivered* energy as nuclear power, and some 5.6 million homes in the US are heated entirely by wood. The city of Burlington, Vermont, converted a 10-megawatt coal-fired power station to burn local wood, commercially unmarketable, from dead, dying or diseased trees. (A larger plant proved less successful.) Co-generation also offers opportunities to many communities; that is, production of both heat and electricity from the same source. It is estimated that co-generation could extend to 15 per cent of US electrical output by 2000; by the same date, renewable sources could supply 20 per cent of US energy needs.

The Lovinses emphasise that the values of self-reliance, imagination and confidence in local initiative are more certain guarantees of local regeneration than waiting for large-scale economic rescue packages from outside. In any case, these usually manage to filter disproportionate quantities of the wealth produced away from the places where it is created. Although most of the examples in which Amory and Hunter Lovins have been involved are rural communities, similar experiments would be possible within inner-city areas, or the big outer-urban estates in Europe — Tor Bella Monaca in Rome, Creteil in Paris or Castlemilk in Glasgow. There are few sights more desolate in the Western world than these great concentrations of the poor, whole communities waiting for rescue from elsewhere, dependent on welfare cheques, charity, big employers or crime, that caricature of mainstream enterprise.

Amory Lovins is an enthusiastic proponent of the market as the most effective means of allocating resources, at least where there is a reasonably fair distribution of income; although clearly, the market cannot produce social justice or a system of ethics. Indeed, he points out that, for all their proclaimed devotion to the market system, the US, Japan and Europe have no compunction in suspending market forces where these run counter to their interests, notably in defence, energy and agriculture. If a truly free market were to operate in the area of energy, Lovins believes the situation would be transformed. However, this would require what he calls 'economic glasnost', or 'prices that tell the truth', that is to say, prices which internalise costs not currently included in the point-of-sale price of commodities and services. Just how this might be achieved, and what the consequences might be for the existing economic paradigm have yet to be determined.

Amory Lovins says that if energy were the principal constraint on development, its more careful use could permit the whole planet to be industrialised to the level attained by the (then) Federal Republic of Germany in 1975, using only one-third of the energy the world presently consumes.

Energy is the LAST constraint on population and economic growth if properly applied. Since the publication of Soft Energy Paths, we have broadened out from energy issues into work on the relationship between energy, water, agriculture, security and local economic development. We learned that end-use, least-cost approach is crucial. Instead of seeking to expand the supply of something you are short of — energy, transport or whatever — you start off by asking, 'What are we really trying to do? What is the best tool for the job?' For example, how much energy, of what kind, from what source, at what price, on what scale, is going to do each desired task in the cheapest way? Instead of looking for *more* energy, you say, 'What is the best way to get hot showers and cold beers?' You reason from ends to means, instead of the other way round. And the next thing is the importance of scale, the right size; and then the power of market economics to solve a lot of problems at once, if you know how to use it right. Of course, the market isn't good for other things. It will not produce sufficiency, nor social justice, for example. It's not meant to.

Seeing interconnections is vital. If you don't see how things are connected, then often the cause of the problems is the apparent solution. If you do understand connections, then often the cause of the solutions can be the solution. Market solutions are more efficient than any government regulation.

Amory Lovins reacts strongly to some of the European Greens, particularly those who urge a change of life-style and reduced consumption. 'Privation, discomfort, curtailment. Hair-shirts!' He is committed, rather, to 'aikido politics', that is, where 'you don't fight with an adversary, but dance with a partner'. Indeed, he sets great value on honouring other people's feelings, as he hopes they will honour his, even when he believes them to be wrong.

You don't get fixed into a single rigid position, but move around, seeing things from another point of view, even while you stick with your own values. You're committed to a process, not to an outcome. From a good process, a better outcome will emerge, and then, whoever needs to take credit for it can do so, whether deserved or not. It is a Taoist, insidious sort of politics.

Hunter Lovins adds that although they are interested in using market mechanisms to solve social and environmental problems, there could be a conflict between what is economically viable through the 'least-cost energy' approach, and what is environmentally sound.

It may be that things fundamental to the market are unsustainable. If it comes to it that there needs to be a basic change in life-style, then if we say that there is a technical fix for everything, we may not have done the world the service we are trying to do. And we owe it to ourselves to be honest about these things. Market theory is, of course, very different from what is currently practised. If what is practised is unsustainable, then maybe we have to say, 'Here's how market theory ought to be.' What we may come out with is a rethinking of market theory, which includes the physicist's concept of entropy, and which will accommodate all externalities and give us a GNP which measures true welfare.

Amory Lovins came to respect market forces and the private sector, not out of prior ideological commitment, but through direct experience. He has observed constructive change in what had always been thought of as 'inflexible' institutions. He cites the example of the American utility companies, trying to sell *less* electricity, more efficiency; of water suppliers actually conserving water.

The socialist economies, while they had no mechanism for regulating prices, were simply machines for eating resources. Profits tell people what is worth doing for material reasons. Of course, what they don't tell should also be kept in mind. There is, I believe, plenty of good news overall. Although the human ego is strong, the love of life may prove stronger. At present, however, it seems that our powers are developing faster than our wisdom.

PATRICK VAN RENSBURG, RIGHT LIVELIHOOD AWARD WINNER 1981. Patrick van Rensburg resigned his post as South African Vice-Consul in the Belgian Congo in 1957, in protest against apartheid. In Britain in 1959, he became involved with the movement to boycott South African goods. Returning to South Africa, his passport was confiscated, and he was forced to flee the country following the State of Emergency after the Sharpeville shootings. He went to Bechuanaland in 1962, which on independence from Britain became Botswana, of which he became a citizen in 1973. In Botswana, he founded the Swaneng Hill School, the Swaneng Consumers' Co-operative and the Brigades Movement. His experience with the schools and brigades through the 1970s, led to his establishment of the Foundation for Education with Production; an approach to education radically different from usual practice, which integrates practical with academic instruction, and values of self-reliance and building upon indigenous wisdom and practice. The Foundation for Education with Production spread both within Botswana and internationally; projects were set up in Zambia and Zimbabwe. It devised and held workshops, conferences and seminars in many parts of the world, published a Directory of Projects, newsletter and journal.

PATRICK VAN RENSBURG, in a very different context from that of the Lovinses, also has faith in the mobilising of popular resources for self-reliance. He views as malign the fragmentation of labour into mental, manual and menial activity, with the stratification that this brings, and the hierarchies of elites, experts and advisers. These effectively inhibit others from using their own skills and capacity to do things for themselves and for each other. Van Rensberg's combination of education with production has a resonance far beyond Botswana, where it was conceived.

Rensburg's practical experiment on an alternative educational model took place in a country which in the 1960s saw only 15 per cent of its young people in secondary school. The aim was to introduce productive activity into school life, to upgrade and develop the skills of urban workers and rural producers, by linking educational programmes to their real life conditions and prospects. It involved, too, the setting up of producers' co-operatives, with appropriate training and education programmes that would strengthen their ability to manage and control their enterprises; and the development of those co-operatives as the future work-places of those in training.

It is a non-elitist education, one that continues beyond the school in both place and time, that is, in the community, and throughout life: education should not be enclosed or appropriated. The Foundation for Education with Production (FEP) founded the Serowe Brigades, young people who would build schools for themselves, because it was clear that the demand for education in Botswana far outstripped anything that could be provided. As well as building, the young people learned to provide their own food, as well as the equipment they needed, and at the same time, to provide goods and services that would yield enough income to pay the salaries of their teachers; a model of participation and self-provisioning in education.

Botswana has been a prime example of a dependent economy, where a few primary products, principally diamonds, but also cattle, earn foreign exchange that pays for the growth of enclaves of privilege, where elites are educated in ways that will ensure they strive to perpetuate a hierarchical system. Such elites always serve as a kind of Trojan horse for exogenous, deterministic and inappropriate forms of development. Western-inspired education, as well as being a major buttress of global inequalities, also creates a class of semi-educated imitators of the elites, psychologically oriented towards an alien culture, and lacking the skills and insight to be able to respond to their country's real needs.

Van Rensburg encourages young people to use their own energies and abilities, first of all to satisfy their own basic needs, a process which is itself a potent satisfier of other, less tangible needs. Self-reliance demands that education be multi-dimensional — economic, political, cultural, psychological and intellectual — so that the young may not only combat the subtle and manipulative forces of dominance, but also counter these with their own proud, capable and self-confident alternative. In the Serowe Brigades, 400 young people were trained in a wide range of different skills, which enabled them to produce vegetables, milk, eggs, cooking oil, and gave them skills to build houses, repair engines, produce clothes, and make and operate printing presses. The integration of so many diverse skills is an intensely empowering experience. It is the opposite of a division of labour into incomprehensible fragments, which renders the work of specialists unintelligible to each other and to everyone else. The international linkages of FEP are valuable, because they reveal the importance of *human* resources. The proper use of human resources avoids dependency on material resource-depletion, which is characteristic of the dominant development model in the world.

As a refugee from South Africa, and committed to the struggle against apartheid and racism, Rensburg learned also that there are other systemic injustices that have nothing to do with racism.

> It isn't possible to say that we would like to have some more benign form of capitalism in South Africa, free of racism, because in that manifestation of capitalism, racism is actually inherent. The whole system of migrant labour is built upon the exploitation of people. The creation of the so-called homelands began with the need of mines and farms to have cheap labour at the mercy of employers, without the obligation to feed the workers' wives, children and old people. It represented the cruellest separation of all — the sundering of labour from life.

And that is the antithesis of van Rensburg's work of integration at all levels. It is clear that one of the reasons why South Africa's capitalists were converted to the abolition of apartheid is that they would prefer the impersonal and colour-blind logic of economic forces to designate who will be the subordinate classes, rather than the grosser triage of race. Institutionalised injustice is a more discreet instrument that institutionalised racism. The need for alternative and transforming models of education has fresh urgency as the structures of apartheid are taken down: without such models the scars cannot be so easily healed.

15. LEARNING FROM THE SOUTH: REVITALISING THE NORTH

The Third World appears in the Western media principally as pathology, associated with war, violence, hunger, disorder, brutal rulers and corruption. The people, when they figure at all, appear as helpless victims of human-made or natural disasters. When the TV images are not of emaciated limbs or bellies swollen by kwashiorkor, they are of charred and mutilated bodies on the streets of some unhappy Third World capital. The dead bodies of white people are never shown; only blacks bleed on TV.

The principal function of this charnel-house iconography is to serve as a focus for its privileged recipients to realise how lucky they are. The lesson is unmistakable. They want what we have. They provide a formidable object lesson to the rich in the virtues of solidarity.

The range of possible responses is limited by the brutal insistence of the imagery. There is bound to spontaneous human sympathy, a desire to help. But the lachrymose elation that accompanies the charity concerts, the phone-ins and the conspicuous giving, merely conceals the fact that for all the open-heartedness, the problems which call it forth are rarely illuminated and never solved. The assumption remains that the West alone can rescue the people of the Third World: *our* know-how, *our* technology; *our* generosity. There is a second sub-text, namely that the poverty and social injustice of the South are the fault of greedy, tyrannical and dictatorial rulers. That most of these received instruction in the academies of the West, and are infinitely prepared to subordinate the needs of their people to the necessities of the Western financial system, rarely receives great prominence. This readily merges with the view that they are incapable of running their own affairs, that things have gone from bad to worse since they emerged from the protective tutelage of the Western colonial system. Imperial nostalgia, in turn, only makes more acceptable the colonising prescriptions that issue from the IMF, the World Bank, GATT, the transnational corporations and Western governments, to 'cure' the pervasive sickness of the Third World.

The Third World, then, is a locus of disease, horror and oppression. Almost every day in the newspapers there are a few lines of a Reuters report telling of a train that plunged into a ravine in India, a ferry that sank in Bangladesh with great loss of life, a fire that raged through a Cairo slum. It is clear that even nature hates these countries: typhoons, hurricanes, volcanoes, earthquakes regularly tear through their wild landscapes, in sympathy with the political and economic turbulence which sometimes barely differentiate themselves from the forces of nature. Religious strife, civil war, communal conflict, are reported to sweep through them in the same language as that used to describe killer storms or tidal waves.

In the West, where images now speak louder than its debased and discredited words, the ubiquitous pictures tell their own ideological story. Many people say they are upset by the juxtaposition in glossy magazines of photographs of extreme poverty and starvation on one page, and on the next, advertisements for the most supremely dispensable vanities. Yet here is a lesson for which words would be too crude a vehicle: in the markets of the world, our rate of resource consumption directly confronts their survival. It is our appetites versus their populations; our wants their needs. We are at the heart of the taboo that hangs over the real relationship between North and South.

The people of the South rarely speak for themselves in the Western media. In Sri Lanka, where the brutal aftermath of an old colonial violence still makes daily headlines of atrocities and violence, we seldom hear of those who persist in the quiet pursuit of social justice and creative development.

PARTICIPATORY INSTITUTE FOR DEVELOPMENT ALTERNATIVES (PIDA), RIGHT LIVELIHOOD AWARD WINNER 1982. PIDA is a non-governmental organisation, established in 1980 for the purpose of promoting grassroots participatory development in Sri Lanka. PIDA's approach grew out of the pioneering work of Asian scholars in the mid-seventies (Published as *Towards a Theory of Rural Development* by de Silva et al., Progressive Publishers, Lahore, Pakistan, 1988), centred on the UN Asian Institute of Development in Bangkok. These scholars initiated a process of reflection on the reality of Asian poverty and the failure of past developmental efforts, and sought to develop a conceptual framework for an alternative development in Asia. To turn this theoretical work into practice, the Sri Lanka government and the United Nations Development Programme began a Change Agents Programme in 1978, which in turn led to the foundation of PIDA.)

S.P. WICKREMAARACHCHI of PIDA recognises not only the political obstacles to what has been called 'creativist' development, but also the structural inequalities within village society where PIDA works.

> On the one hand, there is a minority of dominant interests. There are the traders and moneylenders and the big landowners, even the village-level bureaucrat, who all benefit from the status quo. On the other hand, there is the majority. These are the small and marginal farmers, landless

workers, small fisher-folk, rural artisans, most of whom live in poverty. The rich are able to control the very survival of the poor.

It works like this: a considerable portion of the value of the product of the small producer (whether farmer, fisherman, artisan or wage-earner) ends up in the hands of the dominant interests, through low prices paid for produce, high prices charged for inputs, high land rents, low wages, exorbitant interest rates and corruption. It may be noted, in passing how, at the micro-level, this replicates the wider system of global injustice. The drain of economic surplus through dependency links further impoverishes the poor, and maintains their productivity at a low level. This, in turn, is reflected in the mental attitudes and existing social structures of the village.

However, the poor themselves are not a homogeneous category. They are divided on caste, religion and other issues, and they compete with each other for limited economic opportunities in the village. These factors prevent them from taking initiatives to improve their condition, and result in non-innovative, non-experimental attitudes. This is why it is difficult, if not impossible, for self-reliant rural development to be generated spontaneously, and why catalytic introduction is, more often than not, a necessary initial input to stimulate the poor to self-reliant action.

Under these circumstances, a delivered 'neutral' or technocratic intervention by government or even non-government organisation only adjusts to the village society, and often ends up benefiting the dominant interests.

The role of the catalyst with small producer peasants has been to focus upon the income losses they suffer as a result of their dependency on traders, money-lenders and landowners. The people then move away from a sensory perception of their poverty, and a fatalistic response to it. They begin to see it within the social and political environment. The small producers then explore the means within their collective power to retain the surplus of their production, to protect it from exploiters and to use it for their own consumption and investment. They form a group to initiate action that will release them from dependency. It is clear to them that as individuals they are too weak to start such moves towards self-reliance.

The work of PIDA was conceived as a reaction against models imposed upon an overwhelmingly rural society that were fundamentally anti-rural. Some PIDA catalysts began in the late 1970s to look at projects that offered no financial resources to the beneficiaries. Some coir workers got together and analysed their economic dependency, and looked for a way in which they could build up a savings fund which would free them from the village traders. They could not save out of their pitiful earnings, so they hit upon the idea of saving in kind. The trader who supplied them with raw materials calculated that a certain quantity of yarn should be returned from them to him. The source of the saving was the slight excess which the producer was able to make, over and above the trader's calculation, and which had traditionally been handed over for no extra payment. The producers decided they would withhold that modest excess. Within a short time, they had saved far more than they expected. They sold this surplus on the open market, by-passing the trader, and making more money from it. The essential breakthrough was made.

The *collective fund* is almost always the first step. It was discovered that it could readily be extended to many other village workers. As the fund grew for the coir workers, self-reliant activities became possible — the purchase of capital equipment for the use of group members, which saved on the hire of equipment; small loans for help at times of sickness; the bulk purchase of basic goods, rice, kerosene, coconuts; mutual exchange of labour in cultivation work for subsistence.

The range of activity can then be widened. Greater bulk purchases of goods for consumption become possible. People can cultivate common plots of land, as a means of adding to the collective fund. They can diversify crop patterns in order to reduce specialisation and introduce greater stability into incomes. After a time, technologies can be reversed — tractors replaced with animal power, chemicals with organic fertiliser. Eventually, wider marketing collectives can be formed, ousting the few traders who had previously dominated. Then they are able to obtain credit, which means that they are no longer compelled to rely on money-lenders.

One of the most successful initiatives was with the vegetable growers at Ranna, a village about 250 kilometres from Colombo in the south of Sri Lanka. Of the total population, more than 90 per cent are subsistence farmers, peasant farmers who cultivate highlands, without irrigation, and those cultivating paddy in settlement areas with irrigation facilities. The plots of the vegetable farmers are only one to one-and-a-half acres, where they grow snake-gourds, bitter gourds, okra, brinjal, tomatoes, beans, chillies, while the main crops are cowpea, green gram, groundnuts, maize. The money-lender traditionally provided loans, not only to cover inputs, but also as living expenses. The small farmer never repays the debt and remains dependent. As soon as the rains begin, work is so intensive that he has to hire additional labourers. Their wages are also borrowed from the money-lender. The family must also borrow for basic living needs — rice, coconuts, sugar, tea, kerosene, onions, spices for curry. The total borrowed was, on average, Rs 6,750 per season, and the interest on it came to Rs 4,056.

When the farmer marketed his crops, he had to pay the commission agent eight per cent, and the market fees collector three per cent. The buyers falsify the scales, and deduct about two per cent of the value of the produce. The brokers also kept about four to five per cent from the actual prices. This reduced the farmers income by about 17 per cent, that is, a further leakage of Rs 2,550. A farmer who cultivated one acre of land could expect a return of about Rs 15,000 a season, but debts, consumption and leakages came to around Rs 13,366.

The position of the paddy farmers was even worse, because they had to repay loans in kind; and since that happened immediately after the harvest, when the price of rice was low, the creditor could keep it and resell at far higher prices long after the harvest.

S. P. Wickremaarachchi worked with the farmers, and he calculates that groups of 10-20 are capable of breaking out of the cycle of poverty when they work together. They began by sharing their own labour rather than hiring it. They started a small collective farm. This generated an income which became the basis of a common fund. Once this was achieved, it became possible to talk to the banks about loans for cultivation. This had never happened before. The people were on their way to being free of the money-lenders.

Together with groups from other villages, they were able to buy the town market centre, where their produce was sold, thereby extending their control over the marketing of what they grew. As self-confidence rises, groups can federate, expand and turn their attention to wider questions of development. They can begin to think of providing community amenities — sanitation, drinking-water wells, schools and health care.

Initial actions are usually defensive, aimed at protecting people's means of livelihood against the predations of other interest groups. If these initiatives are followed up by further activities aiming at self-reliance, the lives of the people can continue to be enhanced. Groups can unite with each other to formulate and propose alternative development plans, over which they can negotiate with government and public agencies.

Even in very poor communities, there is often scope for small savings in one way or another. Mobilising the poor to answer their own needs is always more creative than waiting for economic growth to raise their level of living (it rarely happens), or to expect basic needs to be provided from elsewhere, let alone placing their hopes in an even more dubious and indefinite wait for social revolution. By focusing on *what people do not have*, there is already an in-built orientation towards dependency, which is the very opposite of motivating the community to engage constructively in imagining and inventing its own way of fulfilling need with what it *does have*. While such endeavours include an urgent need to work for economic improvement, the very fact that people mobilise and pool resources is of far greater importance than the immediate material gains. This in itself creates a practice, and for those who come after, a heritage of expertize and self-confidence to be passed on, even if initially it is thwarted by superior and more powerful interests. Wherever aspirations — whether these are articulated as 'needs', 'entitlements' or 'wants' — are dissociated from the immediate creative possibilities of the community, their potential is immediately neutralised. The problem of poverty, as traditionally defined, concentrates on *deficiencies* rather than on *opportunities* for producing or commanding the things needed or desired through people's own creative actions. Anisur Rahman, Bangladeshi critic of development, says:

> Even definitions of 'basic needs' — food, shelter, medical care, education — are, in some form or another, also the needs of animals, who do not create, except by instinct. The distinctive characteristic of human beings is the alliance of our creativist need with our fulfilment of other needs.

Revitalising participation is not merely a distant aim for poor societies, but is an increasingly urgent concern for the West, where democracy has come to mean passive spectatorship at a political spectacle, and a vote once every four years in a gladiatorial context, in which the most proficient manipulators of the economy are guaranteed success.

FRANCES MOORE LAPPE, Institute for Food and Development Policy, RIGHT LIVELIHOOD AWARD WINNER 1987. Frances Moore Lappe's book, *Diet for a Small Planet*, published by Ballantine in 1971, sold three million copies, and first gained public attention for her ideas. In 1975, Lappe and Joseph Collins founded the Institute for Food and Development Policy (IFDP) in San Francisco, a non-profit education and documentation centre. IFDP has become internationally recognised as addressing the political and economic roots of world hunger, and demonstrating how ordinary citizens can help to end hunger. IFDP now has 20,000 members, a staff of 17 and an annual budget of over $1,250,000. With Collins, Lappe co-authored in 1977 *Food First: Beyond the Myth of Scarcity*, which demonstrated that hunger is a political and economic phenomenon, caused neither by scarcity nor by over-population. The theme is elaborated in *World Hunger: Twelve Myths*, published in 1986 by Food First, the imprint of IFDP.

THE INTENTION OF IFDP is to understand and publicise grassroots, non-governmental strategies that work, democratically controlled initiatives through which the poor are able to transform their lives. IFDP and Lappe have conducted searching investigations of food issues in the Philippines, Cuba, Mozambique, Tanzania, Bangladesh and Nicaragua. Their books and reports are widely used by grassroots groups in both industrial and non-industrial countries.

More recently, Lappe has been working on a project which explores the underlying ethical values of US society. It is intended to be a long-term philosophical inquiry into American political values, to offer a redefinition of such concepts as 'freedom' and 'democracy'.

Frances Lappe is now devoting her energies to the furtherance of what she calls 'an active political culture'. This seems to her a natural development of her work on the politics of food.

> If people don't eat, something must be seriously flawed. Food is, after all, not only a basic need, but around it cluster so many other needs — emotional, cultural and spiritual. You have only to think of fertility rites, the symbol of the breaking of bread, of holy communion. Whole cultures have evolved around traditional crops and staple foods. But now, world dietary patterns are being rearranged, partly by the effects of the transnational companies involved in agribusiness and food-processing. Areas that have been long-term regions of food security are now net importers of food.

(In Bombay recently, there was a promotional event called 'Hamburger Fortnight', which suggests that if hamburgers can be marketed to Hindus, there can be no cultural tradition on earth that is proof against the higher necessities of Western salesmanship.)

As a consequence of the shift from providing liberating economic analysis towards the re-creation of a positive and participatory democracy, Lappe has set up the Institute for the Arts of Democracy. This is a partner organisation of Food First, and will concentrate on revitalising US democratic values. This change in emphasis comes from her perception that, however different the problems of North and South may appear, they derive to a considerable degree from the same root cause: the absence of, or limited space for genuine democratic participation by citizens. It had been assumed for a long time that economic development preceded democracy, and that the creation of wealth was of the first urgency; the implication being that true democracy could be put more or less on ice until the conditions were more propitious. But the fall of dictatorships in Latin America and Africa, and the insecurity of authoritarian regimes in the newly industrialised countries of Asia, have made it clear that there is an inseparable connection between development and democracy. The problem in the US and Europe is somewhat different.

There, the danger is that formal democratic institutions become ossified, and that people lose faith in them, because the real power moves elsewhere — to autonomous and apparently unbiddable economic forces. This makes people cynical and fatalistic, aware of their own *impotence*, which is deeply damaging to a system whose supreme virtue is supposed to be that it empowers people. It serves little purpose to get issues on to political agendas, if people no longer believe in politics.

Frances Lappe believes that democracy and equity are indivisible. But these are not the only attributes of a development that would both respond to the needs of the Third World and be capable of continuous renewal: such development must also protect and preserve the environment. Food First sees the contradiction, not as one between people and the environment, but as between unequal social structures and the environment. Inequitable social structures promote ecological disequilibrium, and the absence of democracy intensifies this condition by stifling popular responses to the impact of government and corporate policies.

Revitalising a democratic culture is a harder task than analysing economic injustices. Democracy is a process beyond formal democratic institutions. It requires an empowering framework, in which alternative economics can be practised. It is relatively easy to do the analysis. The *why* of the problem is always easier than the *how* of building participatory structures for achieving change.

The fundamental problem is that political discourse is itself dead. Political culture is dying, because of the mass media, the tempo of life, the role of experts. This became more clear to me as I turned from focus on the Third World to focus on the USA. Working in and on behalf of the Third World can be a form of escapism. Things are clearer there, and then the people endure so much, with such a positive and co-operative spirit.

The level of wealth here just separates us from one another, and it becomes hard to imagine any group process accomplishing anything. And the worldview that sees people as 'atomised creatures' is very powerful. We breathe in this idea of ourselves, and it shapes our perception of reality. This can be very destructive, not only for us, but also for the rest of the world to which we are exporting it. To see ourselves in this way is to pull out one piece of the potential of human nature and to universalise it, the competitiveness, the individualism; and we construct our world out of it. The values underlying this material culture, this fragmented, over-busy world, in which it so hard for people to connect, creates a profound suspicion of any group process.

It is significant that Hobbes said '*Homo homini lupus est*'; man is a wolf to man. That pervasive animal imagery has pervaded our thinking.

We need to shift from seeing ourselves as masters of a threatening world, to members of a biotic community; from seeing a threat we have to conquer to seeing a family we can join. Our social nature is both our salvation and our undoing. We want people to approve and understand us, so we shape and censor ourselves to the status quo in order to gain approval. Yet it is as social beings also that we have the potential for empathy, the potential for seeing our own interests as linked to those of other people. So the same social nature which motivates us to change is in conflict with our social nature that wants approval. Fear is the greatest inhibitor of change: fear of embarrassment, fear of being different, fear of not being understood, fear of being wrong.

At the same time, people are hurting more in the world. Hunger is worse, the debt crisis is worse. Misery in the United States is up by any measure. Yet that misery itself, homelessness, debt, unemployment, drug addiction, all serve as a living warning to everyone else to go for a well-paid job and all that entails. On the other hand, people's understanding of the problem has grown. People know the causes of hunger now, which is a great gain.

It is important to bring together groups who do not normally encounter each other. This helps to overcome the fragmentation that keeps people in ignorance of each other's needs and struggles. If we bring together major grass roots organisations in the United States — the educators, the YMCA, political theorists, journalists, librarians, diverse interest groups whose paths would not otherwise cross — we shall be astonished to see how much common ground there is. Part of the problem is that you cannot create what you cannot name. And we cannot name *an active democracy*. It doesn't exist anywhere. So part of what we are undertaking in what we have called Project Public Life is developing a language.

One idea in the furtherance of this is a Public Achievement Programme, where students would train with experienced community activists to set up a project that would address a specific problem within their community. Then there would be public recognition for the work achieved. Project Public Life focuses on democracy in the classroom, and that is part of my work. 'How do we do the art of public life?' Everything is dealt with, from coping with embarrassment, to being able to express yourself, from analysing problems to participating with others to resolve them.

There are openings now that I've never seen before. People are hungry for something. They are upset about the alienation of youth, social problems within their own communities. The alarm level has risen across the political spectrum. But we need to relate our analyses to the social movements. It is almost like starting over again. Writing the exposé isn't going to be enough any more. It is a very ambitious project, but there are strengths, even myths in American culture, on which we can build.

We are living through a moment that is similar to that of the 17th century, a period of fundamental challenge to the worldview we have lived with. In the 17th century, we let go of an interventionist God and a mystified universe, in favour of the notion of absolute laws, and the idea that everything could be reduced to its parts. Now we are back full circle. We have learned that reducing everything to its parts leads to death. Fullness, integration, wholeness, must be learned all over again. I'm hoping that what we are living through is really a period of death for rebirth; it is the throes of that we are experiencing.

I would like to focus on the creation of a true democratic process, which represents *diversity* and is *empowering* at the same time. The single-issue organising of the 1970s and 1980s alienated people from politics. It was too self-righteous and too confrontational. We have to learn to listen to other points of view, not present ourselves as pure, sole possessors of the truth, whilst those who disagree with us are seen as absolute sinners or idiots. Issue-work will not change the world. We have to change the political culture; focus on people's experience of public life, wherever this may be — in schools, churches, youth organisations. Unless we can address these *precursors*, places that allow people to imagine that they can make a difference, that their opinion counts, how can we imagine that we can make a real difference simply by seizing an *issue*?

Democracy is not what we *have*, but what we *do*. It is a fundamental question. If people are enabled to get in touch with their innate capacities for empathy towards others, joy in learning and developing together, with their connectedness to others, we would have a healthier society. People are deeply offended by poverty, homelessness, injustice and environmental degradation. But they feel powerless. Project Public Life goes back to the fragmentation, and is an attempt to heal the lack of effective group processes.

I may see my work as a spiritual concern, but I express this in a secular vernacular, which is also useful in communicating across a range of faith groups. Democracy is a profoundly spiritual question. I feel I have no choice but to do what I do. I also love learning. It is a privilege to be alive at this time, when things are so *evident*. Life on earth is at stake. It is an extraordinarily charged moment to be living.

16. EMPOWERMENT: UNITY OF INTELLECTUALS AND ACTIVISTS

LOKAYAN, RIGHT LIVELIHOOD AWARD WINNER 1985. Lokayan means 'Dialogue of the people' in Hindi. It is a research and documentation initiative, which provides a forum for non-party political activists, through dialogues, workshops, working groups and lectures. These activities involve a large network of concerned intellectuals, activists and opinion-makers. Through these, Lokayan has evolved a systematic critique of established development models and to promote political action towards a new ideological crystallisation suited to the needs and hopes of the people. Drawing upon the large variety of small initiatives that are struggling to achieve a just society, Lokayan aims at building a body of knowledge, opinion and strategies of intervention at the 'macro' level, that will promote a decentralised, democratic order, enhance respect for cultural and social diversity, including the most marginalised, and empower them for participation in the larger movement for social transformation. The popular social movements are, says Rajni Kothari, one of the founders of Lokayan, 'the deep stirrings of consciousness, an awareness of crisis that can be turned into a catalyst of new opportunities'. Lokayan publishes its own influential bulletin, of comment, analysis and reviews. Lokayan has played a significant role in the coming together of the wide variety of popular initiatives under the Harsud process, after the meeting in Bhopal in 1989, when in 1990, activists and grassroot movements resisting various development projects all over India, came together for the first time.

THE PURPOSE OF LOKAYAN has been to feed academic research into the work of activists in various social movements, and to create a flow of information between researchers and grassroots. It builds bridges, and at the same time seeks to heal one of the major separations brought about by 'modernisation' and 'development' — the isolation of intellectuals from the people.

Smitu Kothari is co-editor of Lokayan's journal. He speaks of the function of Lokayan as a 'creative midwifery', whereby the implications of damaging development projects are disseminated into mainstream political discourse. The proliferation of micro-movements all over India were in the 1980s, were, he believes, a response to a deeper malaise.

More than this, those movements provided the rudiments of an alternative. The problem has been to articulate these into a consolidated and considered critique of established development models, and into frames of action for change. There is a long list of issues that must be linked into a coherent whole: unrest and violence (much of it created by an alliance of upper castes, corrupt politicians and 'lumpen' elements fostered by the informal economy — liquor, gambling, prostitution and drugs), bonded labour, ecological damage, oppression of women, forest policy and the position of tribal people, farm policy, science and technology, human rights, effects of irrigation dams, protective discrimination, organising the rural poor, Dalit ('untouchable') organisation, communal tension; the whole nexus of crime, casteism and corruption in local politics.

It has been the aim of Lokayan to discuss the findings of its research, not only with academics and activists, but also with those immediately affected by them. A macro-vision is needed that can be satisfied only by a growing partnership between activists, people and intellectuals in the process of social transformation.

Lokayan began in the early 1980s at the Centre for the Study of Developing Societies in New Delhi; the centre itself remains one of the most dynamic and vital generators and co-ordinators of new ideas in the South. In the beginning, Lokayan received foreign funding. It was resource-intensive, its activities widely dispersed throughout India, with its representatives travelling in eight or nine states. Later, it was decided to renounce all money from abroad.

We were the first group in history to say after three years to the Konrad Adenauer Foundation, 'We don't want money.' Based on the ethics of self-reliance, if the project is relevant to our country, we should be able to sustain ourselves.

The core group may be small, and much of our work invisible to outsiders. Once an initiative has been taken, we prefer to step back. We value effectiveness above publicity. Dialogues are participatory. We translate the concerns from where they are experienced to where people are numbed and unknowing through their remoteness from them. It is a sensitising process. We seek to break the boundaries of the established knowledge system, to confront universities and colleges, to let them know of the vast reality out there, the people whose voices and struggles and pain are a more fundamental Indian reality than that projected in places of learning. To some degree, we get cast as spokespersons. That is inevitable. But the important questions is whether we have correctly represented the struggle of the key actors in it. As long as they recognise themselves in what we say, then we have done our work properly.

The modern project of *integration*, whether into the world economic order, the technological market-place or the global strategic order, has effectively split society in two; and the greater the integration of one segment, the less the care, the understanding and knowledge about the other. In other words, the poor are reduced to being stateless in their own state. The poorest have lost both worlds: uprooted and displaced from traditional local habitats and a modicum of security (however exploited), they yet find no place in modern political and social structures, except in the form of workers, masses, targets of new forms of social oppression and violence; they pass from exploitation and poverty into unmitigated destitution, hunger and terror.

The unique partnership between intellectuals and grassroots in Lokayan was active in promoting a meeting in Bhopal in 1989, which sought to create a national forum for alternative development. This was the Harsud meeting, the first time that representatives of major struggles had come together — those fighting the establishment of a missile site at Baliapur in Orissa, the anti-Narmada forces, those resisting the Tehri dam, the people against the Singhroli complex of super-thermal plants, the anti-nuclear struggle — in a common forum. We also have two national working groups, one on the displacement of people, those ousted by 'development'; and the other on India's water, the most precious and most threatened of all our resources. There is such relentlessness in the violation of all the values that we stand for, that there must be an equal relentlessness in the firefighting we have to do just to contain the damage that has already been caused by malign development projects.

We have regular links with the struggle in the West, but there are certain problems in that relationship. First, the more we intervene in our own society, the more we realise that our practice and thinking must centre primarily on our own space, that is, first, Indian, and second, South Asian. There is so much to be done here that playing a wider role sometimes slips from our priorities.

Then there is the frustration we feel at the universalism imposed by the North in its own interpretation of the world. By default, this undermines the uniqueness of our own civilisation, our traditional knowledge system, our positive indigenous traditions. For instance, on *environment*, the priorities defined by the North are the pollution of its own system — air, water and ozone layer and by the eventual non-availability of resources. For us in India, the central issue is how every act of environmental degradation cuts brutally into the heart of *survival*, not just of our people, but of their cultures in the ecological context. It impinges upon and destroys livelihoods, life-ways and life itself. Therefore, the environment is not an issue that can be resolved by conservationist concerns, nor by the protection of non-renewable resources from pollution. Environment is indivisible from issues of equity and social justice. This is not felt with the same intensity in the West. Common property resource removal centrally affects tradition and the ability to sustain the next generation: inter-generational sustainability is a major question for us. We do not want the North to set its own environmental agenda and impose it upon us. We don't want them 'managing' our forests under the guise of 'global conservation'; that is the recipe for green imperialism, and we have had enough imperialisms.

The many people who come here from the West are genuinely concerned, but why are they not doing more in their own societies? The majority of those exercised by the Third World ought to focus on the issues too rarely raised by their own culture. Rather than preoccupation with population in the South, it would be more pertinent to address the issue of sustainable populations in the North, for they are the ones using up disproportionate quantities of resources. Language remains a problem, when everything must pass through English. English is a filter that cannot possibly represent the depth and nuance of the local experience. Most people who come from abroad are exposed only to this filtering English translation, editing, censoring, distorting meanings. The nature of discourse is inevitably determined by those who control it.

Other major themes that concern us are cultural diversity and religion. In the alternative development groups now, the best are talking of spiritual regeneration, a movement away from anthropocentrism, a position that sees humanity as simply one element in a complex web of natural processes. There is, however, rarely a full appreciation of either the possibilities or the problems created by and inherent in religion in our societies. There is an assumption that you can have a peaceful society if you divorce religion from politics, if you divorce religion from economics. Gandhi said, 'Those who speak of separating religion from politics understand neither religion nor politics.'

The crisis is multi-dimensional. If a secular homogenising ethic is imposed on a nation, this de-legitimises multiple identities, cultural and religious. If these are seen as archaic and regressive, if the manipulation and logic of the secular ethic seeks to marginalise these identities, then the ground no longer exists for a reaffirmation of the spirit. The pressure then is on the *religious institutions*, to make them play the positive role in people's lives. Religion gets hi-jacked by fundamentalists, so the regeneration of the spiritual life increasingly passes to them, which distorts the impulse towards renewal. The challenge is within religion, to decommunalise itself and restore its spiritual content. Disregarding religion, or fulminating against it because of fundamentalist activity, neglects what a majority of people in our society relate to, and continue to relate to. An homogenising secularism only reinforces this process. Religion can be liberated. Sikhism was originally a powerfully reformist sect, a reaction against hierarchy and ritual; Sufism was a powerfully reforming movement. What we should look to is neither secularism nor fundamentalism, but a true spiritual liberation.

There are, however, many positive developments. For one thing, the devaluation of politics among the advocates of alternative development. If we reaffirm our faith in the planet and in humanity, the economic and political structures that are anti-planet, anti-humanity, will crumble. Of course, there are clear possibilities of convergence in a distorted form — the integration of the European Community, for example, Eastern Europe and the Russian republics being swallowed up by the Western system. But what is of unquestionable value is that dialogues of great depth and understanding are now possible between large sections of people in North and South. This would not have happened 20 years ago. For us, the euphoria of independence obliterated all other questions. Nation-building took supremacy over everything. But now, we are reaching a historical juncture, where we have tremendous opportunities, and the responsibility for widening and deepening the dialogue. The coming of the Greens in Europe reopens the questions of lifestyles, industrialism, relationships with the South.

We have the chance at this time to seize the initiative and elaborate further the radical alternative philosophy. We do need to formulate the elements of a new theory, not for the sake of theorising, but to strengthen our analyses and our practice. We must build more, and do that with confidence, so that we are not always on the defensive. Those who oppose us come out with a new bomb, a new missile, a new drug, a new disease, new pesticides, new crises all the time, and 95 per cent of our energy is used up devising a defensive response. Many of the things that Lokayan talked about six or seven years ago are becoming major issues today. We have played something of a prophetic role. And if we remain sensitive, in touch with the pulses and impulses of society, there is no reason why we should not continue to do so.

There are, all over India, many thousands of examples of alternative practice, and to articulate the underlying patternings has been the work of Lokayan. One such example is the regeneration of the village of Ralegaon-Siddhi, near Ahmednagar in the State of Maharashtra.

By the mid-1970s, the village was threatened with desertification. The agro-system was collapsing, as has happened to many others in this drought-prone area, which has a rainfall of less than 400mm a year. Most of the rain that did fall was lost, and the people were unable to make a living from the land and had become dependent on money-lenders, permanently in debt. The principal economic activity had become the brewing of illicit liquor: ecological degradation was accompanied by social dislocation.

The principal force behind the rehabilitation of Ralegaon-Siddhi has been a Gandhian, Annasaheb Hazare, who had been a truck driver in the army. He came from a poor family in a nearby village, and had joined the army during the Indo-Chinese war. Later, he had survived a truck accident in which many of his companions were killed. He had taken this as a sign that he should devote his life to *janseva*, service; and it seemed to him that this lay in effort to the regenerate this parched rainshadow area of Ahmednagar: the vegetative cover had practically disappeared, and the surrounding landscape, around the main Pune-Ahmednagar highway, a scene of human-made desolation.

The most important element in the process of restoration was the simultaneous rehabilitation of the landscape and the economic activity of the people. Watershed management went hand-in-hand with social upliftment. The scanty rainfall had to be conserved, harvested and stored: by means of small check-dams and percolation tanks in the barren hills around. Hazare called together all the youth of the village to control the manufacture, trade and consumption of liquor; and at the same time, to find alternative employment, while replenishing the productivity of the soil by reforestation. The species of trees were local, traditional and productive — tamarind, guavas, mango, neem, bhimal. Water-harvesting and community reafforestation became the source of renewed soil-fertility, and this has led to a 60 per cent increase in the productivity of the land. There has also been a several-fold increase in animal wealth.

It was a long and arduous job to break the addiction, not only to brewing liquor, but to drinking it, too. This was achieved by exposing to public shame those who did not give up the *bhattis*, or illicit stills. Most of the people in the village owned land, but few cultivated it; within a few years, every family with land was producing both *kharif* (monsoon rainfed) and *rabi* (winter) crops. Fields of *bajra*, beans and sunflowers offer a dramatic contrast to the surrounding countryside, where miserable huts and skinny animals cling to the denuded hillsides.

The village is clean, the houses, although of traditional stone, are modern and stand apart from the ruins of the earlier, degraded village. The members of the village *panchayat* ('village council') are all female, and this shapes the people's priorities towards food security and education. The secondary school has a hostel which attracts children from all over Maharashtra; in addition to the state timetable, there is a heavy stress on revaluing rural life and village tradition, on practical agriculture and animal husbandry. There is now nothing for the young in Ralegaon Siddhi to flee from. Perhaps the greatest secret of the rehabilitation comes from the fact that the labour for water management, school- and house-building has been done through *shramdan*, voluntary labour. This has saved what is normally the highest proportion of expenditure in villages — the cost of wages, which is so open to corruption and malversation.

The village now has 28 biogas plants, of which three are community based. Two villagers employed by the community collect the animal dung for the gas-plants. Human wastes are also managed to produce biogas. The land remains privately owned, and the only restriction on crops is that sugar-cane and eucalyptus trees are forbidden, because these require too much water.

Caste and communal tensions that have grown with destructive and inequitable development elsewhere have all but disappeared in the village. There were a few landless families, but the rest of the village built houses for them, also through *shramdan*, and the landless families make a livelihood through making and selling brushes and other artefacts of palm-leaves. The castes mix freely. The higher level of social security which the people enjoy means that birth control follows as a natural process, without any need of incentives or threats. It is a living example that the poor need security before they need advice on how not to have children.

The village, with its 2,000 or so people, has evolved in such a way that politicians, and agents of enforced 'development' have become marginal to its own version of self-reliant development. They no longer depend on 'aid'; they rely on collective social benefits, rather than private profit; on a secure sufficiency, rather than the intensive mining of the resource-base for the sake of monetised surpluses.

Bringing together grass-roots movements with researchers and intellectuals has been one of the great achievements of the International Organisation of Consumers' Unions, and Friends of the Earth Malaysia (see p.44) both based in Penang.

ANWAR FAZAL, International Organisation of Consumer Unions (IOCU), RIGHT LIVELIHOOD AWARD WINNER 1982. Anwar Fazal has worked on consumer affairs since 1968, for the Government of Mauritius, the Hong Kong Consumer Council and the United Nations Food and Agriculture Organisation (FAO). In 1978, he was the first person from the Third World to become President of the International Organisation of Consumers' Unions, an independent, non-profit group, which links the activities of consumer organisations in half the countries in the world. Over the following four years, Fazal galvanised the international consumer movement, founding a number of global consumer networks, which enabled and empowered people to deal with transnational corporations whose practices are, more often than not, impenetrable to those who buy their products.

ANWAR FAZAL INITIATED Consumer Interpol, a global citizen alert system on hazardous products, processes and wastes. Consumer Interpol was the first organisation to speak of 'commerciogenic malnutrition', the ability of unscrupulous corporations to displace traditional child-feeding practice by publicity for largely worthless and often damaging substitutes. One of its studies showed that in some countries, anabolic steroids were being promoted as the answer to malnutrition and low weight in children: because so many people in the South are exposed to constant sickness and disease, the side effects of such drugs would be masked by other symptoms. Consumer Interpol intervened in countries where petfood was being sold for human consumption; alerted them to the dangers of clioquinol; and the risks from lead and mercury in face creams and skin whiteners. It has exposed the lengths to which some transnationals will go in the promotion of its goods: one was even offering architectural advice to hospitals, which in effect, meant designing maternity units so that mothers and babies would be separated after birth, thus facilitating routine artificial feeding, using its products, rather than breast-feeding.

The International Babyfood Action Network followed a coalition of groups active in the infant formula campaign. 'If the freely given and abundant nourishment of mother's milk can be interrupted and substituted by commercial products, there is no limit to the potential for dislocation and re-arrangement of natural practice anywhere in the world.' Health Action International (HAI) is a coalition of action groups working on pharmaceutical issues, and the pesticides Action Network was effective in alerting the South to the transnationals' dumping of dangerous products which had been banned in the North.

Malaysia, a relatively small country, has been industrialising at great speed. It has one of most 'open' economies in the world. Here, market forces rule with the rigour of an army of occupation. The triumphal emblems of the transnationals are branded on the night sky of Kuala Lumpur and Penang: Mitsubishi, Sharp, Sanyo, Bosch, Siemens, Hoechst, Maggi, Bata, Pepsi, Toyota, Carlsberg, Brother, Cadbury. The Free Trade Zones are wired-off, alien compounds, where the nimble fingers, pliability and deteriorating eyesight of young countrywomen contribute so conspicuously to the international competitiveness of those they serve. It is fitting that Malaysia should become a focal point for resistance to some of the world's most flagrant corporate excesses.

The Consumers' Association of Penang (CAP) is affiliated to IOCU. This was set up in 1969 by S. Mohammed Idris, a Penang businessman, who also founded Friends of the Earth Malaysia, and the Third World Network, an influential alternative and South-oriented news service.

The CAP has been a vigilant monitor of losses and gains in the transformation of Malaysia. As time goes by, says M. Idris, the nature of the work changes: things become more clearly defined. What often began as campaigns come to be seen as part of wider thrust against systematic dispossession and loss.

Agricultural employment declined from over 50 per cent of the people in 1970, to less than 40 per cent by 1985. The biggest export earners are crude oil, tropical hardwoods($1.6 billion in 1986), palm-oil and rubber. In 1986, 25 per cent of Malaysia's GNP was sucked abroad, 14 per cent through adverse terms of trade, and 11 per cent on debt servicing. The shining light of equitable and modest life-ways is being extinguished in Sarawak; and in their place, the imported Western paradigm is accompanied by an upsurge of new social problems, the costs of which are not borne by those who make profit from them. Malaysia now has an estimated 200,000 alcoholics, especially among Indians on the plantations. Smoking is increasing at the rate of about five per cent a year, consumption of sugar is among the highest per capita in the world. Consumption of fruit, vegetables and fish-protein has declined, as more land is taken for cash crops. The category of the *sufficient* is basic in traditional societies. Once you start to measure wealth in cash, then *enough* ceases to exist, for it cannot be found in the realm of monetised riches.

CAP began publication in 1989 of two new periodicals, *Third World Resurgence* and *Third World Economics*. It has its own publishing imprint. Among recent books are Frederick Clairmonte's and John Cavanagh's *Merchants of Drink*, an account of transnational control of beverages in the Third World; and Evelyne Hong's See *The Third World While It Lasts*, an indictment of the consequences of tourism in the Third World, and its power to divert resources from local people, and its power to compel hundreds of thousands of young women into the sex industry of South-East Asia; and *Recolonisation*, Chakravarthi Raghavan's account of how the Uruguay Round of trade negotiations under GATT is an attempt by the West further to disadvantage the Third World and to usher in a new era of economic colonialism.

I went with members of CAP to visit some of the people involved in the social and environmental issues on Penang and the immediate hinterland.

Environmental degradation has a long history in Malaysia, notably in the legacy of the colonial rubber plantation. There are desolate landscapes of rows of identical rubber trees, which create long arcades of gloomy shade. Each tree has a diagonal wound in the bark, and a clay pot to catch the milky latex as it bleeds from the trunk. In places, weedkiller and pesticides have withered the sparse vegetation under the trees to a dusty ash. Paraquat and DDT are still freely available at sundries stores. Paraquat has other melancholy uses: it contributes to the maintenance of the high suicide rate among those who have lived and died on plantations for three generations; mostly Tamils, brought to Malaysia by the British at the turn of the century.

At the Barlow and Bousted estate in Kedah, the rubber trees are being doubly tapped. This will kill them. The sites will then be cleared and replanted with oil palms. Many of the workers on these estates are elderly; the rest little more than children. The workers of CAP call them 'green ghettos'. A large proportion of young women and men have gone to work in factories in the Free Trade Zones. A woman of about 60 works slowly through the grey forest. She takes a stepladder from tree to tree, and with a curved knife, makes an incision in the bark. She must tap 600 trees a day to make up the 30 kilos of latex that will earn her a daily wage of $M8.50 (about $3.50). The people here are relatively favoured; management has constructed houses which they can buy. This is a great advance on the barrack-like structures of other estates.

S. Jayarman is a former president of the rubber-tappers union. He earns $M227 a month ($80), and the company takes $M72 for the mortgage. The house may be occupied only while at least one member of the family works on the plantation. If he or she loses the job, even through accident or sickness, the whole family is evicted. Mr Jayarman's two sons are working in a radio assembly plant in a Free Trade Zone. Their pay is $M7.50 a day — even lower than on the plantations; but the work is associated with the modern sector, and draws the young to it.

The work on oil-palms is even more arduous. The clusters of orange-red seeds grow at the base of the palm branch. The workers must remove the branch with a long pole tipped with a metal blade. The branch falls, a ponderous green feather; it is in fact so heavy that if a worker is immediately beneath, it will cause serious injury. Then the seeds must be dislodged, and those that have scattered collected. The worker is paid 30 cents a bunch from the tall trees, 15 cents from the squat ones. The piles of dead branches are a work-hazard; they shelter snakes, especially cobras, and snake bites in these isolated places can be fatal.

The acreage under oil-palm is growing. Since there is a shortage of labour, the owners have recruited workers in Indonesia and Bangladesh to work alongside the Tamils. In the early morning, before it is light, groups of dark Tamil children gather to wait for the buses that will take them to their ill-equipped and run-down schools. Indians are the most disadvantaged group in the country. They make up about 11 per cent of the population, as against 57 per cent Malays, and 30 per cent Chinese.

There are other brutal scars of development on the landscape. At Ayer Itam, a few kilometres from Georgetown, principal city on Penang Island, the hills have been blasted for building materials; red wounds of landslips appear on the wooded slopes. A new urban centre is being constructed on what was some of the most fertile soil in Penang. It was an area occupied by vegetable growers, who sold their fresh produce in the local market. There were 500 families here, several thousand people. They have been displaced by construction work. Most have migrated to Ipoh, 150 kilometres away. There, they are buying fresh vegetables and transporting them by truck to Penang, where they sell them in the market to which they once took their own produce. This raises the price of fresh food to the people of Penang.

The growers tried to resist. There were demonstrations and protests, supported by CAP and Friends of the Earth Malaysia. The police shot and killed a demonstrator, a young woman. Most people then accepted that there was nothing they could do. Chong Gek Sim, however, a determined woman in her fifties, refuses to move. Her family came here from China when she was a child. Her self-built house is a sizeable structure, with concrete base, wooden walls and corrugated metal roof. It stands barely two metres from the soaring stone cliff of a 12-storey apartment block under construction. Builders' rubble falls in a constant cascade of stones and cement on to her roof. On the day I was there, a piece of rusty metal had pierced the roof and fallen into her kitchen. Chong Gek Sim still grows vegetables, but the area is now liable to flooding. You can still gain an idea of how it was — bougainvilleas in flower, crimson canna lilies, orange hibiscus. There is sugar-cane, a papaya tree, plantain and rambutan, with beds of green leaf vegetables. All around is the wreckage of other people's homes, the concrete floor, old chairs, a discarded fridge, children's toys, gardening tools, dismantled pig-pens and chicken runs, with which the growers used to supplement their income. Chong says:

> After the retreat of the Japanese, people were given land which they cleared and made into productive gardens. I used to work with my children. Now my sons are in an electronics factory, my daughter in a garment factory. But I won't leave unless I am given the equivalent of the 25 years' earnings which my children could have expected from this land, if they had been allowed to work our 11 acres.

In front of the hut is a little Buddhist shrine, where incense sticks are burning. Blue and saffron-coloured butterflies flit over the declining patches of vegetation, and the traces of family burial plots, where grass grows over the red-painted Chinese characters on abandoned headstones.

Penang island is heavily urbanised. Marketed to tourists as the Pearl of the East, there are now over 6,000 hotel rooms, colonising the opal beaches, stripping away the trees. Tall condominiums, rented mostly by Japanese businessmen or by rich Taiwanese seeking a refuge from their own ravaged island, are replacing the peeling colonial bungalows, with their cool spacious interiors, their terraces and ancient frangipani trees.

The fishing village of Jelutong is now almost completely enclosed by the colour-washed arcades of Georgetown's streets. A narrow lane leads from the congested main road, past a *kampong* of substantial Malay houses on stilts, with ladders leading to the upper storey, and shaded by soaring angsana trees. Ashim, in his sixties, comes from a fishing family living at the water's edge. The fishing people still use the traditional sampan, two men to each craft. They now have a Yamaha outboard motor, because they must go further out from the shore for their modest catch of senegin, jenhak, kerapu. Pollution has destroyed the in-shore fishing grounds. There are now only about 60 sampans left in the community. Some of the fishermen work part-time, and also have factory jobs. Of Ashim's eight children, only three still work in the traditional occupation.

The village itself is crowded on to the foreshore, built mainly over water. An area of stinking mud soon gives way to contaminated water, full of rusty cans, plastic bags and garbage. The houses are on stilts, all of wood, with rickety jetties the only walkways between them, the slats of which yield perilously as people step on them. Beyond the village is a narrow causeway, alongside which the sampans are moored. In the sheds, some men are baiting a long line of hooks with silver shrimps. Hosein says they must go further and further out to sea, because industrial and toxic wastes are being dumped into Penang River, which flows into the sea a few hundred metres from Jelutong. In any case, the best fish is taken industrially, and goes for export: high-protein fish goes abroad, and Malaysia now imports food.

The government has plans to 'reclaim' this area, but the people do not want their homes 'upgraded', because this will certainly mean they will be ousted for some prestige project, luxury apartments or the redundant new toll bridge that now joins Penang to the mainland, and which, according to the calculations of CAP, will not pay for itself for another 200 years.

Friends of the Earth have been fighting a plan to transform Penang Hill, the highest spot on the island into a multi-million dollar leisure complex. This spot, 800 metres above sea level, is a ramshackle collection of former colonial buildings, where the British came to escape the heat of Penang; it is a neglected and melancholy site, overlooking virgin forest on one side, and with a wide range of unique flora and fauna, especially delicate ferns. The hill is reached by tortuous paths through the trees, and there is also a funicular railway. The new plan would turn the area into an industrialised 'pleasure-resort', with five-star hotel, an acropolis, a moonwalk and a 'banyan tree-top restaurant'. There are no banyans in Penang, despite the abundance of tropical trees, so the company planning the scheme would build one in concrete.

Martin Khor, economist with CAP, says that this kind of development is suicidal for the Third World.

We see here in microcosm a development that is articulated to the needs of the rich and which mimics the West. The West tries to make this acceptable through rhetoric about 'freedom', 'free trade' (not fair trade), liberalisation, opening up, free markets. All this has a positive sound, and it has the advantage of making them sound as though they are on the side of liberty. This makes those who oppose them — and that means the Greens now, sound as though we stand for controls and restrictions. They can frighten people into thinking we stand for unfreedom, because we are against the effects of the market. If we are not careful, we shall see a replay of the defeat of socialism; already the ideology of the TNCs and Western laissez-faire has cast us in the same role once occupied by the Red menace: destroyers, spectres at the global feast, wanting to spoil everybody's good time. This is why we must articulate what we *do* want, not only what we *don't* want. So the groups and activists who are fighting development need also to go on the ideological offensive. One example — when the West talks of the horrors of a planned economy, we can say the West itself does have a planned economy. The only difference is it is planned by advertisers and salespeople. People may believe they have what they want, but everything is structured to ensure that they want what they can have.

17. LESSONS FROM A DECAYED ALTERNATIVE

The West has been swift to draw the conclusion that the fall of Communism in Eastern Europe and the former Russian empire proves that there is only one way in the world, and that is embodied by 'Western values', which naturally includes the sagacious and universally benign Western economic system. Rejoicing over the death of tyranny quickly shaded into a celebration over the death of all alternatives to what the capitalist project stands for. The 'lessons of history' have been invoked; although as we are now seeing, history has no lessons. Humanity is destined to receive only a permanently repeated, and nearly always bitter, instruction from an eternal present.

Those whose work was to define alternatives to the majestic certitudes of Communism have seen themselves submerged by the only system remaining and the new world order which flows from this happy arrangement of providence. Many of those courageous people who resisted the monolith in Eastern Europe when it seemed invincible now find themselves in the position of being equally marginalised. The spaces which they worked to open up have been unceremoniously occupied and occluded by the economic forces of the West.

Duna Kor and Janos Vargha, Right Livelihood Award Winners 1985. Duna Kor means the 'Danube Circle', and was set up in 1984, as an environmental movement, opposing the construction of an enormous dam and hydroelectric complex on the Danube. Its founder was Janos Vargha, a biologist who had earlier worked for the Hungarian Academy of Sciences. The $3 billion complex was to have been built jointly by Hungary and Czechoslovakia, with considerable financial input from Austria, and involved drastic interference with nearly 200 kilometres of river; the flooding of 50 islands and 120 square kilometres of forests and fields; and the loss of valuable wildlife habitats. It had also incalculable implications for the groundwater of the region and the drinking water supply of some three million people. It also had no economic rationale, and was opposed for this reason by the Presidency of the Hungarian Academy of Sciences in 1983. But the Hungarian government was determined to proceed.

DUNA KOR WAS a social innovation as well as a protest movement. Duna Kor networked informally, opposition to the project in scientific, professional and literary circles increased, and some ten thousand signatures were collected against the dam. Despite harassment and intimidation, Vargha and his colleagues persevered with their protests. It was not until February 1989 that Duna Kor was able to register officially. In 1988 it organised a 130,000 signature petition for a referendum on the power plant. With the fall of the Communist system, the legacy of environmental ruin created by the urgency of industrialisation in Eastern Europe during the Communist era has been revealed. What Vargha said of the Danube project remains as relevant and dissenting in the new order as it did in the old. 'What I am fighting for is something that no system with a central idea of power, whatever its ideology, will accept: self-limitation by mankind.'

The projected dam was a huge scheme, conceived before the First World War in its original form in that section of the Danube between Bratislava and Budapest, when the region still belonged to Austro-Hungary. Its parentage, therefore, was rooted in the heroic industrial age of capitalism, to which tradition, at least, the socialist heresy remained true.

It was not until after the Second World War that the possibility of co-operation between Czechoslavakia and Hungary under the occupation of the USSR became realistic. In the early 1950s, it was proposed that there would be storage lake of 60 square kilometres and a lateral canal 30 kilometres long, rising up to 18 metres above ground at a peak power station at Gabcikov. Vargha says that such projects were an object of dispute between various sectors of the economy. In this case, the water lobby was set against the energy lobby.

Communist countries were supposed to be centrally planned. It isn't true. Sure, they made beautiful plans, but they were useless. The production was based upon the share of central budget each sector received. The political influence of each sector was the chief determinant on how much it got. Behind the curtains, around the wide tables of hunting lodges, they debated. This was in the early sixties. What gave it the final momentum was the oil crisis of the seventies. The two countries signed a treaty in 1977, and started preparatory work, building roads. It was a time of economic stringency in the Eastern bloc, so Hungary had to cut its expenditure, and work was halted. They suggested to Czechoslovakia that they should postpone it for ten years. It was only shortage of money. They had no idea of the other problems that would arise, for instance, that the storage lake would become a trap for polluted sediment and a source of eutrophication. This would have created an explosion of the plant system of the river, and when the organic materials died, they would have overburdened the decomposition system.

Then they planned to leave only 2.5 per cent of the original flow of the

Danube in the river, which would have dried out the adjacent forests. Some of these are original ecosystems with rare species. The problems of the dam were quite well-known, and I'm sure the hydro-engineers who planned the project didn't publicise them because they had an economic and political interest in building large dams.

Janos Vargha had been a biologist, working on genetic engineering; and he changed his career to become an environmental journalist, in order to create awareness of the consequences of such projects.

My first article was forbidden. That was my first encounter with censorship. I had to educate myself and become familiar with hydro systems. I became very involved, and as I pieced the story together, I couldn't understand why such a project was under consideration at all, given the environmental and economic problems. When my first article was banned, I became both angry and interested. That was my incentive to learn more. Most journalists learned to accept self-censorship, a closed mental universe which works very effectively. In Communist countries the limits of publicity were never precisely determined, it was a wall of fog. You have to find your own limits and not exceed them. If you wrote something too strong, you were punished, so you learned to keep well within the borders, and stay there, which is a form of mental illness. It begins to destroy your critical capacity.

I often thought it would be easier to give up. But once you have started, you cannot live with yourself if you abandon the struggle. Later, it became an issue inside the Party. We had great help from the international press. Without that, we would have been treated worse than we were by the Communist authorities.

The environmental movement played an important role in the changes in Eastern Europe, although since the change-over, capitalism has been seen as the rescuer; and it is clear that the West sees economic failure as a greater sin than environmental disaster.

The more flexible part of the nomenklatura tried to modernise the economy, but it became clear that political control also inhibited economic development. It seems that once this process is set in train, it cannot be easily halted. There are no intermediate solutions between the reign of terror and the moderate, soft manipulation which is used in the Western countries. It is true that in Hungary, the environmental movement added some pressure to the leadership, which pressed against the limits of the system. But there is also another reason that increased the numbers of those participating in the environmental movement, and that is that despite the fact that it was regarded as an enemy movement, hostile to the state, it was more softly handled than the hard political opposition.

Then the political opposition used environmental issues to blame the Communists, quite justifiably, of course. But the political opposition also sought to incorporate the environmental movement. I was against this at the time, because I argued that the environmentalists would pay a high price if the political dissidents came to power, because no political ruling parties are ever friendly to the environment. This all gave a higher profile to the environmental movement, and made it appear both more effective and more influential than it was.

Judit Vasarhyeli, also a member of Duna Kor, has a somewhat different perspective on what happened in Eastern Europe. She says that the first feeling of everyone was one of enormous relief that the transition occurred without bloodshed, at least until the violence in Yugoslavia. In Hungary, because it all happened so peacefully, she says, many of the officials of the old regime are still in place in the administration. It would, in any case, have been difficult to find replacements for them: there simply are not enough people in the former opposition with the necessary experience and education.

Of those remaining, some would be loyal to any government. Another type, those committed to the old regime, are now re-established in their fortresses. One result of this is that we had thought the hydro-electric project on the Danube had been settled once and for all, but now we are not quite so sure. The Ministry of Environment and the Ministry of Water Management were previously the same, but now they have been separated. The new Environment Minister has been receiving more and more letters in favour of the dam. The old guard feel a little more confident now, and in the confused circumstances created by the change-over, can show their true feelings. There is nothing in the altered ideological landscape that is inherently anti big dams.

We are concerned that in the shadow of the monolithic state, there was no civil society. Non-government organisations, civil society, this is all new for us. Previously, we had been seen simply as a handful of crazy individuals. We are still overwhelmed by the catastrophic inheritance of socialism, not only in the area of pollution, but even more in the destruction of the identity of the people. There is a need to rebuild family, community and local strengths that had been broken by the system. It is hard to foster healthy emotions in the wake of this distortion of our identity. The Communist system involved such a *waste of human resources*, a destruction of human capital, as well as its material waste. Many people in the West say, 'Yes, we too have alcoholism, drugs, crime.' Well, we have that as well as the cruel political legacy.

One of the worst things is the scepticism of the people. They are intolerant and impatient. They tend to think that whatever is wrong is the fault of the present government, even though it only recently came to power. They don't see it as the postponed effect of 40 years of Communism. People have never been used to taking part in decision-making. Revitalising is not just a question of economics, but also of social and mental hygiene. In spite of the change, people are not happy. There was little celebration here. The economic situation will, in any case, get worse. Next year will be worse than this; after that, it may improve. Unemployment will go on rising, because of the closedown of unproductive factories whose losses were concealed for years in the state budget.

Then there are the environmental consequences. Air pollution is the main concern; that is highly visible, and amenable to treatment. More serious is the lack of potable water in many rural areas. Many villages have to be supplied by tankers or plastic bags. Country people are highly exposed to nitrification of the water from fertilisers.

We are still addressing the issue of a post-socialist economy. We welcome Green entrepreneurs, but not sharks moving in after the liberation: these are only adding to the degradation in the name of economic progress. We don't want obsolete or dangerous technologies. The French government, for example, wanted to build a nuclear power station. There is a surplus of energy in France, so they will get the business and we will get the pollution.

We are discussing Green economics and energy conservation with our friends in the West. The Democratic Forum originally talked of the Third Way, but that has now been abandoned for straightforward liberalism. We urgently need to talk about environmental auditing, legislation for environmental protection, as well as social healing of the scars of Communism.

The Duna Kor activists are well aware that the competition between biological and technological systems is a worldwide phenomenon, and that the latter are everywhere gaining ground. But at least in the West there was a space for the environmental organisations to respond, even though governments too easily called themselves green and paraded policies that were mainly symbolic and cosmetic. In Eastern Europe, the totalitarian social-economic systems could not react. The crises of several decades there had been 'solved' by strengthening totalitarian structures and continuing with the use of aggressive technologies. This was built into the ideology of Communism at source, and is part of the distant inheritance of Marx's admiration of the powers of 'bourgeois' industry, which impressed him more than the powers of a natural world which was there only to be conquered.

Vargha acknowledges that the extension of the Western model to the East will not solve the ecological problems, because the governments of the democratic countries also represent the interests of the technological/industrial concentrations of power, not those of either humanity or the biosphere. In any case, the developed countries 'export' much of their environmental destruction to the Third World. It is this escape route that has permitted the West to express its righteous horror at the devastation wrought in Eastern Europe.

After escaping the tyranny of Moscow [says Vargha], these countries are now seeking to enter the Western orbit; although Western resources are proving to be not so bountiful after all. Eastern Europe, instead of becoming full members of a united Europe, may become a bad copy of the Western model, or even the back-yard and dumping ground of the West, because of its cheap labour and because its citizens are unable to defend themselves.

The civil society of Eastern Europe and its independent movements are far weaker now than they seemed at the time of political change. The immense weight of state ownership restricted their sources of finance. Their competence was reduced by a lack of independent experts and the inefficiency of the information systems; public support is being eroded by the constant rise in the cost of living. After elections, political organisations, as well as the state, turn away from environmental problems, as economic issues appear to overwhelm them.

PETRA KELLY, RIGHT LIVELIHOOD AWARD WINNER 1982. Petra Kelly was one of the founders of the West German Green party in 1979, which she described as 'a non-violent ecological and basic-democratic anti-war coalition of parliamentary and extra-parliamentary grassroots oriented forces within the (then) Federal Republic of Germany'. In 1983 she was elected to the German Parliament as one of 28 Green MPs. She concentrated her political work on four themes closest to her heart: peace and non-violence, ecology, feminism, human rights, and the links between these. She believed in civil disobedience and participated in many such actions in various parts of the world. She also founded and chaired a Europe-wide citizen action group against childhood cancer, set up after the death from cancer at the age of 10 of her sister, Grace. Kelly's first book, *Fighting for Hope*, was published in English in 1984 (Chatto and Windus.) She has written subsequent books on Hiroshima, childhood cancer and Tibet.

THE GREEN PARTY has been much concerned with the changes in Eastern Europe, the end of the Communist era: because the Greens' vision of an alternative was supremely relevant to the East, Petra Kelly bitterly regrets the speed with which the reunification of Germany took place. The alternative was quickly submerged.

At the same time, the takeover effectively stifled any critical self-examination in the West. It might have been thought that the triumph of the West would make Western society more secure, and therefore more able to look at its own flaws and failings. The opposite has been the case. Indeed, it seems, in its assertiveness, triumphalism and self-confidence, to have learned a thing or two from the system it has defeated. A distinct intolerance, a renewal of racism, a recurrence of old xenophobias suggest a darker side to the victory of the sole system remaining in contention in the world. In the same way, the liberation of the East and the dissolution of the former Soviet Union has merely uncovered old hatreds, virulent nationalisms, antagonisms suppressed for a time under the frozen Communist system.

It was sad how in Germany, Kohl simply took credit for everything, even though without Gorbachev nothing would have happened. Kohl decided to buy Gorbachev off, so much money he couldn't refuse. The East had to jettison all its social legislation, including its more liberal abortion laws. Women couldn't fight it; as a result women are losing ground in Germany right now. The revolution that had such an abundance of creative energy has eaten up its women. Within the space of a decade, it seems, women have gained and lost power. The promise has not been fulfilled.

The West claims that everything that happened in Eastern Europe vindicates their strategy of 'negotiation through strength'. They have tried to devalue our non-violent social defence policy, our idea of building-down threats.

The Greens made the error of taking the reunification clause out of our policy barely a year before it happened. We thought Kohl was crazy, but then he did it. I feel unhappy at the thought of a German centralised unitary state. We find it difficult to draw the limits, to practise self-restraint. To see the hatred on the streets of Germany once more is so frightening. There is such intolerance of foreign workers and refugees. We have seen migrant hostels firebombed, refugees assaulted in public. Some of those who originally came to Germany for asylum have already fled to other countries to escape the persecution of what was to have been a haven of refuge. And then there has been an upsurge of anti-Semitism; Jewish monuments have been daubed. How can we prevent nationalism from becoming violent and aggressive? With the breakdown of the East, how can we deal with the revival of nationalisms in a positive way? Self-determination, but not determining the lives and deaths of others. After 40 years of repression, suddenly the lid is off. It is always easy to see what you are being liberated *from*, but what people are being liberated *into* is rarely thought about until it is too late.

But in spite of that, the Greens have brought a renewal of hope in the world. We may have been eclipsed electorally in Germany for the moment, but we have offered the only alternative in the world to the decayed dogmas of Communism, and the equally threadbare limits of social democracy. The Greens have brought something of lasting value to both East and West. We have added energy, commitment, idealism to politics. Whatever happens, those values will not disappear. The SPD in Germany seemed more concerned to marginalise the Greens than to defeat the Right. They have been so anxious to become respectable, moderate. Willy Brandt said to me when I left the SPD at the end of the seventies, 'The Greens won't come to anything, and if they do, we will take them over.' And that is what has been happening. But social democracy has become such a conservative force in Europe now. What an irony that the Greens saw parliamentary extinction through reunification! The nineties were to have been our decade. All the things we had warned about — worldwide catastrophe, it is not for the future, it is now. Yet the urgency has gone out of the issue. There is already no way to heal the soil and the forests. The rich are telling the poor to stop damaging the environment — don't chop down the forests; even though they are doing it with German chain-saws.

The Greens became more middle of the road after the early parliamentary successes. Some of the transforming impulse was muted. Representation in legislatures is not, of itself, going to change the direction of the world. But neither would it be wholly true to say that the failure of the Greens to achieve parliamentary representation at all in 1990 means that Germany has become inward-looking, preoccupied only with unification and materialism; the deep impulse of concern that has gone out from here in the past 20 years and influence Green initiatives everywhere has not decayed, although it may take new forms.

The annexation of the East was a tragedy. There was a revolution through people's power. The Greens had had a vast input into the ten years of planning the revolution and dreaming of the new society that would be created. But the West's money moved in and all alternatives were marginalised. Under Honecker, the CDU in the former East Germany never opened their mouths; and then, when it was safe, they never closed them. How painful it is for those who were in opposition all those years to find themselves sidelined again! Now they are dissidents once more, in back rooms and attics all over again. The only thing you can say is they had a lot of practice. The revolution was stopped, caught off guard. The economic disaster has been the excuse for subordinating everything to instant takeover. There has been such a disregard, a diminishing of popular struggle. Many people from the former DDR feel they have lost their identity. They feel schizophrenic, victimised. They felt they had nothing to offer. The idea that we had of a better alternative, a better East Germany, never stood a chance.

And then the Western conservative leaders moved in and claimed that all the changes in Eastern Europe had come about becaause of their policy of maintaining their nuclear strength. They took responsibility for things which had nothing to do with their efforts. All the work we had done, in urging the building down of tension, of seeking security through fewer weapons and non-offensive defence, was nullified. It is clear now that there will be very little rebuilding of the East: the West will dump technology and dangerous products on them; because the level of technology is higher in the West, people think anything emanating from there is progressive. Those parts of Eastern Europe that are too damaged to be rehabilitated will become a dumping ground, the site of 'garbage imperialism'. They will build nuclear reactors in the East, and all the work we did will have to be started all over again. When I went with Gert Bastian to Czechoslovakia, the foreign minister met us. He had spent three years in jail under the Communist regime, and he said, 'We are going to build three nuclear power plants.' The nuclear lobby were the first to jump in after the changeover, offering help, know-how. The people wanted to do something different, but they are being forced into a development they don't want, because they have no option. The bankruptcy of the East — in every sense — means they are ripe for forms of domination and colonialism which they may not like, but which they must submit to because they have no choice.

The triumph of the West serves to obscure the deeper crisis of industrial society. It hides the fact that the Western way itself is the source of the most monstrous abuse of human beings and of the resource-base of the earth. The Greens are the only political formation in the West who are concerned with both global social justice and a more prudent use of natural resources. Racism in Europe is a refraction of the global injustices that sustain our precarious and damaging culture. That is the great theme of the 21st century, and the Greens are the only ones who have engaged with it.

PART 4: TOWARDS A NEW PARADIGM

18. THE SPIRITUAL DIMENSION OF GREEN POLITICS

Most of those working for a hopeful alternative agree that this must be put forward with humility, in a non-dogmatic way, preferably by practical example.

New movements and fresh ideas often enjoy a certain success in their early stages. It is only later that resistance becomes stronger, when they strike against the vested interests of the social forces opposing them. This happened with the phenomenal rise of the Greens, and the slower advance, once people had taken stock of the implications of the changes they were proposing.

The objections to the alternative by those in power have been both vociferous and, in their way, effective. The logic of 'common sense', 'reason' and 'realism', has led to an unparalleled unanimity between Left and Right in their attack upon the Green movement. ('They want to turn back the clock'; 'They want to take us back to the Middle Ages'; 'They don't live in the real world'; 'They will throw away everything we've achieved'; 'These are fine ideals, but they go against human nature'; 'These are privileged people who want to prevent others from enjoying what they have' are just a few of the taunts with which many in the Green movement are familiar.) One of the most urgent tasks is to devise an alternative common sense to oppose the triumphal negations of the received wisdom. The Greens evoke such powerful responses because they are challenging the management of exhausted conflicts that are embodied in existing political formations. The barrenness of revivalist zeal for market forces as the supreme guides of human affairs is matched by the emptiness of a social democracy which is in permanent subjection to the wealth-creating powers of capitalism.

In spite of the attempts to block the Greens, and the setback in the German elections in December 1990, their emergence in Europe has been of a piece with the rise of other social forces which have, at intervals, radically changed Europe, and indeed, because of the European imperial tradition, the world. The Greens are not a random assemblage of malcontents and dissenters, who have appeared arbitrarily in the richest societies the world has ever known. They embody vital interests, and are as much part of the late 20th century as any other of the component groups of 'advanced' industrial society. They represent currents of feeling and forces as real as those which, in the early industrial era, challenged landed and aristocratic interests with all the energy of an impatient and disfranchised middle class demanding recognition of its contribution to the wealth of society. The appearance of the Greens is as epochal, too, as the rise of the organised working class towards the end of the 19th century, which also refused any longer to be excluded from the benefits of an industrial life to whose workings they were indispensable.

There are, of course, crucial differences. The objective of the Greens is not merely to gain a share of the wealth of industrialism, but to modify radically the way in which that wealth is created, measured and distributed. The self-interest to which they appeal is longer-term, the rewards less immediate, the benefits apparently less tangible, certainly less selfish, although scarcely less real.

It is true that the Greens in the West do, on the whole, constitute an intellectually privileged group, the equivalent, perhaps, of the clergy at an earlier historical moment, in the sense that they are living from a 'cultural' rather than an economic or political capital. It is not by chance that many adherents of the Green movement come from the realm of the arts, teaching, academic and administrative sectors, or that the Greens have unlocked much of the energy of women, as well as many minority groups who do not identify with any of the existing, and now conservative, political parties. Perhaps it is the appeal to non-immediate less material interests that helps to account for the strong spiritual content of Green values, in the appeal to planetary integrity and survival, pluralism, diversity, peace and social justice. To those who see the Greens as a permanent minority, unlikely to influence the industrial juggernaut, the words of Murray Bookchin, in *Towards an Ecological Society*, may be of comfort:

> Success and popularity, in the sense of massive human commitment to an ideal, are matters of growth, painstaking education, development, and the ripening of conditions that render the actualisation of human and social potentialities the real epochal changes in the individual and society.

One of those who have most consistently contributed to the rekindling of spiritual values in our time is Sir George Trevelyan.

GEORGE TREVELYAN, RIGHT LIVELIHOOD AWARD WINNER 1982. Born in 1906, George Trevelyan was an agnostic until he attended a lecture by Rudolph Steiner in 1942. Thereafter, his study of anthroposophy profoundly altered his philosophy of life, and laid the basis for much of his future work. After the Second World War, he went into adult education as principal of Attingham Park, Shropshire, where he first started giving courses on the spiritual nature of man and the universe. On his retirement in 1971, he founded the Wrekin Trust to continue his work. An educational charity, the Wrekin Trust is not affiliated to any particular doctrine or dogma, nor does it offer any one way to 'the truth'. Rather, it helps people find the disciplines most suited to them, organising conferences on the holistic view of the world, and offering a curriculum for ongoing spiritual training. Trevelyan has written three books: *A Vision of the Aquarian Age* (1977), *Operation Redemption* (1981) and *Summons to a High Crusade* (1985).

SIR GEORGE TREVELYAN has been a major influence on the emergent 'New Age' sensibility. He describes the New Age as

The holistic picture, the realisation that the earth is a living creature. And this runs over into the spirit: most people can accept it very easily now. The earth isn't just a mechanical structure — Gaia is a living being. You cannot conceivably think about the planet holistically without thinking of it as a spiritual thing. Of course, we can stop doing the monstrous things we are doing, like cutting down the trees, and realise that we are killing the earth; but it is much more powerful if you can realise that we are killing a living being. And furthermore, that there are other beings: this being of earth is part of a wonderful creation for the experiment of man, to develop with freedom of choice, of free choice to come back to God as co-creator, which will give an impetus to further creation and exploration of the universe . . . And we, who ought to be the consciousness of the earth, the guardians of nature, are doing these monstrous things for greed and war and passion. We are immortal, spiritual beings in a death-ridden culture. We are truly the stewards of the planet, because we come back again and again to compensate for the damage we have done, and to learn the lesson of a new epoch, until we have got so far that we can be co-creators, able to leave school and go to university, the universe.

We need to identify with the totality of humanity, as one huge being, of which we are each a droplet of intelligence. That is the change that is coming, and that is what the younger generation are increasingly able to understand.

The earth is certainly going to get into trouble. Earth changes are bound to come, as a result of what we are doing. But on the other plane, there is the realm of light. There is such concern on the higher plane for the redemption of the planet, the spiritual forces are rallying. The planet is so important an experiment, an absolute key-point, carrying a being who can consciously become a co-creator with God. And this planet is being flooded now with the Christ — with that aspect of God which is sheer love. This is the great excitement of the age.

Even if very drastic things have to happen to the poor old earth, everything has to die in order to become. Remember Goethe:

Und wenn du Dies nicht hast,
Dieses Sterben und Werden,

> *Bist du nur ein truber Gast*
> *Auf der dunklen Erde.*

The earth has to change, in order that something more splendid may come to birth. But in order to be involved with that, we've got to have thought enough to say 'yes' to the idea. That, I think, is what I'm about. We've got to wake up and think this, and act as if it were true. Goethe was once asked if he could explain the secret of life. He replied, 'You want to know the secret of life? That which the planet does unconsciously, do consciously. That is all.'

If there is a significant spiritual content in the emerging world-view, this is not because it has developed in reaction to a world dominated by either materialism or reason. For the values which animate and pervade industrial society are also based upon faith, a faith which, moreover, from its Judaeo-Christian origins, has undergone many mutations through time. The economic system of the West long ago freed itself from the constraints and inhibitions imposed by religion; a process described by Tawney in *Religion and the Rise of Capitalism.* The people of the West, so awed by this epic act of self-emancipation, and the energies that made it possible, subsequently transferred their orphaned faith to the economic 'miracle' itself, and the dynamic forces this released into the world. This is what Jose Lutzenberger means when he speaks of Western consumer-industrial society as a 'diabolic religion'. For, in the pursuit of ceaseless economic growth, the continuing conquest of nature, the profusion of technological fixes, the creation of wealth as redemption and spending as sacrament, we find ourselves in the presence of fervours and ecstasies once prompted by less material promises of salvation and transcendence. Those who propose, in its place, a holistic and more humble reverence for creation, a more balanced integration with Gaia, are actually taking sides in an undeclared war of religion.

For there are no secular societies. It is simply that objects of worship undergo some strange metamorphoses, and faith, evicted from its familiar sanctuaries, goes, exposed and shivering, in search of new abodes. We may wonder whether, in order to counter a dogmatic and unyielding faith in industrialism, material progress and the revelations of economic reason, the most effective response may not lie in an equally strong act of faith. It is surely not by chance that the only force to have turned back the tide of Westernisation in the world has been fundamentalist Islam. This is not to argue for or against the desirability or relevance of this model, but merely to indicate the levels of energy and commitment required to break radically with existing forms of development, and the apparently irresistible power with which they sweep over the earth. Mohammed Idris of the Consumers' Association of Penang pointed out that the assumption that Iran would soon collapse after the revolution because of 'economic breakdown' revealed more about the fundamentalism of Western economic ideology than about the condition of Iran: the people there had other things to sustain them than goods and services; among them, shared hopes and hardships, and the life of the spirit. 'These things are a more real social and psychological cement than anything indicated by the "fanaticism" attributed to the people by the West.'

Yet if the Green Myth, the new paradigm, the emerging worldview, whatever we may call it, is also based upon an act of faith, there is nonetheless a radical difference in the way that faith is conceived. It is not a blind, unreflecting belief, subsequently installed in the realm of reason and imposed upon a world already immemorially injured and tormented by a succession of absolute creeds. On the contrary. The new sensibility looks rigorously at the evidence of the damaging irreversibilities of our actions upon the planet that must bear us; and upon that the act of faith is made, faith in the capacity of humanity to change rather than perish. It is a more modest and temperate belief than any traditional faith in salvation. It merely holds out a hope of survival. Therein, perhaps, lies its greatest strength. An informing belief, yes, but one which knows itself, does not harden into dogma or seek to impose its revelations upon others, but remains fluid and flexible, open and welcoming. It does not compel living flesh into its rituals and observances; a humble faith, if such a thing is possible on earth.

19. HUMAN SCALE DEVELOPMENT

MANFRED MAX-NEEF, RIGHT LIVELIHOOD AWARD WINNER 1983. Manfred Max-Neef is a Chilean economist, who taught economics at the University of California (Berkeley) in the early 1960s. He has worked in projects in Latin America, as a specialist in social development with the Pan American Union, as a general economist with FAO and as a Project Manager with ILO. He has written extensively on development alternatives. In 1981, he wrote the book for which he is best known, *From the Outside Looking In: Experiences in Barefoot Economics*, published by the Dag Hammarskjold Foundation the following year. Late in 1981, he set up his organisation CEPAUR (the Center for Development Alternatives) in Chile, where he still works. CEPAUR is largely dedicated to the reorientation of development in terms of stimulating local needs and, more generally, to advocating a return to the human scale. To do this it acts as a clearing-house for information on the revitalisation and development of small and medium-sized urban and rural communities in the region; researches new tools, strategies and evaluative techniques for such development; assists with development efforts aimed at greater local self-reliance; and communicates the results of its researches and experiences. In 1987, the Dag Hammarskjold Foundation published in Spanish *Human Scale Development*, which has had a major impact in Latin America. It is now available in English.

HUMAN SCALE DEVELOPMENT sets forth the outline of a new paradigm of development. Much of the basis of this involves a new understanding of the well-worked theme of human needs. Max-Neef and his colleagues at CEPAUR demystify, clarify and liberate the debate about need.

Human needs are, as they always have been few, finite and classifiable. They remain constant through all human cultures and all historical periods. What changes over time and with societies, are the *satisfiers*, the ways and means whereby those needs are met, and the sometimes complex, and occasionally self-cancelling interplay of those satisfiers themselves. Any fundamental need not satisfied is a human poverty; and this is as true of an unfulfilled need for affection or identity as it is of the need for subsistence. Moreover, each poverty generates pathologies. The economistic proposition that below a certain threshold of disposable income poverty begins, has always been an unsatisfactory indicator, and accounts for the elusive, shifting frontier of the 'poverty line', much sought after but rarely defined by those who would find a remedy for the corrosively intractable poverties of the West.

The taxonomy of Max-Neef is daring and imaginative. Needs, he says, indicate both deprivation and potential: that is, both the absence of certain things, but also the impulse to do, to create, to build and to anticipate. *Human Scale Development* describes needs as existential (having, doing and being), and as axiological (values). These are classified, not definitively or dogmatically, as the need for Subsistence, Affection, Understanding, Participation, Idleness (in the sense of leisure, time to reflect), Creation, Identity and Freedom. The satisfiers of all these are not necessarily dependent upon, or commensurate with the kinds or quantities of economic goods available in any given society. Indeed, it is possible that some means of answering one or more need may impair or destroy the satisfaction of others in the process, and even, in extreme cases, undermine the satisfaction of the very need they are thought to supply. Max-Neef and his colleagues look critically at satisfiers that are destructive of the satisfaction of other needs; at pseudo-satisfiers; inhibiting satisfiers; and single satisfiers. In contrast to these, they offer examples of synergic satisfiers, which promote and extend satisfactions beyond the immediate needs they answer.

Satisfiers that violate other needs occur spectacularly in the need for protection: the arms race, for instance, which, as it protects, actually destroys subsistence, participation, the need for affection and freedom. Censorship, again ostensibly to satisfy a need of protection, also undermines the need for understanding, participation, idleness, creation, freedom and identity. Among *pseudo-satisfiers* are aggregate economic indicators which seemingly answer a need for understanding, but which cloud any true perception of well-being; formal democracy, which is supposed to suffice for the need to participate, but which both alienates and depowers; prostitution, which appears to respond to the need for affection, but is both exploitative and itself a generator of other deep dissatisfactions. *Inhibiting satisfiers* might include unlimited permissiveness, which, while apparently providing freedom, at the same time, inhibits the need for protection, affection, identity and participation. Commercial television, while responding to the need for idleness, also interferes with understanding, creation and identity. *Single satisfiers* are those which offer partial and limited satisfactions — insurance systems provide a form of protection, the ballot-box ensures a kind of participation. But *synergic satisfiers* are those which complement and enhance each other, lead to multi-layered satisfactions that engender others: breast-feeding, while answering the need for subsistence in a child, also stimulates the satisfaction of the need for protection, affection and identity. Popular education answers the need for understanding, but it contributes also to protection, participation, creation, identity and freedom. Barefoot medicine also offers protection, but equally, subsistence, understanding and participation.

This richly suggestive, but non-prescriptive way of looking at need is liberating, and indicates a possible direction for the realisation of self-reliant, human-scale, autonomous initiatives. Max-Neef acknowledges that sympathetic global planning is also required for their enablement: development in the local spaces is inadequate unless complemented by macro-policies that will improve, and not worsen, the precarious living-conditions of the most dispossessed. But the abundance of these local spaces is a source of great hope and opportunity. Many popular initiatives already take place in the interstices of the formal economy — self-build settlements, self-employment, community supports and popular resistance to grandiose development projects, squatter occupations, alternative forms of production. Once again, they allow for the free play of non-conventional 'resources': the intangibles of popular creativity, the ability of people to organise for the satisfaction of their own needs (itself also a basic need!). Needs, says Max-Neef, should be seen as a system, the dynamics of which do not obey hierarchical linearities: they are a complex web of simultaneities, complementarities and constant trade-offs.

In the rich countries, 'development' means, at the level of popular experience at least, a rising income. This sets up an increasing dependency upon money, so that people are able to *buy-in* satisfactions which they no longer provide directly or freely for themselves and each other. This loss of control deeply undermines a basic need, a human freedom; and the cure for it is seen to lie in an exacerbation of the social and psychological cause — more money. This is how the *need* of the economy to grow and to expand constantly is internalised by human beings, so that they come to experience this as their own need. This makes it more and more difficult for human beings to define the frontiers of identity. As market-penetration becomes more intensive, human resources fall into decay, in the sense that the ability to improvise, to make and to create, is put to sleep by the very marketed proliferations that are taken to be the ultimate indicators of economic progress. We thus find ourselves in the West living through a double profligacy — not merely the obvious material wastage of natural resources, but the discarding and rejection of human resources. Human-scale development suggests a movement towards a more balanced relationship between the two — a husbanding of natural material resources, and a re-awakening of the human powers.

By countering the logic of economics with the ethics of well-being, as Max-Neef puts it, it is important to win over the present practitioners of economics, for most of them are by no means adamantly opposed to the changes that have to be made. Indeed, many regard these as a liberation, an extension of their sphere of competence. Max-Neef discovered at CEPAUR that the principal contributors of funds to alternative initiatives were private individuals, many of them in business. Institutions and aid agencies have been far slower to respond.

People who are in business take decisions quickly. They have an intuition for survival, and as such, are swift to respond to changes that are in train, far swifter than most other social groups. The hostility towards business of the Left and of some Greens is an error. Of course, in the past, business was concerned only with growth and profits. But profit that no longer yields happiness is not good business.

While the many deficiencies and limitations of the theory that supports the old paradigm must be overcome (mechanistic interpretations and inadequate indicators of well-being, among others), a theoretical body for the new paradigm must still be constructed. But let me make it very clear — and I cannot stress this point enough — I am not advocating theorising for the sake of theorising. Of that we have had enough! What I am proposing instead, is the coherent systematisation of the experience acquired by all those of us who have been working for years on the alternative solutions to the real problems affecting the world today, especially those that weigh upon the poorest and most vulnerable sections of humanity.

Like many others, Max-Neef raises the question of *language* in the formulation of alternatives.

There are two separate languages now — the language of economics and the language of ecology, and they do not converge. The language of Keynesian economics emerged at the time of crisis in the late 1920s and 1930s. The language of Development Economics came as a consequence of the optimism and the spectacular reconstruction of Europe and the affluence of the 1950s. The idea that poverty could be overcome by growth gave rise to a vigorous language- expressions like 'take-off', 'the big push', 'dash for growth'. The 1970s and 1980s have been characterised by disappointment after earlier enthusiasm, but our age has not generated a language to deal with it. The language of growth and expansion is disarticulated from that of social and ecological collapse.

The language of economics is attractive, and remains so, because it is politically appealing. It offers promises. It is precise, authoritative, 'scientific', coherent, seductive. Economic models are beautiful, aesthetically pleasing. Policy-makers apply the models, and if they don't work, there is a tendency to conclude that it is reality that is playing tricks. The assumption is not that the models are wrong but that they must be applied with greater rigour. It is clear that we are in the presence of economics as faith. Indeed, many economists are now undergoing a crisis of faith.

André Gorz has described it thus:

Economic rationality functioned as a substitute for religious morality: through it, man attempted to apply the eternal laws which governed the universe to the predictive organisation of his own affairs. The aim, beyond the material ends it gave itself, was to render the laws of human activity as rigorously calculable and predictable as those of the workings of the cosmic clock.

'This is not to say', Max-Neef continues, 'that economics must be jettisoned; simply that it has to become sufficiently elastic to accommodate all the costs that have hitherto been elided.' It may be that economics proves flexible enough to contain and reflect what Amory Lovins called 'prices that tell the truth'; or it may be that the system must undergo such severe modification that it will no longer be recognisable as itself.

This is why Max-Neef has set up, in co-operation with the University of Concepcion in Chile, the Department of Human Ecology in Edinburgh, and the University of Linkoping in Sweden, a post-graduate degree of a trans-disciplinary nature in Ecological Economics.

Just as it is important to create a congruence with business, so a breakthrough in conventional economics is also essential in the academic world. To acquire legitimacy in the existing structures is necessary, because that is the only way it will be accepted by governments. There is no point in defenestrating the whole paradigm that went before, because, after all, it is rare that everything is wrong with one particular worldview. Serious faults have emerged with time, but when that system was evolving, 100 years ago, such flaws as are now obvious were scarcely visible.

Recognition that crude economic indicators such as GNP are no longer adequate criteria for judging human well-being has gained ground in recent years. Alternative indicators have been sought which will begin to incorporate some of the hidden costs of wealth creation. In 1990, the United Nations Development Programme (UNDP) published, for the first time, a Human Development Index. This at least accepts that economic growth and development are not necessarily synonymous, and as such, is a move in a positive direction. However, even this modest shift is open to a number of questionable interpretations.

The new UNDP Index acknowledges not only purchasing power, but also life expectancy and levels of literacy in its survey of the countries of the world. By this standard, some interesting reversals occur. Rich Middle Eastern countries such as Oman, Saudi Arabia and the United Arab Emirates find themselves demoted from 26th, 23rd and 4th place in the GNP/per capita scale, to 82nd, 65th and 53rd out of the total of 130. This is principally because of their low literacy rates, especially among women. There are some other interesting results: India, which in GNP divided by population is 105th, rises to 93rd, while Costa Rica and North Korea both overtake Brazil.

However, these modified measures of well-being also contain assumptions that cast doubt on the meaning attributed to them. For one thing, countries like the United Kingdom and USA show up with 99 per cent and 96 per cent literacy respectively. These figures bear little relationship to functional literacy in those countries: unofficial estimates in the USA range from 15 per cent functional illiteracy to much higher levels. There is a further problem here: this measure does not take account of the power of oral tradition, indigenous people's knowledge, and the capacity of non-literate peoples to store and transmit enormous amounts of valuable information and knowledge. It ignores the rich familiarity with the natural world, the storehouse of precious understanding they hold in their heads. It may well be that the level of literacy required to read, for instance, the *Sun* newspaper in Britain cannot really be compared with the efficiency of the forest-dwellers of India or the indigenous people of the Amazon, in their understanding of their environment. Such people know the use of thousands of plants and herbs, they know where to gather food, where to find medicines, fibres for building, fuel, and all the resources necessary for the fulfilment of satisfactory ways of living that have endured for millennia. Such an index cannot reach the power of transmission in stories, people's science, law and culture by word of mouth. It capitulates to the Western-dominated paradigm which it purports to be transcending.

Some qualification is also required when it comes to life expectancy. Of course it is true that avoidable sickness and treatable disease is an absolute inhibition on human development in Ethiopia, Afghanistan and many West African countries, for it denies life itself. But to conclude that longevity is, of itself, an absolute measure of well-being may be a false assumption. (The analogy with poverty is telling: while an absolute absence of resources is certainly destructive of life, it does not follow that life is enhanced in direct proportion to an increase of wealth measured by money.) No one who has observed the fate of those in the West who have been the beneficiaries of the vaunted longevity, those whose wisdom has been devalued, whose function undermined, yet whose lives have been prolonged through medical technology through the indignities of Alzheimer's disease, incontinence and social isolation, can say with certainty that longevity is a guarantor of well-being.

As for purchasing power itself, it ignores the capacity of many people in the world to provide for themselves, to make and create outside of the monetised economy. It is interesting to observe that the word 'resources' in the West is more often than not used as a synonym for money. The resource base of the earth must be turned into commodities and priced, and monetary power over these then becomes a universal yardstick to measure the wealth of individuals and nations. Nowhere do the values of sufficiency, stability and conservation enter into these calculations of well-being.

The step taken by the UNDP is both reasonable and well-intentioned. But if it is elaborated in the same direction as it evolves, its purpose will be radically falsified. What began as a departure from superficial and discredited aggregated measures of development can lead only to a reaffirmation of monocultural values which it claims to call into question.

Should people in Britain be pleased that, although in terms of GNP, their country is now 17th from the top, behind Austria, Hong Kong and Singapore, it nevertheless occupies 10th place in the Human Development Index? And can we believe that although Japan is actually 5th in per capita income, on this index it rates as the most desirable place on earth to live?

20. LIMITING CONSUMERISM

Healing destructive divisions has been one of the aims of all those seeking alternatives; divisions between North and South, black and white, women and men, workers of hand and brain, country and city, Muslim and Hindu. What permits so much injustice and cruelty in the world to go unchallenged is the licence it gains from people's *unknowing*, the inability to connect what we do, the way we live, with the consequences for distant, unseen others. The information-rich privileged societies of the West also create enormous ignorance at the same time, a kind of licensed *avidya*, a disregard of our connectedness.

Few more damaging separations occur than that between producers and consumers. This division has become a source of great waste and exploitation; particularly since the new international division of labour has removed many people in the West from any significant contact with production. This makes it easier for them to remain oblivious of the human and environmental costs incurred in the manufacture of what they regard as daily necessities. Goods, once made locally, within sight and touch of communities that used them, are now regularly transported across continents. During that journey, they become divested of the pain, sweat and blood that attended their production. Indeed, the business of *cleansing* them has become the work of armies of promoters, publicists and advertisers, whose function is to render desirable, even irresistible, everything that jostles for attention in the gaudy crowded markets of the West. Indeed, the advertisers, the creative marketers, the copywriters, constitute an elevated caste, whose role in the division of labour is the performance of purification rituals. This is scarcely surprising, when so many of the products and services which they cleanse are profoundly polluting. (By contrast, in India, the traditionally 'polluting' castes are, in effect, those whose function has been to guard and preserve the resource base — agricultural labourers, fishing communities, forest people, leather-workers, recyclers, those dealing with waste and death. The real polluters are those whose zealous imitation of the West weighs so heavily upon the eroded resources of their country; but they are mostly from the higher castes. Such inversions do not make the formulation of alternatives any easier.)

SEIKATSU CLUB CONSUMERS' CO-OPERATIVE, RIGHT LIVELIHOOD AWARD WINNER 1989. The Seikatsu Club Consumers' Co-operative (SCCC) is a unique consumers' co-op in Japan, which combines formidable business and professional skills with strict social and ecological principles and a vision of a community- and people-centred economy, which provides a radical alternative to industrialism. SCCC traces its foundation to 1965, when a single Tokyo housewife organised 200 women to buy milk collectively in order to reduce the price. Its growth has been exponential. It now has 170,000 family members, comprising half a million people. It is also a significant business enterprise In 1987 its turnover was 41 billion yen (approximately $300 million). It employed 700 people and had a member investment of seven and a half billion yen. The business centres on the distribution of 500 different products, carried out through a unique computer-operated advance ordering system to enable producers to plan in advance and guarantee product freshness. When the club cannot find products of adequate quality or which meet its ecological or social standards, it will consider producing them itself. SCCC places great emphasis on direct producer/consumer links to moderate and humanise the market, especially in the area of food production, where consumers regularly visit farmers, to inform themselves about or help them in their work. With the pressure on more women to get jobs, SCCC set up women workers' collectives, to undertake both distribution and other service enterprises, including recycling, health, education, food preparation, child care. About 60 such collectives now employ over 1,550 SCCC members.

THE PURPOSE OF THE SEIKATSU CLUB is to offer a living alternative example of consumption to the rich. It evolved in part as a response to the process of the redundant adding of value to and complicating the consumption of basic necessities. Some Japanese women discovered in the 1960s that it was virtually impossible to buy fresh, pure milk that had not been vitaminised, flavoured, enriched or altered in some way. Indeed, as a visit to any supermarket in Japan immediately reveals, the pathways whereby the food of the people is procured have become increasingly opaque and invisible. Fish and meat come packed with artificial leaves and real flowers inside the plastic wrappers; soy sauce in ornamental bottles resembling cosmetics rather than condiments; the fruit and vegetable departments are like hanging gardens, decked out with the plundered riches of the tropics. School children are reported no longer to believe that apples grow on trees.

One of the more startling developments in the rich world in recent years has been the revelation that even the most envied and wealthy societies on earth are finding difficulty in supplying their peoples with simple nourishment and fresh water. In 1989, for instance, Perrier water had to be removed from the shelves of shops in Europe, because the bottling machines had been contaminated. The product which people had sought as a substitute for unsafe drinking water was itself a health hazard. Similarly, outbreaks of food poisoning in Britain have been rising throughout the past decade. It was revealed in 1989 that bovine spongiform encephalitis had been spread by the practice of feeding the carcasses of sheep that had died of scrapie to cows — herbivores. Industrialised food production it seems, has been turned against nourishment.

A basic premise of Seikatsu is that there are too many important decisions to be made in life for people to waste their time pondering the merits of products which are, to all intents and purposes, indistinguishable.

Seikatsu has given a new impulse to the co-operative movement in Japan. The co-op producer movement had become simply another competitor in the conventional marketing and retailing business. Shuei Hiratsuka of Seikatsu says that the rapid urbanisation of Japan in the post-war period removed more and more people from the production of food. During the 1960s, people were leaving the land at the rate of almost a million a year, in order to provide labour for industry. A generation of what Huratsuka calls 'urban peasants' filled the factories of the big companies. People dominated by a work ethic were transplanted from the traditional arduous labour of farm and field. There was a brusque transition from biosphere to industrial technosphere, in which work habits were one of the few sources of a sense of continuity.

The spectacular economic growth of Japan had other social and environmental consequences, notably the rise of the nuclear family, and an even more extreme separation of male-female roles, in the life of corporation and family respectively. It is no accident that the impulse of Seikatsu came from women, particularly wives of corporation men, women who found their reduced function as shoppers in supermarkets, as well as the indirect servicers of their husbands' employers, both inadequate and diminishing.

What began as a way of buying simple, unadulterated products turned into a network of distribution, and later, a demand for goods to be available in the form women wanted. 'It is important to remember that we are not selling anything; we are *providers*.' Seikatsu has nothing to do with utopia: it is both a practical way of answering need, and, as one woman said, 'a school where you can think, make connections, and see how you can set about the wider work of social transformation'.

The role of consumer has always been thought of as passive. Now the consumer has become proactive. There are two ways of bringing about the change — to buy in such a way as to change the production process, or simply not to buy. Seikatsu uses both. Consumer choice was in danger of becoming a substitute for more basic liberties, as big companies swallowed up their smaller competitors.

The effectiveness of Seikatsu's development can be seen by the early example of milk provision. By collective purchase of fresh milk, it became cheaper. The next step was to set up a milk-processing plant, so that purity could be guaranteed. The next was to discover what the cattle were eating and in what conditions they were being raised. Each move is a logical one, and it breaks the growing monopoly of big corporations over the whole food chain. There are, of course, many things that Seikatsu does not provide. The point is, not to make everything available, but to help people think about and understand the system whereby basic goods are brought to them. A human being should know precisely how her needs are met. Not to know is to be not free. The ideal is a liberation process. In this way, the 'down-stream', represented above all by women, as buyers and consumers, is empowered to regulate the 'up-stream', and its established role in commodity production.

The simplicity of the goods and products in the stores and depots of Seikatsu is refreshing. There are fewer than 500 items, but since so much of supermarket choice is a variant of the same thing, this is actually quite an extensive range. Everything is plainly wrapped, from chick peas, macaroni, eggs, seaweed, soy sauce, dried and fresh fish, tofu, pork, vegetables and fruit (organically grown), to honey, biscuits, chocolate, rice, green tea, conserves. 'When we need products from poor countries,' says Katsumi Yakota, 'we plan a direct transaction with the local producers. We object to the methods and prices of big commercial agents. We created a trade organisation for this purpose.' There is an agreement with a banana-growing collective on Negros in the Philippines, whereby the collective receives three or four times the amount paid by the commercial agents for each kilo of bananas. Coffee comes from a collective in Feripe in Peru. In an attempt to expand direct trade with the South, Seikatsu has created an International People's Exchange Shop, run by a workers' collective, to distribute and sell products and to facilitate an exchange of information and awareness.

The local groups of Seikatsu members consist of *hans*, seven to ten people in each. These come together in branches of 100 or so, which are then organised at the level of the prefecture (the local authority administration). The hans place their orders once a month, a week before the actual purchase. Members themselves deliver and distribute the goods. Monthly contributions of 1,000 yen per person ($6) mean that Seikatsu is now the fourth largest co-op in Japan in terms of investment capital. But because the purpose of investment is not profit, there are no dividends. Everything goes back to the provision of organically produced, sound and socially useful materials at reasonable prices. 'The movement has progressed from being a functional necessity into a philosophy that encompasses the whole of life . . . ' The aim is the creation of a new culture, which depends upon minimal consumption and a rich life. The search for alternative ways of working has led to the setting up of a restaurant, a home catering service, confectionery, care for aged people, a bakery, a translation service, market management, food processing, a transport and delivery service, a building maintenance operation, a domestic cleaning enterprise, a recycling shop, a day nursery, a wedding arrangements business, a cooking school, a community college, video production, a publication and printing centre, an acupuncture service, a fish shop, a nursery school, and the provision of *bento* — traditional boxed lunches — for workers. In recent years, Seikatsu members have entered local politics, and there are now 19 representatives on Tokyo City Council, most of them women. There are others in Yokohama and Chiba.

Seikatsu is not an easy option. Membership requires commitment and effort. It is not always convenient to plan purchases in advance, particularly when you can buy anything you want in Tokyo 24 hours a day. Katsumi Yokota says that the great virtue of Seikatsu is that it preserves and encourages living skills within the local community, and brings a mechanism of direct exchange into daily life.

> This helps to limit the growth of commodities and services provided by the big corporations, which only disable the homely, the local and the familiar. The boycott of various commodities was made possible by collective purchase. This, together with the development of workers' co-operatives, can change the character of the local community and its productive power. It provides for another economic power, represented by citizens' capital and their businesses; although small, if it grows, it can expand and counter the great concentrations of corporate wealth.

The biggest threat to Seikatsu is the danger that comes from success: the risk of becoming too unwieldy, of succumbing to commercial pressures, and of the growth of bureaucracy.

A recent initiative has been a soap-making collective in Kawasaki. One of the early struggles of Seikatsu was against synthetic detergents. Now they have set up a plant for making soap-powder from used cooking oil which was previously thrown away, and which polluted the local water supply. The small factory unit employs about a dozen people. It is barely profitable as yet, but publicity spreads by word of mouth at neighbourhood level, and orders for the product are increasing. The plant uses second-hand machinery which is effective for its purpose. The used oil is collected by members, from restaurants, institutions and private homes. It has to be deodorised, steamed and filtered. The clear oil is then churned to a paste, steam-heated and dried to a solid state.

At Kumagaya, about 70 kilometres from Tokyo, is the factory which produces vegetable oil for Seikatsu. There, they have revived the traditional method of making oil from rapeseed. The more widely used vegetable now is soya, but rapeseed has a 40 per cent oil content, whereas soya has only 16-17 per cent — another example of value-added inefficiency in the modern sector. The extraction at Kumagaya is carried out without chemicals, purely by pressure, and once again, the machinery is archaic but effective. Some 20 years ago there was a scandal when, during the deodorising process in a big Japanese oil-producing company, PCV contaminated the oil, which killed or damaged the health of 10,000 people. The traditional rapeseed is pure, more tasty than its mass-produced counterpart. It has a slightly greenish colour, whereas most cooking oil is bright yellow, and this is said to tell against rapeseed oil in the market place. The owner of the company says, 'Without knowing how products are made, and how they reach them, people have no power over their lives. Big companies are abusing "green", "natural" or "pure" labels. But unless you know whether they are telling the truth, "consumer power" is a meaningless phrase.'

Many members of Seikatsu would have been (and often were) previously in the labour movement. Among them is Katsumi Yokota, President of Tokyo Seikatsu, who says

> The character of the labour movement changed in the 1960s. The unions lost their ideals, began to seek only more money from the system. They gave up their desire to transform it. The sensibility of the workers changed too; the principle of industry began to overwhelm the principle of life.

He speaks of an 'alternative market', where it is not capital that controls things, but consumers. He likens the relationship of Seikatsu to the mainstream to that of the *kobanzame*, a fish that sticks to the underbelly of the whale: far from innocent, it takes its nourishment from the larger creature, draining it of strength. Seikatsu is building 'another economy' in practice, within the heart of the most powerful economy in the world. As such, Seikatsu is of a piece with many attempts, worldwide, to resist the excesses of capital-promoted consumerism, and is probably the most successful.

When I left Seikatsu, I went from Tokyo to the Philippines. The flight provided an insight into an area of consumption that marks a logical extension of its accepted definition. Human beings, it seems, have become the most lucrative cash crop of all. The aircraft is full of young women, going home after a six months' contract in the hotels and clubs of Tokyo and Hokkaido, working as 'entertainers'. The Philippines is now the world's largest exporter of women to the sex industry. Many of them are only 17 or 18 years old. On the night before the flight, they were working until three in the morning. After the show, they just had time to go back to their lodgings, pack a case ready for the flight at 10 a.m. They are wearing hotpants, short skirts, coloured tights, denim blouses, and they carry electric-blue soft toys and pink vanity cases. Throughout the journey, plastic combs work away at their long dark hair, burgundy lipstick is reapplied, fingernails examined for flaws. They are laden with gifts: cassette recorders, Yamaha keyboards, perfume, whisky, cigarettes. There are an estimated 100,000 Filipinas working in Japan, only 25,000 of them legally. Some of the young women have been sending money home, but others found that even $1,000 a month was not enough. Letizia, aged 19, from Bicol, says she had to turn to prostitution for extra income. She says that the working life of many women is finished at 25. Some of her friends have married Japanese men, even though they may have husbands in the Philippines. The girls sleep on the flight, exhausted, sprawled in the seats, or with heads on the table in front of them. The flight is a shipment of sexuality, a cargo of exports, bought in to amplify the already substantial wages of Japanese businessmen, those dedicated servicers of economic miracles. In spite of the freight of possessions which they are taking home — most of it junk — it was impossible to avoid the feeling that these drained and drowsy young women were returned empties.

Because the word 'consumerism' has become a jargon word, it is perhaps time to redefine it. Consumerism is the systematic intensification of dependency on marketed commodities, artefacts, services, experiences, sensations, fantasies, consolations, many of which can well, indeed often better, be provided for ourselves and for each other from freely available resources, both human and material. It is accompanied by a progressive surrender of autonomy. It generates both impotence and a growing fear of loss or change. That the possession of more and more money should pass for 'independence' or 'freedom' is a measure of the inversion of values in Western industrial society. The richer we become, the more deeply are we in thrall to the addiction to money and what it will buy. For the poor, consumerism involves the deepening of a process described by Hassan Fathy as 'the imposition on the poor of the cash-economy without the cash'.

Many of those defining a new worldview have addressed the issue of decreased consumption with insight and imagination. Both Manfred Max-Neef and Amory Lovins speak of a decrease in consumption of *energy*, rather than a decrease of consumption in monetary terms, as the best means to lower the pressure of consumerism. As Max-Neef puts it:

> If the USA, with six per cent of the world's people, can consume almost half its energy, without, for all that, achieving conspicuous levels of social peace, contentment and harmony, then the scope for reduction must be ample.

Others have gone further.

ERIK DAMMANN, RIGHT LIVELIHOOD AWARD WINNER 1982. Erik Dammann began his professional life in design and advertising. Disillusioned with the consumerism his work required him to promote, he went with his family to live for a year in Polynesia, where they shared the life of the villagers in a culture founded on co-operation and sharing. He returned to Norway with the realisation that the West's focus on competition for personal gain had more to do with social structure than with human nature, and with a deep respect for other cultures, which were being destabilised or destroyed by the Western life-style or world-view. In 1972, he published *The Future in Our Hands* (English edition, Pergamon Press), a book which touched a responsive chord in people in Norway and elsewhere. In 1974, Dammann devoted himself full-time to establishing a Future in Our Hands (FIOH) movement, which grew during the 1970s to over 20,000 members. The movement has individual groups, a Development Fund that has funded support for projects in 20 poor countries, an Alternative Bank which gives loans for alternative development projects in Norway, and an Information Centre to promote political, personal and social change towards a more just and conserving society, as described in his later book, *Revolution in the Affluent Society*. (Heretic Books.) In 1987, he published *Beyond Time and Space*, about a more holistic view on Man and Nature, freewill and responsibility.

THE ACHIEVEMENTS OF THE FUTURE IN OUR HANDS movement have been considerable. The Development Fund works by members using part of their income for purposes of international solidarity, rather than for increased personal expenditure. Friendship groups between Norway and countries of the South have been established, and goods are produced by co-operation with local groups in the Third World.

Since FIOH was established, Erik Dammann has continued to monitor the movement and its evolution. It reached a plateau beyond which it could not go; a pattern recorded by many other innovating groups. Initial success reaches a peak, and then the movement appears to stagnate. It is not that the diagnosis is faulty. Quite the reverse: everything Dammann said in 1972, and has reiterated with great force and clarity in his new book, *Your Money or Your Life*, still stands. There is one fundamental problem, that of maldevelopment, which the English socialist, William Morris had already identified in the 1890s, when he wrote of 'a humanity wrecked and wasted, in one way or another, by luxury or poverty'.

The connections Dammann made have been vindicated by, among others, the UN World Commission on Environment and Development, which states that world poverty and unjust distribution of wealth is also the most serious environmental problem of our time. Dammann also saw that the struggle of the global alliance for change was one which, for the first time in history, was not based on economic self-interest, but, on the contrary, has grown in opposition to movements built precisely on those foundations. He suggested that the sicknesses of the rich have grown beyond their welfare systems to deal with them. Welfare, designed to cushion people against the worst existential and social sufferings, has been overwhelmed by the latter, as it tries to cope with unprecedented levels of sociogenic disease — violence, cancers, stresses, addictions, breakdown of relationships and associations, loneliness, the sicknesses of an excess beyond satiety.

Beyond a certain stage, the social forces opposed to change mobilise to block it and those who promote it. Pressure from the mainstream becomes too strong for many of those who would like to practise a more modest lifestyle. Dammann saw that the old politics continued, and the optimism of people in the FIOH movement turned to impotence. The project seemed destined to turn into a tepid reformism, rather than the radical shift he had originally envisaged. It was dismissed by the supporters of the existing order as 'amateurish', 'muddled', 'incoherent'.

Dammann later wrote a proposal for a research group, and a manifesto calling for government funding for a project called 'Alternative Future', where social aims and environmental responsibility would have priority over economic considerations. It was intended to review conditions for *national liberation* from an economic system which forces the industrialised states to compete for increased wealth and further industrial growth, regardless of the ecological consequences. The alternative economy and social structure should make it possible to see the economy, not as an end in itself, but as a means to a future of global social justice and survival. After meetings with people in the alternative movements in Norway, Sweden, Denmark and Finland, NGOs, church, political, scientific and cultural institutions, an application for funding was made to the government of Norway. A sum of $350,000 was granted.

During the 1980s, Dammann became more sceptical about the 'lifestyle' approach to social change.

> The impact of free trade competition has become so strong that the direction of development is no longer a question of opinion or good/bad will: participation in the life-threatening competition for growth has become a question of necessity for nations, companies, labour organisations and individuals in the rich parts of the world. They all *have to* compete for narrow economic self-interest to avoid being excluded as losers. How are the values and ideas we share to be formulated as a political macro-strategy for change? I do not think of a new, complete political ideology. To develop a common political pressure for alternatives to destructive trade competition that dominates the world is

more important now than ever, particularly where the obvious failure of Communism has made the world's leaders talk in terms of 'the final victory' of capitalistic free competition.

Dammann identifies the block to change as the consciousness of 'the common man and woman' beyond the elites. He warns against a phenomenon that others have also foreseen, the emergence of Green activists as another incarnation of 'the vanguard party', those who, claiming a higher consciousness (not, of course, this time, of the destiny of the proletariat, but of the wounded earth), might be tempted to take leadership upon themselves in the name of absent or silent others.

Belief in the deeper values of the common people is our only hope. We cannot judge from how people behave under pressure of a society that forces them to compete for self-interest or to be excluded. We must step out of our narrow social environment, and learn to know the underprivileged who have never participated in our activities. When we have them with us, that will be real change from below.

21. PEACE AFTER THE COLD WAR

HANS-PETER DURR, RIGHT LIVELIHOOD AWARD WINNER 1987. Hans-Peter Durr is Director of the Heisenberg Institute of Physics at the Max Planck Institute of Physics and Astrophysics and Professor of Physics at Ludwig Maximilian University, in Munich. Durr is a committed interdisciplinarian. He has been professionally active in the fields of energy policy (expressing his opposition to nuclear energy), science and responsibility and epistemology and philosophy, as well as in his specialisms of elementary particle and nuclear physics. In the 1980s, he became concerned about Third World, ecological and economic matters, and since 1985 has been a member of the Board of Greenpeace Germany. But his main campaigning has been on the theme of peace. In 1983, he became a member of the Pugwash Conference and was co-founder of the Scientists' Initiative 'Responsibility for Peace', leading to the Scientists' Peace Congress in Mainz, attended by 3,300 scientists, and the Mainzer Appell, a declaration against further nuclear armament. The following year, another scientists' convention in Gottingen warned against the militarisation of space. Out of these conventions came interdisciplinary lecture series in 40 per cent of German universities. Durr has been especially active on the issue of non-offensive defence and, his main preoccupation, SDI (Strategic Defense Initiative). A long article in *Der Spiegel* in 1985 argued overwhelmingly against the feasibility of the SDI concept. In 1986 he proposed a World Peace Initiative, of a similar scale to SDI, to solve the problems of pollution, depletion, Third World poverty and economic injustice. This idea was reborn as the Global Challenges Network in 1987.

HANS-PETER DURR INSISTS that it is no longer enough simply to hinder malign processes, but is necessary also to promote positive practice. This is the impulse behind both the Global Challenges Network, and the more recent International Foundation for the Survival and Development of Humanity.

> There is so much wisdom and intelligence accumulated that does not find its way into public life, because the actors are foreign to each other. Society does not have the appropriate platforms and institutions. The exchange of papers cannot do this work — only contact between individuals can. This is why I am concentrating now on a high-level approach to certain basic issues. My position gives me access to people from industry, ecology, science, insurance, education, politics. I can bring about a dialogue between these groups, be a catalyst, a transmission belt for those at the apex of society. I am able to facilitate their communication with each other. People can be sensitised in a quiet way.

My experience with the arms industry is a good precedent. I went into arms factories, spoke with scientists, engineers, planners. They are not terrible people, they are open to discussion. It is no good adopting the 'You're all bastards' approach. You try to think of the *path* towards *convergence*. You have to acknowledge that you are familiar with their problems. All the big armaments companies are under pressure from below now that the Cold War is over. The conversion aspect is dominant in their minds. We have to reach out to help them, not place them in fear of losing their jobs or losing face. All the debate on the technical feasibility of Star Wars did little to stop the process. Such argument deployed against it merely stimulated its advocates to have their experts devise new and improvised proposals.

The most likely cause of war remains not a breakdown of deterrence but the inability of the military-technical structures to handle a political crisis. The arms race was caused not by vicious people but by an *Eigendynamik*, which strongly constrained the system of armaments on the pernicious trajectory it was already following. We tend to look at phenomena as static. Not enough attention is given to their development in time, as it results from their integration into a more general causal structure. Strong feedback mechanisms cause the system to run out of control, and proceed on its own destructive path. Military *equilibrium* is a nonsense, because of the asymmetries in one's opponent's situation, and the continuous development of technology. Add to that the changing and deficient perceptions of the opponent's strength and intentions, and the ambivalence over offensive/defensive use of weapons, and it is clear that each side will feel safe only if it is certain of being stronger. The data may be complex and secret in such discussions, but you don't need details to make a broad evaluation of the situation.

Similarly, the end of the Cold War has led to a decay of the immoveably belligerent attitudes that formerly froze East and West, but at the same time, it has given rise to fears about new insecurities and unpredictabilities in the former Russian Empire. The argument that the 'firmness' of the West resulted in the dissolution of Communism can easily be used as a reason for confronting new 'threats' to the West in the same way, whether from its perceptions of the assertiveness of Islam or the 'danger' from a Third World pushed to the edge of despair by poverty and social and ecological breakdown.

The only effective answer is *sufficient defence*, with a structural inability to attack. Military-technical measures can only lengthen the fuse. And that helps only if the time gained is used to effect change in the underlying causes of insecurity.

The real problems facing us are in four main areas: 1) economy and economic development; 2) ecology and the sustainability of the ecosphere; 3) peace and international co-operation; 4) in social structure and human rights.

All attempts to solve any of the global problems without a basic revision of the presently accepted economic principles and practised economic rules are futile. Economic theories today perceive the environment as an infinite reservoir which serves, on the one hand, as an infinite source of material and energy resources for all human activities, and, on the other, as an infinite sink for all their end products.

Essentially, all real productive power derives directly or indirectly from nature. 'Capital' and 'plan' in particular are not production factors, but rather organisation factors, which allow the transformation of intrinsic natural values into bargaining or utility values respectively.

1) ECONOMY AND ECONOMIC DEVELOPMENT

Because the value structure of nature is so much richer than the value structure of economy based on money, we actually have to seek ways to include the economy within nature. This is likely to require a long time. Hence it may be more efficient, as a first step, to attempt the opposite, partially to include nature into the price system of the economy.

Policies

Triple or quadruple prices of non-renewable energy resources by additional taxes during the next decade.

Change of production to minimise damage. All-out attempts to close production cycles in order to avoid hazardous end products. Environmental conservation through an extensive repair operation, although necessary in the short term, will aggravate the problem in the long run. The GNP should be augmented by an eco-balance-number to demonstrate this fact.

The interest rate of capital should be related to the actual natural value creation, related directly or indirectly to the creative power of the sun, rather than to the increasing exploitation of the earth or the people of the so-called 'Third' World.

Obstacles

Any change of economic rules leading to a lesser exploitation of nature will in toto diminish the profits, and therefore the power of the people dominating de facto our societies. In general, these powers will never voluntarily yield.

The people will also resist such change because everybody indirectly gains from exploitation of the planet. Only future generations will suffer, but they have no voice at present.

Resolution

Decentralise and empower the people. Democracy should consist in continuous participation and not only going to the polls once in a while.

Strengthen the influence of women in our societies, who overall are less narrow-minded and more strongly devoted to the interests of future generations.

2) ECOLOGY AND SUSTAINABILITY OF THE ECOSPHERE

Our actions should not be primarily aimed at meeting our so-called 'needs', but rather to establish a lifestyle which is compatible with the sustainability of the ecosphere. This effort should include providing for the *basic* needs of *all* people, and not only a privileged group. Since the ecosystem is too complex to allow reliable forecasts, we should employ a 'defensive' strategy in all our actions.

Policies

Exercise moderation, and slow pace in our activities, in order to give nature an optimal chance to correct our possible errors.

Attempt to close production cycles to avoid waste hazards.

Improve energy efficiency and try to return as far as possible to sun-energy as a primary source, and this predominantly in a decentralised form. In the long run, to provide in addition for high density energy, also in the decentralised form of sun-power stations, perhaps with hydrogen storage.

Introduce new energy-efficient integrated transportation techniques in Central and Eastern Europe, rather than the outdated unsustainable one we use at present in the West.

Obstacles

Strong vested interests prevent genuine protection of nature, but prefer the expensive and unsustainable repair approach, which allows additional industrial activities in a saturated market.

The car industry is one of the strongest lobbies, and will do everything to prevent any move away from road transportation.

Resolution

Try to get people, especially children, in direct contact with the natural environment, in order that they can experience personally the degradation. This will create a strong incentive to prevent it in future.

Networking people to enhance this experience and to strengthen mutual assistance and solidarity.

3) PEACE AND INTERNATIONAL CO-OPERATION

Emphasis on economic and ecological issues will automatically strengthen the peace issue and international co-operation. In addition, strenuous efforts must be made to reduce armaments and prohibit the export of arms.

Policies

A comprehensive test ban of nuclear weapons should be observed by all nuclear power states. This will have an important effect on decreasing the relevance of nuclear weapons.

Non-provocative defence posture for all conventional armaments.

International exchange of experience on conversion of arms industry to civilian production.

Obstacles

High profit rate in arms production.

Power play still of major importance.

Growing insecurity because of unresolved 'Third World' problems, including economic disparities and a decreasing resource-base.

Resolution

Public pressure to reduce arms expenditures, and to transfer these to ecological issues.

Fostering worldwide solidarity by direct contacts with individuals or groups at the community level.

4) SOCIAL STRUCTURES AND HUMAN RIGHTS

The unequal economic status of people within countries and between countries, in particular of North and South, but also of East and West (especially since the brutal change-over to the free market system), represents a serious instability which, in the long run, will lead to disaster. The steadily increasing number of economic refugees to Western countries is an index of this dangerous development. It can be curbed only by dramatically improving the life conditions in the poor countries by a transfer of resources on a far greater scale than anything we have seen.

Policies

Cancelling all foreign debts of the poor countries.

Giving financial help, mainly via the women in these countries.

Offering advice in solving problems, as comprehended and stated by the people in those countries, rather than by trying to solve the problems for them.

Obstacles

The industrialised countries are not genuinely interested in offering help to the poor countries, but are more concerned to open up new markets for their products.

The rich countries are interested in keeping a low-wage labour force for cheaper production.

They consider the people of these countries and their cultures as inferior.

Resolution

It has become obvious to everybody in the rich countries that this imbalance cannot be kept up indefinitely, and will become more explosive the longer it remains unresolved.

The cultures of the so-called undeveloped countries may give us in the North decisive hints for sustainable lifestyles, since ours are most certainly not.

Durr advocates the use of investment money for social innovation. He says that finance has never been a constraint on his research on Elementary Particle Physics at the Max Planck Institute.

There is always money available for what is seen as an important investment for the nation and the world. In science, technology and economics, they realise that they must invest, to reap later benefit. If only they would think of social research in the same way.

I had the idea of starting an Environmental Academy with the help of *industry*. It could start on things we can all agree on — Energy and Transport. In the former DDR, in Poland, in what was USSR, they need an integrated transport system. We had a discussion with the Bundesbahn, Lufthansa and the car manufacturers. Couldn't we get together at the top level and *imagine* a new traffic system? Systems are already planned in the West, on shelves and in safes, because it is known that existing ones are untenable in the long run. Couldn't we pull those plans out now in the East? Rather than begin a construction programme of roads that will litter the countryside, ruin the landscape and lead to the same failures as in the West. Imagine something optimal — tracks for high-speed trains, and small non-polluting cars for short distances. Set an example that other countries will want to follow.

It was such a take-over of the DDR! All the people there have seen their initiatives marginalised. 'We know how to run a country, we'll handle it.' Yet there are many things we do wrong in the West. For example, the approach of pricing the environment to protect it is mistaken. But perhaps we have to make wrong approaches in the beginning. We should not be adapting the environment to economics, but economics to the environment. Take the sustainability of forests. You say, 'We must not take out more than we can grow.' But you will soon see that forests have other functions — retention of water, soil preservation, protection of diversity, as well as an aesthetic value. It won't fit into the economic paradigm. Pricing is only a start — it isn't the answer. In a competitive society, maybe it could be made competitive to preserve rather than to waste. On the other hand, if you price everything, if you say, 'This bird is worth $5' people will ask, 'Can we afford it?' which is the wrong question. That simply reserves environmental damage for those with the deepest pockets. But at least if things are costed, perhaps people will begin to ask why.

Scientists have overestimated their wisdom and knowledge. Technology can answer questions that are relatively precise, but not moral questions. Scientists understand simple things, but they don't always see the complexity of natural structures. The apprehension of the *Gestalt* is as important as the detail. I see *exactness* and *relevance* as opposite poles. The analytic is important, but so is the unfocused, the fuzzy, the overall context. Science takes things apart, and in doing so, can lose sight of the structure. Art and religious rituals have traditionally had the other, more general purpose, but these have decayed in recent times, as science and economics have become paramount.

Durr uses a telling image for the role of science in our culture. He says we are like a community of fishing people, who use nets of say, five centimetres. We have caught all the fish that those nets will hold for hundreds of years. We know intimately, and in great detail, every species the nets can catch. We are so sure of what we know that we deny the existence of anything else in the sea. That there is a whole world unknown to us, beyond what our nets will hold, is inconceivable.

We have to learn to be less proud of our technology. We feel we are more clever than nature. But nature has been conducting tests for four billion years. Her mistakes are no longer around. That is not to say that nature is stupid! Humility; we need to relearn traditional wisdom and knowledge. Combine the intuitive with the analytic, the vision with the detail.

Nor should the ecological movements limit themselves to biological ecology. What about cultural ecology? The diversity of cultural heritages. Some say, 'Don't emphasise that, look what it's doing to the former Yugoslavia and USSR.' But what is happening there is a consequence of a long period of the suppression of diversity. Once the presure is off, that wider diversity will be appreciated. What is visible is diversity; what is hidden is that such diversity is part of a higher structure. As it is with nature, so it is with human ecology.

JOHAN GALTUNG, RIGHT LIVELIHOOD AWARD WINNER 1987. Johan Galtung has had an international academic career spanning 30 years, five continents, a dozen major positions, over 30 visiting Professorships, 50 books and more than 1,000 published monographs. After initial work as mathematician, Galtung turned to the social sciences, and in 1967 he published his *Theory and Methods of Social Research* (Allen and Unwin). In 1959, he set up the International Peace Research Institute in Oslo, and remained Director for ten years. He founded the *Journal of Peace Research* in 1964, and edited it until 1974. He was professor of Conflict and Peace Research at the University of Oslo from 1969-77, during which period he also helped to found the Inter-University Centre in Dubrovnik, Yugoslavia, as a meeting place for East and West. High ranking university positions followed in suceeding years, interspersed with consultancies to the whole range of UN agencies: UNESCO, UNCTAD, WHO, ILO, FAO, UNU, UNEP, UNIDO, UNDP and UNITAR. His most recent university position is Professor of Peace Studies at the University of Hawaii USA, working on an integrated agenda with four main strands:

1. comparative civilisation theory, exploring the underlying implications for peace and development of occidental and oriental civilisations;

2. the generation of textbooks in general peace theory and general conflict resolution;

3. development theory, including issues of ecology, health and peace;

4. a new approach to economics which can more comfortably accommodate such major world goals as peace, development, human growth and ecological balance.

Galtung's publications reflect his position as one of the founders of peace research. They range from the early *Gandhi's Political Ethics* (Tanum, Oslo, 1955), through the five volumes of *Essays in Peace Research* (Ejlers, Copenhagen, 1974-80), to *The Two Worlds* (Macmillan, New York 1980), to his most recent book, *There Are Alternatives* (Spokesman 1984).

JOHAN GALTUNG'S WORK has been characterised by commitment to a goal that received wisdom declares impossible — the abolition of war as a social institution. Much effort has been expended in demonstrating the folly of such an ambition. Galtung points out that precisely the same arguments were deployed against those who have sought an end to other damaging social institutions: the defenders of slavery, for instance, always insisted that this was an outcrop of something mysterious and unchangeable called human nature. Vestiges of slavery, of course, remain, but not as a legitimate social institution; and so, it will be one day with war.

In 1959, Galtung set up the International Peace Research Institute, the first such foundation to create a significant impact on the academic world. Now there are over 100 colleges and universities in the USA alone which teach peace studies. There are, Galtung explains, three major determinants which propelled him towards what has been in effect the creation of a systematic study of the conditions leading to peace. The first was the occupation of his native Norway. When he was 14, he saw his father hauled off to a concentration camp. Secondly, obligatory military service led him to formulate the question of whether there might not have been a non-violent, peaceful alternative to armed resistance to the Nazi violation of so much of Europe. The third was the propitious social and moral environment of Norway, with its tradition of commitment to social justice.

Galtung's first work was on the political ethics of Gandhi; and he soon realised that the cause of peace could be advanced not only by theory and writing but that it required also the building of institutions. Over the years, he has not only refined and deepened the arguments for peace, but also elaborated the practical steps that may be taken for its realisation and maintenance. If peace means a reduction of violence, then a more subtle and complex understanding of it is required than its use as the opposite of 'war' He distinguishes between three types of violence. First, the naked expression of military power and conquest. Second, structural violence, often by means of economic power, which damages and destroys less directly; and third, cultural violence, which legitimises the other forms and persuades its practitioners that it is their right and duty to do so, since the victims invariably belong to some out-group of diminished humanity — unbelievers, outcasts, savages, social or racial inferiors. Of all forms of violence, this last is the most intractable.

In the early 1980s, Galtung wrote *There Are Alternatives*. This was the most persuasive response to the posturings of those who sought illusions of 'equilibrium' in the inherent instabilities of the arms race, the chimera of 'peace through strength', a strength that had to be so overwhelming in order to prevail that it was unattainable. As well as analysing the deep cultural roots that fed the recrudescence of the Cold War at that time, he also demonstrated that there was a potential source of constant renewal of conflicts in the underlying ideological universalism that informed the great monotheistic religions in the world, and whose offspring are 20th century economic ideologies.

Galtung pointed out that it was the common philosophical roots of both Marxism and liberalism that made the East-West conflict so menacing. Both were based upon universalism (validity for the whole world) and singularism (validity of only one system.) Since the dissolution of the Cold War, the shape of this conflict has undergone a mutation that was, perhaps, predictable. One of the questions facing us now is whether the vacuum left by the decay of the 'Communist threat' has not been filled by the resurrection of an even more antique 'enemy' of the West — Islam. In the past decade, the most prominent objects of hatred in Western ideology have all been leaders of Islamic countries. Further, the intense demonising of Saddam Hussein after Iraq's invasion of Kuwait, and the levels of licensed public loathing, quite disproportionate towards a leader whom the West had, until that moment, been pleased to conciliate, offered material for some disturbing reflections. The United Nations was 'rehabilitated', when it was discovered it could become an instrument of US foreign policy once more. The Gulf War was the first overt 'resource-war', and served to gain a foothold by the US in an area containing resources indispensable for the only future conceivable by the West. It served as a kind of living arms-bazaar for Western weaponry, and demonstrated the 'folly' of winding down 'defence' expenditure in response to the diminished threat from Communism. But perhaps the most alarming feature was the rhetoric, supported by the metamorphosis of the Communist *Feindbild* (the image of the enemy), and the remembrance of even more potent Western crusades than mere missions against the upstart godless creed of Communism. Many of the symmetries of a familiar enmity towards Communism are already present in the opposition to what is described in the West as 'Islamic expansionism'. This is particularly dangerous now that the West sees itself as having triumphed in the world, and can see no further obstacle to the spread of its own economic creed. One has only to look at the 'conditionalities' being imposed on countries in eastern Europe and the Third World by the IMF, World Bank, Western governments, to realise that the universalising mission of the West has not gone away, but merely deserted the traditional Bibles, scriptures and holy writs, and taken up its abode in the single-minded promotion of an economic system which has served the West so well. The fact that that system is not replicable in the world, based as it has been upon the plunder of resources, the flow of wealth from poor to rich, and institutionalised global inequality, does not disturb the serene propagators of the only way in the world. It is clear that the era of peace may be delayed. Much of Galtung's analyses of the rivalry between Marxism and liberalism have vibrant echoes for new, or rather, the reassertion of old enmities.

Galtung said that liberalism and Marxism acknowledged their common pedigree by their expectation of similar reactions from one another. 'The East expected capitalism, when in crisis, to develop fascistic characteristics, and hence to become totalitarian and also belligerent; the West expected Communism — and not only in crisis — to develop totalitarian characteristics, to be dictatorial and repressive at home and expansionist abroad, in order 'to divert attention from domestic problems'.

Galtung sought to show the absurdity of the doctrine of security through strength, a balance which, given the multiple forms of weaponry, and the constantly evolving technology, could never be maintained. It is always bound to be disturbed by renewed attempts to level-up in those are perceives itself to be in deficit in relation to the other. Galtung showed the inutility of existing fora devoted to disarmament, and advocated instead a policy of *transarmament*. This meant pursuing neither so-called 'multilateral' nor 'unilateral' policies, but seeking a measured transition from offensive defence to a truly, unequivocally defensive posture, whereby a country would use a combination of conventional military defence, para-military defence and non-military defence, in order to make its territory untenable by its putative antagonist; and under conditions of peace, to draw closer to the adversary by means of strengthening the ties of trade and commerce, and so on. This option seems even more desirable with the relaxation of tension between East and West.

Security and invulnerability cannot be attained through 'strength', when what this really means is the proliferation of destabilising weaponry. Galtung identified 'offensive capability' as the common enemy, and 'defensive capability' as the common good. The goal must be sustainable and unthreatening security, rather than the total abolition of armaments. Forswearing unilateralism does not mean that Galtung is yielding to those arguments often put forward by conservatives about human nature and its unchangeably violent and aggressive impulses.

> It is true that there are strong human needs that must be fulfilled, and around which most activities are centred, notably food and sex. The ways in which these are expressed are very different from society to society. If there were the same drive for war, however, we would not see such variation in the world in different social structures through time and from place to place. In nomadic and so-called primitive societies, war is almost unknown. But as societies become more complicated — industrial, unequal and dependent — there is an increase in violence. And add to this the cultural reasons, especially the inheritance of monotheistic religions — Christianity, Judaeism and Islam — not because they are monotheistic, but because they insist upon their singular validity, their universality, and they claim their votaries as a chosen people, an elect, and you have powerful reasons for aggression, violence and incontinence.

In spite of the loss of credibility of the threat of Communism, there remains the *Eigendynamik* of the military-bureaucratic-corporate-intelligentsia complex. Johan Galtung draws the parallel between the long chain of organisation in military production with that in more conventional economic activity. The use of intellectual and military power, the research and development, the testing, production, stockpiling, training and deployment, and finally, the use of weapons, have their counterparts in the processes leading up to the production, distribution and marketing of everyday economic goods, consumption being the analogue of the actual use of the weapons, the orgiastic release. This suggests that such processes are inextricably entwined; and indeed, the more unabashed apologists of increased weapons research often make explicit the 'benefits' which have accrued to society as by-products from military research.

There is something more. The omnicidal possibility which Galtung associates with nuclear war (for such a war threatens not only personal survival and the human-made environment, but also genocide, sociocide and ecocide), creates a sense of permanent menace over the lives of the people. One popular response to this has itself become a means of feeding the economic growth-and-consumption machine. That is to say, the pervasive fear and possibility of annihilation, and the conviction that there is nothing much individuals can do about it, create a nihilistic recklessness in Western society, a devotion to living in the present, to the search for immediate pleasures, which lead to an accelerating tempo of production. This may be disagreeable for the prospects of humanity, but it certainly helps to promote the economy. Thus, even the threat of extinction can become yet another business opportunity for the entertainers of the people. The disturbed and unquiet hedonism of Western society comes, not simply from the fact that life is short (that has always been the case), but that it may be rendered even shorter by those who have only to press a button. Such anxieties contribute to a deepening addiction to the available consolations. They lead to a greater desire for escape and distraction from what are possibly the most systematically escapist and distracted societies in human history. This, in turn, only exacerbates forms of economic growth and expansion that compound the danger to the planet and to the unstable societies it must contain. There is a congruence between a high-consuming perspectiveless present shadowed by an uncertain future, and what is good for the economy. Indeed, that human beings in the rich world should have come to think of themselves primarily as 'consumers', suggests that human purposes have become identified with the using up of things, the destruction of resources, which is itself a kind of everyday warfare against the planet itself. Nothing clarifies more dramatically how we have exalted economic systems above humanity; the survival of those systems is given priority over Creation itself.

In response to this, Galtung speaks of the *inner security* of societies, and this is equally true for the individuals within those societies. By building up self-reliance, harmonious internal relationships (which also means greater equality), the need is reduced for amplified external armouries, and for the elaboration of the symbols and display of power.

Galtung also offers new tasks for the Peace Movement.

Historians will have a difficult job sorting out the events of 1989-92, deciding exactly what happened and why. But I will advance one single hypothesis at this stage: without the peace movement in the West and the dissident movement in the East, nothing much would have happened. The movements both gained momentum in the early eighties, and both carried the same message: we are sick and tired of Stalinism (in the East) and nuclearism (in the West.) It is an irony that the dissident movement which did so much to shake the system has been by-passed by power in the East; and of course, the peace movement is not in power in the West.

So the struggle of the peace movement continues. Even with no ostensible competitive threat, there is a constant pressure for the expansion and refinement of armaments: space-based weapons, generating powerful beams in space, or reflecting them with geo-stationary mirrors. The peace movement has to insist on much deeper demilitarisation, uprooting the ideologies and institutions that still protect the dynamic of the arms race, even though there is only one competitor. Secondly, the peace movement should argue for a totally new military doctrine. The best would be to abolish the army, going in for a combination of non-military defence, with UN peace-keeping forces (with handweapons only), and a massive mobilisation of youth and others for social development and environmental service, both nationally and internationally. The second best, but still much better than the offensive, genocidal weaponry the more aggressive countries possess today, would be non-provocative defence, based on short-range armed capability. The second best can be a good stepping stone on the way to the best, as the example from Switzerland in November 1989 showed, when a surprising 35.6 per cent of people voted 'Yes' to abolish the Swiss army by the year 2000.

The third task is the healing of Europe. With *pax sovietica* gone, cracks open; the resurrection of old hatreds, xenophobias and racisms can be the popular responses to the vacuum, especially if allied to the poverty and inequality of naked market economics. German reunification could lead to the Fourth Reich, even with nuclear weapons. The European Community will become the European Union, with the Western European Union as its military arm. Economically, the strong West is about to 'thirdworldise' the weak East, a sure recipe for future upheaval. The peace movement has to warn and to propose alternatives. Its role is as vital as ever.

22. IMAGINING THE FUTURE

ROBERT JUNGK, RIGHT LIVELIHOOD AWARD WINNER 1986. Robert Jungk was born in Berlin in 1913, emigrated to Paris in 1933, lived from 1936 to 1938 in Prague, where he published the anti-fascist paper *Mondial Press*. He fled to Switzerland when the Nazis entered Prague, and stayed there till 1945. Then as freelance journalist he worked for several papers, including the *Observer* in London. During the 1950s, he began to explore the themes which have dominated his life: the future, peace and anti-nuclear activity. His first book was *The Future Has Already Begun*. In 1953 he founded the first Institute for Research into the Future, and in 1967, he set up with Johan Galtung the International Conference on Futurism, out of which emerged the World Federation for Future Research. He began to develop Futures Workshops, in which people envision desirable futures and the means whereby these can be achieved. In 1987, he founded the Futures Library in Salzburg. Scholarship and activism characterise his peace activities. His book, *Brighter Than a Thousand Suns* was followed by several others on the nuclear theme, including *The Nuclear State* in 1978.

BEING ABLE TO IMAGINE alternative futures is a recurring theme, the necessary step beyond the warnings and the analyses. Robert Jungk, with his Futures Workshops has been doing that for a quarter of a century. His *Internazionale Bibliothek fur Zukunftsfragen* (International Futures Library) opened in 1986; located in Salzburg, a city that symbolises high culture, tradition and exclusiveness, the library looks to a future culture based on the release of popular creativity and imagination which will help people to regain power over their own lives and destinies.

Robert Jungk has himself known the meaning of powerlessness: in Switzerland during the war, he had sought in vain to alert the Allies to the scope and extent of atrocities against the Jews.

He knows that what pass for apathy and indifference in people are often simply a logical response to a world which offers them no space to express what they think and feel, and provides them with no outlet for any creative contribution to the work of society. Apathy, in this context, is not a moral failing, a kind of social accidie, but a considered withdrawal of constructive energy when this has little scope for action, even though formal arrangements of 'democracy' may exist.

Any discussion of the future is made more difficult by the fact that it has become the province of large numbers of charlatans, seers and colonists. Murray Bookchin in *Towards an Ecological Society*, observes 'Futurism has abolished the future ... by assimilating it to a present which thereby acquires a stagnant eternality by virtue of the extent to which it permeates the eras that lie ahead.' Robert Jungk has devoted much of his life to a retrieval of the future for the people, out of the hands of deterministic soothsayers, a future for liberation and not domination. Economic, scientific and military decisions reach far into the future; and it was in the think-tanks of the United States military and industrial establishment that Jungk first perceived the lineaments of a violent and predictable futurism — attempts to control and manipulate future conflicts as well as markets, in which the people would have no say.

Jungk is not a methodologist of futurism. One of his great abilities has been to communicate, in an understandable way, that which is normally sealed within academic, scientific and military fastnesses. He does not believe in the exclusive ownership of information or expertise, but practices a constant giving, exchange and transfer of knowledge.

As a generalist in a time of extreme specialisations, Robert Jungk has sought to break the monopoly of experts through Futures Workshops, where the slumbering and discarded creativity of the people may be rekindled and given practical expression. In the 1960s, when talking with Viennese factory workers about their wishes for tomorrow's world, he was shocked to discover that they tended to repeat what they had heard from advertisers and publicists. He realised that it takes a long time for the buried imagination to re-emerge through layers of suspicion and thwarted self-confidence.

> The future is coloured by visions we have of it — if we are sombre and fearful, that is how it will be. The workshops embody the idea of *social innovation*, as opposed to the research and development of the technological establishment.

The earliest alternative workshops were the private property of intellectuals. Futures Workshops released a flood of imaginative popular ideas for the future we want, rather than the preordained extrapolations from the present that have been imposed upon people. (It is significant that 'what the people want' is a battle-cry of the defenders of the existing order; yet what the people want, as exhibited in patterns of consumption, is, more often than not, an expression of their resignation to wanting what they know they can have.) Futures Workshops aim to awaken the deeper needs and desires, and to find spaces for their partial realisation in the interstices of society.

> There are three phases in the Futures Workshop: the critical phase, where the participants identify the aspects of contemporary society that are abhorrent to them; then a period of unbridled fantasy, where they imagine what the future could be like; and finally, the phase of implementation, where the likelihood of its realisation is assessed, and pathways towards its achievement explored. At the same time, by drawing up lists and examples of existing projects and initiatives that have been undertaken

elsewhere in the world, great encouragement may be derived from actual, living possibilities. In addition, people also gain an insight into the constraints upon their visions and dreams. They are able to 'fight back', which in this context means not aggression but the liberated imagination at work.

Futures Workshops have been the birthplace of a multitude of initiatives. They are 'serious, purposeful games, which restore the spiritual strength depleted by consumerism'. Some of the insights offered by ordinary people have been extraordinary: for instance, one workshop asked why the West did not seek aid from Third World countries which have stability and balance in their human relationships, to help the West deal with its problems of social dislocation and psychological disorder.

Robert Jungk insists that there is a crucial difference between the function of Futures Workshops and psychological therapies. People do, of course, want tenderness, warmth and support, but not only as individuals. We need these things also as part of lived, shared social experience. While personal therapies focus on the disordered individual, Futures Workshops look for ways of transcending damaged or distorted social relationships.

'Futures Workshops are not a new instrument of social engineering, but the midwife of a democracy, frequently debated, often announced, but nowhere yet delivered.' Jungk speaks of 'socionauts', venturing into uncharted social space. At the same time, the participants in the workshops are all securely anchored in, and shaped by, contemporary society. 'It would be jumping to conclusions to think that nothing new could ever come out of working with the existing society. The question should be, rather, on what terms to co-operate with it to achieve real progress?'

Among projects that have grown out of Futures Workshops is the Self-Help Network, for alternative and political initiatives. This is established now in Germany, Austria and Switzerland. Its purpose is to provide support to individuals and groups working on self-organised alternative schemes. The fund receives monthly contributions from over 5,000 individual sponsors in many areas of life — the traditional left, trades unions, green and alternative movements, artistic, scientific and professional circles. This makes available about $20,000 a month for small-scale projects, mostly for help with the purchase of essential equipment or subsistence. A group is eligible if it practises democratic self-management, offers alternative models for working and living, or provides assistance to those not caught in the state welfare net, or if it is oriented towards emancipation or enlightenment, if it operates on a non-profit-making basis, is prepared to co-operate with similarly oriented groups and shows evidence of becoming self-supportive eventually.

Jungk says that mobilising the masses no longer means storming Bastilles or Winter Palaces, but involves instead the release of spiritual and creative energies. Futures Workshops have nothing to do with adult education in conventional terms, that is of absorbing existing knowledge. They signify an inexhaustible flow of ideas and experiments, visions and projects, which find their way into the rifts in the petrified structures of society. They are catalysts of social transformation.

Robert Jungk's most recent book *Projekt Ermutigung* (*The Politics of Encouragement: resistance to resignation*) is an essay to give heart to those who work for change and improvement in the world. He says that the ghost of resignation haunts the bearers of social hope, particularly in the aftermath of the decay of the Marxist alternative. Because that failed, it is easy to draw the conclusion that the formulation of any other way of being in the world is also doomed. There is, says Jungk, so much to celebrate. The technocratic paradigm is tottering. The powerful are weaker than they seem, and the powerless stronger than they know. The 'failures' of 1968 sowed the seeds of the social movements of the 1980s; and they are far from having achieved their fullest expression.

Indeed, these social movements should now extend their operations to all areas of society. It should not be merely a question of demonstrating outside atomic power plants, but should mean also resisting industrialised agriculture, the centralising of consumption, the suppression of human rights in the name of economic progress, the assault on the habitat of indigenous peoples. He says that the old militaristic paradigm of hostility towards an opponent is an inappropriate model for those in the social movements. 'There is no point either in waiting for social breakdown, and then saying, "I told you so"; we should be demonstrating desirable alternative practice that works and that inspires others with hope.'

Among the reasons for optimism he offers are:

1) doubts on the part of the elite itself; dissenters high in the power hierarchies who 'blow the whistle'. Formerly, elites enjoyed both privilege and security, while the poor were out of sight in their slums and factories. But the elite, too, are now at risk, their children's future is not exempt from the effects of pollution and radioactivity, which are not discriminating in their victims. This creates a new situation between the powerful and powerless, and opens the possibility of previously unthinkable alliances. This is another reason why the Freund/Feind model has outlived its usefulness.

2) The fresh awakening, not only of some students, but also of professional organisations — the mobilisation of dissident lawyers, doctors, officials, teachers, managers.

3) The renewal of spirituality, the revival of the intuitive, visionary, affective elements in our nature, those borne especially by women.

4) The overthrow of ideas of 'value-free' science, the non-existence of 'dispassionate observers', and the growing realisation of our connectedness with the natural world.

5) The absence of a new priestly caste in the new movements, and the emergence of long neglected popular energies.

6) Social creativity: 'the *possible* is not a hostile opposing force of what is actual, but is its living essence: what is possible within the actual is the living reservoir out of which reality is constantly evolving.'

7) The fragility of the existing order: the 'indestructible' monoliths of Eastern Europe crumbled overnight; the seemingly impregnable structures of Western dominance are no less wracked by crisis, doubt and anxiety.

8) The thousands of points of hopeful growth, experiments in community living, new family constellations, environmentally friendly energy sources, socially useful production, satisfying work, inspirational education. Whenever the mainstream adopts our ideas, this should be regarded, not as piracy or co-option, but as a tribute to our wisdom and prescience.

It is not to be expected that unanimity should emerge from the practice and testimony of those looking for another way. If that were to occur, it would suggest the growth of yet another ideology. There are, however, common threads. We can discern the outlines of a new worldview, one which cherishes diversity, tolerance, the indigenous, the local and the traditional, allied to the sustainably innovative, one which values popular creativity, decentralisation, and an empowerment beyond existing democratic forms. The celebration of our human diversity is buttressed by a new appreciation of the variety and connectedness of the natural world with humanity. This perception of a change of relationship does represent a different paradigm from the prevailing values of industrial society, with their exploitative domination of nature by human beings, and all the hierarchies within society, the power of men over women, of rich over poor, white over black, North over South, strong over weak. It is a change of relationship that requires neither dogma nor theory, but is nourished by living, growing practice, of which a handful of representatives appear in this book, but which is an already existing worldwide movement of hope and emancipation.

POSTSCRIPT

AT THE TIME OF THE EARTH SUMMIT in June 1992, it appeared for a moment that many of the ideas, practised as well as preached by the people in this book, would come together in a common and explosive recognition by North and South of what must be done in order to change the dominant pattern of development in the world. It seemed that the need for profound and radical change in the way we measure wealth, development and well-being, was going to be acknowledged by the most comprehensive assembly of world leaders in half a century. What happened was that another agenda did emerge; the words of an alternative reverberated around the earth — sustainability, diversity, empowerment, justice, human rights. Some of these words rang awkwardly in the mouths of those who were employing them for the first time. But having absorbed the rhetoric, it soon became clear that the rich had as their intention business as usual. The treaties on biodiversity, on the curbing of greenhouse gases were weak and permissive; the treaty on forests was non-binding; there was no agreement by the North that the level of aid to the South would reach 0.7 per cent of GNP within any foreseeable timespan. Agenda 21 at least signalled something of the complexity and depth of the crisis, and it may serve as a measure of the commitment of individual countries to environmental integrity. But the fundamental question of whether the earth can continue to bear the pressure of an economic system which has become global and has been sacralised, was not seriously addressed at all.

Each of the issues was isolated and made the object of a separate treaty, convention or plan. The idea of the profound and multiple interconnections was lost; thus 'development' was seen as the need of the South, sustainable no doubt, but not differentiated from the patterns and forms of development we have seen in the North. That the present development model is inappropriate to the South was acknowledged; that its extension and establishment there is indispensable to the continued supremacy of the North was passed over in silence. The connection between insecurity and population growth was scarcely touched: mainly because to stabilise populations, a decent level of social security is required, and to attain that would involve levels of distributive justice that the rich cannot contemplate. The need for high-consuming Northern populations to moderate their predations on resources was adverted to; but the President of the US, George Bush, announced he would do nothing to jeopardise jobs or low taxes in his country. Social justice and the environment alike must, in the last analysis, be subordinated to the necessities of the economy.

This means that we must continue to live in an awkward dual consciousness:

aware of the urgency of survival in a spreading and ever-expanding economic system, and aware too of the increasing pressure with which this bears upon the poor and upon the resource base of the earth.

That the Earth Summit should have occurred at the moment when the North was busy declaring that there is no alternative to the unalterable principles of the market economy had a profound influence on the discussions. A majority of the countries of the South represented at Rio had fallen under the tutelage of the Western financial institutions in the conduct of their economic policy; increasingly dependent, insecure and subordinate, they gave no sense of a locus where a truly alternative form of development might emerge, even in those countries where it might have been expected. In spite of the growing solidarity of the Group of 77, and the clarity with which the North-South divide appeared as the major global problem after the end of the Cold War, the possibility of disengagement by the South from a global system dominated by the North was not seriously discussed.

Much was made of the amount of money required by the South to compensate for its ruined environment, its depleted resources, the legacy of colonialism and continuing patterns of unjust appropriation. As long as argument rages over the quantities of money that the rich will disburse, the circle remains closed. For money is the symbol, the final product, as it were, the profit from the wastage, the using up, the erosion of the natural treasures of the earth — including human resources. Money can never replenish the reservoir of natural riches of which it is the symbolic substitute. To accept all argument on these terms means that the South is doomed to remain locked within the Northern paradigm; which can never emancipate its captive peoples.

Instead of celebrating the invasive, destructive and distorting incursions of the market economy into the deepest recesses of both the fabric of the planet and the depths of human need, we should be talking about areas of human experience that can be liberated from market dependency. We should be revaluing all the things we can make and do, and create for ourselves and each other freely outside of systems, ideologies, transnational companies, global institutions. Instead, what we see is more and more of our needs passed over to a market system that is itself the greatest engine of destruction that could ever have been devised by humanity, had it been our purpose to waste and destroy the riches of the earth and the resources of human beings: in the poor world, through abuse of energies and in the rich world by their neglect. It was not to be expected, at the Earth Summit, that world leaders would confront the depth and intensity of the crisis, let alone its origins, nor yet speak of the remedies that might be needed if rich and poor are both to survive in an habitable world.

This is why the energies of the initiatives in this book remain vital: open, questioning, affirming different paths, indicators of another way, representing inspiration and hope. When the leaders of the world finally are compelled to a recognition that their scenarios for the future are played out, that they have followed the sunlit paths to despair, these projects and efforts will show that the answer to the questions that have baffled and confused us have all the time been close at hand.

It is significant that the fate of a number of people in this book should be symbolic of the efforts that the existing order has made to incorporate them — only to find that what they are saying is too uncomfortable and too abrasive to be contained within the system. Lutzenberger in Brazil was dismissed as Environment Minister in March 1992; Wangari Maathai was harassed and arrested for her part in the democracy movement of Kenya; in India, Ela Bhatt and Rajni Kothari ceased to serve on the Planning Commission when the Congress(I) government was returned in 1991. This is not because they are too idiosyncratic or individualistic or incapable of working with others but simply because what they are saying is too stringent a critique of the tottering and unsustainable global system. That system accelerates its destructive establishment ever more extensively over the face of the earth and ever more deeply in the hearts and imaginations of the people. Yet the liberated future already exists; it shines out from the examples and initiatives of these pioneers of change. It tells us that, however sombre and sad the 'real world' may appear, transition to a more hopeful and humane alternative need not involve terrible loss and sacrifice (necessary though these may be); the alternative is within reach, beckoning to us not only through ideas, which can sometimes be too ghostly and intangible for the material urgencies of the present, but also through the practice of living flesh and blood in the here and now. The existence of these pioneers then becomes a power and a passion, which provide us with the confidence and the energies we need in order to change.

Addresses of Right Livelihood Projects

Sunderlai Bahaguna
Chipko Movement
P.O. Box Serain va Tehri
Pin. 249001
Uttar Pradesh
India

Walden Bello
Food First
145 9th Street
San Francisco
CA 94103
USA

Dr Rosalie Bertell
International Institute of Concern for Public Health
830 Bathurst St
Ontario M5R 3G1
Canada

Mrs Ela Bhatt
Self-Employed Women's Association
SEWA Reception Centre
opp. Victoria Gardens
Ahmedebad 380 001
India

Dr Mike Cooley
Thatcham Lodge
95 Sussex Place
Berkshire SL1 1NN
UK

Erik Dammann
The Future in our Hands
Loftuvelen 48-1456
Nesoddhogda
Norway

Professor Hans-Peter Durr
Werner Heisenberg Institute
Fohringer Ring 6
D-8000 Munchen 40
Germany

Cary Fowler
Rt. 5, Box 1029
Pittsboro
Nothern California 27312
USA

Free Legal Assistance Volunteers Association
Room 207, 2nd Floor, Mingson Building
Cor. Juan Luna & Zamora Street
Cebu City
Philippines

Johan Galtung
HSFR
Sveavagen 166 16th
S-11385 Stockholm
Sweden

Stephen Gaskin
Plenty International
41 The Farm
Summertown TN 38483
USA

Inge Kemp Genefke
Juliane Maries Vej 34
RCT
Dk-2100
Copenhagen Denmark

High Chief Ibedul Gibbons
PO Box 428
Koror
Palau via USA 96490
Caroline Islands

Mohamed Idris
Consumers Association of Penang
87 Cantonment Road
Penang
Malaysia

Robert Jungk
Steingasse 31/IV
A-5020 Salzburg
Austria

Petra Kelly*
Die Grunen
Bonn
Germany

Iman Khalifeh
c/o Beirut University College
PO Box 13-5053 F 83
Beirut
Lebanon

Professor Leopold Kohr
170 Reservoir Rd
Gloucester GL4 9SB
UK

Rajni Kothari
Lokayan
13 Alipur Rd
Delhi 110 054
India

Hunter & Amory Lovins
Rocky Mountain Institute
Drawer 248
Old Snowmass
Colorado 81654
USA

* Sadly, Petra Kelly died in October 1992 as this book was going to press.

Professor Wangari Maathai
National Council of Women of Kenya
PO Box 43741
Ragati Rd
Nairobi
Kenya

Dr Manfred Max-Neef
Cepaur
Casilla PO Box 27001
Santiago 27
Chile

Bill Mollison
Permaculture Institute
PO Box 1
Tyalgum
New South Wales 2484
Australia

Pat Mooney
RR No 1
Beresford
Brandon
Manitoba
Canada R 7A 5Y1

Harrison Ngau
SAM Sarawak
PO Box 216
98508 Marudi
Baram, Sarawak
Malaysia

Helena Norberg-Hodge
Ladakh project
21 Victoria Square
Clifton
Bristol BS8 4ES
UK

Evaristo Nugkuag Ikanan
Presidente COICA
Sr. Almargo 614
Lima 11
Peru

Patrick van Rensburg
The Foundation for Education
with Production
PO Box 20906, Gaborone
Bostwana

Dr Alice Stewart
The Medical School
Department of Social Medicine
University of Birmingham
Edgbaston
Birmingham B15 2TH
UK

Sir George Trevelyan
The Old Vicarage
Hawkesbury
Badminton
Avon GL0 1BW
UK

Theo Van Boven
Kantoorweg 5
6218 NB Maastricht
The Netherlands

Mordechai Vanunu
Ashkelon Prison
PO Box 17
Ashkelon
Israel

Janos Vargha
Duna Kor
ISTER
Ucta 4
H. 2097 Pilisboroszeno
Hungary

S. Wickremaarachchi
Participatory Institute for Development Alternatives
32 Gothami Lane
Colombo 08
Sri Lanka

BIBLIOGRAPHY

Arendt, Hannah (nd) *Between Past and Future*.

Alvares, Claude *Homo Faber* (1979) Allied Publishers, Bombay; English edition: *Decolonizing History: Technology and Culture in India, China and the West*. Zed Press, London.

Behn, Mira (1949) *There is Something Wrong with the Himalayas*. Mimeo.

Benedict, Ruth (1934) *Patterns of Culture*. Mentor Books, New York.

Bertell, Rosalie (1985) *No Immediate Danger*. Women's Press, London.

Bookchin, Murray (1982) *Towards an Ecological Society*. Black Rose Books, Canada.

Clairmonte, F. and J. Cavanagh (1991) *Merchants of Drink*. Third World Network, Penang.

Cooley, Mike (1987) *Architect or Bee? The Human Price of Technology*. Chatto and Windus, London. (First published by the author, 1980).

Dammann, Erik (1972) *The Future in Our Hands*. Pergamon Press, Oxford.

—— (1984) *Revolution in the Affluent Society*. Heretic Books, London.

—— (1987) *Beyond Time and Space*. Heretic Books, London.

—— (na) *Your Money or Your life*. Heretic Books, London.

de Silva et al. (eds) (1988) *Towards a Theory of Rural Development*. Progressive Publishers, Lahore.

Fathy, Hassan (1973) *Architecture for the Poor*. University of Chicago Press, Chicago.

Fowler, Gary and Pat Mooney (1988) *Development Dialogue 1&2*. Dag Hammarskjold Foundation, Uppsala.

—— (1989) *Shattering: the Diversity of Life in the Age of Biotechnology*. University of Arizona Press, USA.

Galtung, Johan (1955) *Gandhi's Political Ethics*. Tanum, Oslo.

—— (1967) *Theory and Methods of Social Research*. Allen and Unwin, London.

—— (1974-80) *Essays in Peace Research* (5 vols.). Ejlers, Copenhagen.

—— (1984) *There are Alternatives*. Spokesman, Matlode.

Hong, Evelyn (1987) *See the Third World While it Lasts*. Third World Network, Penang.

Jungk, Robert (nd) *Projekt Ermütigung* (The Politics of Encouragement: Resistance to Resignation).

—— (nd) *The Future has already Begun*.

————(1970) *Brighter Than a Thousand Suns.* Penguin Books, Harmondsworth.

————(1978) *The Nuclear State.* Calder, London.

Kelly, Petra (1984) *Fighting for Hope.* Chatto and Windus, London.

Kohr, Leopold (1957) *The Breakdown of Nations.* Routledge and Kegan Paul, London.

————(1973) *Development Without Aid.* Christopher Davies, Swansea.

————(1977) *The Overdeveloped Nations.* Christopher Davies, Swansea.

Kothari, Rajni (1989) *Re-thinking Human Rights.* Lokayan, New Delhi.

Lappé, Frances Moore (1971) *Diet for a Small Planet.* Ballantine.

Lappé, Frances Moore and Joseph Collins (1980) *Food First: Beyond the Myth of Scarcity.* Souvenir Press, London.

————(1988) *World Hunger: Twelve Myths.* Earthscan, London.

Lovins, Amory (1979) *Soft Energy Paths: Towards a Durable Peace.* Harper Colophon, New York.

Max-Neef, Manfred (1982) *From the Outside Looking In: Experiences in Barefoot Economics.* Dag Hammarskjold Foundation; (1992) Zed Books, London.

Mollison, B. (1978) *Permaculture One: A Perennial Agriculture for Human Settlements.* Tagari Publications, Australia.

————(1979) *Permaculture Two: Practical Design for Town and Country in Permanent Agriculture.* Tagari Publications, Australia.

————(na) *Permaculture: A Designer's Handbook.* Permaculture Institute, Tagari Publications, Australia.

Mooney, Pat (1979) *Seeds of the Earth.*

————(1983) *The Law of the Seed: Another Development and Plant Genetic Resources.*

Norberg-Hodge, Helena (1991) *Ancient Futures.* Rider Books.

RAFI (1988) *The Laws of Life: Another Development and the New Biotechnologies.* RAFI.

Raghavan, Chakravarthy (1991) *Recolonization: GATT, the Uruguay Round and a New Global Economy.* Zed Books, London.

Rose, Kalim (1992) *Where Women are Leaders: The Self-Employed Women's Association.* Sage Publications, India; and Zed Books, London.

Shiva, Vandana (1991) *The Violence of the Green Revolution.* Third World Network, Penang; and Zed Books, London.

Schumacher, Fritz (1973) *Small is Beautiful: Economics as if People Mattered.* Blond and Briggs, London.

Tawney, R.H. (1989) *Religion and the Rise of Capitalism.* Penguin Books, Harmondsworth.

Trevelyan, George (1977) *A Vision of the Aquarian Age.* Gateway Books.

———(1981) *Operation Redemption.*

———(1985) *Summons to a High Crusade.* Findhorn Publications, UK.

Turner, Bertha (ed) (1988) *A Third World Case Book.* BCB.

Turner, John F.C. (1966) *Uncontrolled Urban Settlement: Problems and Policies.*

———(1972) *Freedom to Build: Dweller Control of the Housing Process.* Macmillan, London.

———(1976) *Housing by People: Towards Autonomy in Building Environments.* Marion Boyars, London.

van Boven, Theo (1982) *People Matter: Views on International Human Rights Policy.* Meulenhoff, Amsterdam, The Netherlands.

Index